D0438345

THE TRENCH

Also by Richard van Emden

TICKLED TO DEATH TO GO: THE MEMOIRS OF A CAVALRYMAN
IN THE FIRST WORLD WAR

VETERANS: THE LAST SURVIVORS OF THE GREAT WAR

PRISONERS OF THE KAISER: THE LAST POWs OF THE GREAT WAR

THE TRENCH

EXPERIENCING LIFE ON THE FRONT LINE
1916

RICHARD VAN EMDEN

BANTAM PRESS

LONDON · NEW YORK · TORONTO · SYDNEY · AUCKLAND

TRANSWORLD PUBLISHERS
61–63 Uxbridge Road, London W5 5SA
a division of The Random House Group Ltd

RANDOM HOUSE AUSTRALIA (PTY) LTD
20 Alfred Street, Milsons Point, Sydney,
New South Wales 2061, Australia

RANDOM HOUSE NEW ZEALAND LTD
18 Poland Road, Glenfield, Auckland 10, New Zealand

RANDOM HOUSE SOUTH AFRICA (PTY) LTD
Endulini, 5a Jubilee Road, Parktown 2193, South Africa

Published 2002 by Bantam Press
a division of Transworld Publishers

A catalogue record for this book is available from the British Library.
ISBN 0593 049756

Typeset in 12/18pt Ehrhardt by Falcon Oast Graphic Art Ltd.

Printed in Great Britain by
Clays Ltd, Bungay, Suffolk

1 3 5 7 9 10 8 6 4 2

This book is dedicated to all the men of the 10th Battalion East Yorkshire Regiment, the 1st Hull Pals, and to the four surviving veterans interviewed for the television series:

Arthur Barraclough, 1/4th Duke of Wellington's, born 4 January 1898
Andrew Bowie, 1st Cameron Highlanders, born 3 October 1897
Arthur Halestrap, 46th Division, Royal Engineer Signals, born
8 September 1898
Harry Patch, 7th Duke of Cornwall's Light Infantry, born 17 June 1898

CONTENTS

ACKNOWLEDGEMENTS

I would like to thank Jane Root, Controller of BBC2, and David Mortimer, Deputy Controller of Documentaries, for their support and belief in the documentary series, as well as all those from BBC Bristol who have worked ceaselessly on the project: series producer Dick Colthurst, creative director Tessa Finch, production executive Liz Wilson and the production team of Wendy McCombe, Julie Richardson and Sam Simmons. The production research was undertaken by Sally Dyas, Jennie Fazey, Adrian Lambert and David Olusoga. I am very appreciative of the support given by those connected with the series at BBC London, including Dan Phelan, Sally Turner, Jilly Beresford, David Crockford and David Parsley.

Thanks also go to the series director, Stephen Trombley, and directors Dominic Ozanne and Mike Kleinsteuber, assistant directors Jane Hamlin and Nick Justin, line producer David Higginson, art director Diarmuid Ryan-O'Connor, location manager John Tuite, construction manager Alun Lewis and special effects supervisor Dominic Wigley.

I am particularly grateful to Taff Gillingham of the Khaki Chums, and the many Chums who supported the production with their heroic efforts prior to filming and their steadfastness in the trench during late October and early November 2001, including Dickie Ingram and Captain Rob Yuill.

Very special thanks go to my parents Wolfgang and Joan van Emden, who, as always, have assiduously edited my writing, and to my partner Anna Branch, whose patience and support have been greatly appreciated. A big thank you, too, to Doug Young and Sheila Lee at Transworld for all their help and patience, as well as to Matthew Parker, the book's expert editor. I would also like to thank friends who have helped in various ways, including Johnny and Susie Keating, Sanjeev Ahuja and Vic and Diane Piuk.

I am also indebted to those who helped in various stages of the production, including Peter Barton, David Bilton (author of *Hull Pals*), Nick Fear, Malcolm Mann, Andrew Robertshaw and Julian Farrance from the National Army Museum, and Col. Prof. Ian Palmer, Ministry of Defence psychiatrist.

In France I would like to thank Philippe Gorczynski, Jean-Luc Gibot and Bernard Lesniak, whose local contacts and knowledge helped secure essential local endorsement and co-operation; Alain Jacques, M. Bertrand de Valicourt, and the villagers of Flesquières.

A great thank you to all the Hull Pals Circa 2001. Without their dedication and commitment to this series, the entire project would have fallen at the first hurdle. And very lastly, my deeply felt appreciation and thanks to all the Great War veterans whose support for the series has given *The Trench* genuine credibility. These veterans, whose average age is 104, have given us a final glimpse into a war that has all but been consigned to history.

Line illustrations reproduced in the text are taken from the following sources: David Bilton, *Hull Pals*, Pen & Sword Books, 1999: p. 38; *British Trench Warfare 1917-1918*, The Imperial War Museum in association with the Battery Press, 1997: pp. 46 (both), 48; Martin Middlebrook, *The First Day on the Somme*, Penguin, 1971: p. 63 (© Leo Vernon and adapted); *Blighty*, 1916, reprinted by The Imperial War Museum, 1997: pp. 133, 153, 221 (top); Advertising Archive: pp. 137, 148; Imperial War Museum: p. 175 (HU 63253).

The endpaper photographs were taken by Private William Smallcombe and are used courtesy of Dr and Mrs Smallcombe. All the half-tone images were supplied by the author, except where otherwise credited.

The publishers have made every effort to contact the copyright owners of the illustrations. Where they have been unsuccessful, they invite copyright holders to contact them direct.

THE TRENCH

INTRODUCTION

There is a photograph in the Imperial War Museum that shows men retreating from an attack made on a village called Beaumont Hamel. It was taken on 1 July 1916 and shows the aftermath of the unsuccessful attempt to seize the German trenches and the village. On the photograph, it is clear that while the men are still in full view of the heavily armed German defenders, they are walking or at best jogging back. Why were they not running? Under fire, within easy range of both rifle and machine gun, one would have thought these men would tear back at full speed. It was a question that perturbed me for several years until last July, when, dressed in the full battle order of a Great War soldier, with a helmet, an extra bandolier of ammunition, a rifle and a water bottle to carry, I was invited to run about for a couple of minutes in the cool evening air. I was, while not exhausted, certainly very tired. On 1 July 1916, these men had attacked on a warm sunny morning over two or three hundred yards, had fought, possibly hand-to-hand, while heavily laden, and then been forced to retire. I had been taught a good lesson. The physical exertions these men had undertaken, regardless of the energy used up in nervous tension or the adrenalin coursing through their bodies, was the reason why they were walking. They couldn't have done anything else.

It was a group of historians known as the Khaki Chums who had lent me the kit. When I met them, they had been marching for three or four days around the Somme Battlefield, sleeping out at night, living, as far as it is now possible to live, the experience of the First World War soldier. These men, from all walks of life, get together at different times of the year and travel to France and Belgium using only authentic kit, right down to the watches on their wrists and the laces in their boots. On every trip they have learnt new things about Kitchener's army, and how they managed to survive. Veterans' experiences are fascinating, but veterans have rarely been asked about the minutiae of daily existence. Contemporary training manuals are detailed and specific but, equally, they never reveal, without experience, the corners that can be cut, the improvements made from trial and error, or the simple utilization of common sense and intelligence to overcome problems. Figures collated by the army show in cold fact how it was supplied with water, but statistics are often hard to comprehend. But when twenty-four Khaki Chums consume forty gallons of water on one hot sunny day, then, to my mind, that is a far better insight into the problems of supplying an army of two million men in 1916.

For better or worse, the Great War has become a prolific

industry. More than a quarter of a million people now make pilgrimages to the battlefields of Ypres, the Somme, Arras and Mons, underlining the public's fascination with a war fast receding into history. And it is not just the middle-aged or elderly who visit France and Belgium. Our secondary schools ferry busloads of children over to see the sites, bringing home to those who study the events of the past that the war is not just national curriculum History but a part of their heritage, too.

Perhaps when eight-year-old Simon Barraclough gets his chance to visit the battlefields in five or six years' time, he too will see where his own ancestor served. It is not his great-great-grandfather, nor even his great-grandfather who fought, but his grandfather. Arthur Barraclough, wounded three times in action, is alive and aged 104. He may just be on hand to offer some tips on what to look for when his grandson makes his pilgrimage. Arthur Halestrap, born in 1898, still visits the battlefields. Last October, he was sitting enjoying a cup of coffee in a café when a tour group arrived. Arthur was ignored until he pointed out that he was a hundred years older than one three-year-old who was running around. The response was interesting and immediate: reserved and respectful gawping, as the whisper circulated. It proves that history is never quite as distant as it sometimes appears to be.

Given the heightened awareness of the First World War, it was hardly surprising that, when news leaked out that the BBC had decided to make a documentary series about life in a trench, there would be frantic press speculation as to how this would be portrayed. The war still pushes deep-seated buttons in the public psyche. There was understandable concern that this would, in some way, belittle the experience of the real First World War soldier, trivializing the suffering.

Some First World War veterans have reservations about the series, but intend to watch and judge the programme on its merits. Harry Patch, veteran of the Duke of Cornwall's Light Infantry, who lost three friends during the fighting around Ypres in 1917, agreed to be filmed for the series but eloquently voiced his concerns on camera. 'You can make the programme, you can imitate a shell burst by a thunderclap firework, but unless you have been there, you will never create the fear and apprehension we had about being hit by shrapnel. You can make them dirty, you can give them all the lice you want, give them all the water tasting of petrol. You can improvise everything, except the fear.'

Royal Engineer veteran Arthur Halestrap, while agreeing that mortal fear can never be reproduced, was more up-beat about the programme and its aims. 'Not only am I encouraged but I feel very grateful to the men for putting up with it all and volunteering, giving their time to let other people know what was happening to their forebears, for their good. What we did was for the benefit of posterity and posterity is modern life. I have no reservations whatever about the programme, in fact I would applaud it because it is trying to represent to people what we would tell them by mouth. It is a picture to them, as from a book, a living illustration of what happened. And if it causes people to think, then so much the better, and that will be the object of it, to make people think.'

There are natural sensitivities in making a programme about

warfare, and there are many justified concerns. One million British and Commonwealth soldiers died in the war in great suffering and often alone. To try to replicate the suffering of the seriously wounded, the moans and screams of the dying, or to recreate the fear of those who survived would be impossible and reprehensible.

No-one can replicate mortal fear, and the aim never was to try to do so. The objective was to portray, with all the inevitable generalizations, restrictions and modifications, life in the line during a quiet period before a major offensive began. There could and would be no fighting.

But there was still much else to learn about life in the trenches. As Taff Gillingham, one of the Khaki Chums, puts it: 'Detractors would say that we do not experience the fear, but it was never about that. This is about the everyday life, the trials and tribulations of the soldier. You get up, it's pouring with rain, your blanket's soaked, your tunic's soaked, you can't get your Tommy cooker alight so you can't get a warm cup of tea – all that everyday stuff which, when experienced for real, is as good a way as any of gaining an in-depth knowledge of the soldier as a subject.'

Arthur Halestrap, who had been a signaller in the Royal Engineers, travelled to France and visited the trench a couple of days before filming and gave it his seal of approval. This gave the location a credibility that would have been lost had the producers waited to make the series until all the veterans had passed on. To miss the input of old soldiers would have been an opportunity gone for ever, and who was to say that they did not wish to make their contribution? While many have spoken on camera about the great battles in which they took part, until now most have talked less about the day-to-day activities, such as wiring parties, trench revetting, eating and sleeping. The image of soldiers going over the top is one of the most enduring of the First World War. But in reality, many thousands of soldiers never saw, or rarely saw, a German (except as prisoners), let alone climbed a ladder and advanced across no man's land. Most soldiers' lives revolved around a routine of going in and out of the front, support, reserve or rear trenches, during which time days and weeks on end would be filled with the monotonous repetition of carefully prescribed rules and regulations, from cleaning equipment to carrying supplies up to the line. Now stories of the veterans' 'normal' activities gave focus to the experiences of the men who volunteered for the documentary; sometimes comparisons could be made that, for the first time, brought to life the daily routines of the trenches.

I have quoted from interviews, conducted over many years, with the following veterans, of whom, sadly, only one, Smiler Marshall, is still alive: Frederick Francis, Joe Yarwood, Norman Collins, Ted Francis, Walter Popple, Richard Hawkins, Smiler Marshall, Ernest Ford, William Smallcombe, Walter Green, Jack Rogers, Hal Kerridge, Ben Clouting, Fred Tayler, Bill Eaton, and nurse Marjorie Grigsby. Wherever possible, I have let their families know about the use of quotations; where I have not been able to trace their relatives, I have used the veterans' words in the hope that their families will be pleased to keep their memory alive.

In this book, I have presented snapshots of life in a First World War trench, but it would be a mistake to see these incidents as necessarily representative of the whole war, or the entire Western Front. Standards and practice changed as tactics evolved and new weapons were developed. but, as far as possible, I have presented evidence of life in 1916, with back-up, where it is needed. from earlier or later years. As tactics changed, not least in response to enemy developments, so the life of the men necessarily changed too; there is no definitive history. Some aspects of 1916 warfare have had to be glossed over for reasons of space but I hope that this book will give a personal picture of life in the trenches.

RICHARD VAN EMDEN, DECEMBER 2001

CHAPTER ONE

RECRUITMENT AND TRAINING

The documentary's original remit was to find and name each man in a platoon (sixty men), drawn from one of the hundreds of Kitchener battalions formed in 1914. The volunteers who had joined up in the war's first months would then be shadowed by new volunteers drawn from the same geographical area and of similar ages. These 2001 volunteers would be interviewed, trained and then sifted down to a final twenty-four men who would be taken to France. There they would take over a trench system specially built for the filming of the documentary series. A pre-ferred date was October or early November 1916, a period roughly mid-way through the war.

Finding such an infantry unit was not straightforward. There were two initial problems: first, it was conceived that the battalion should still be reasonably intact, in other words that most of the original battalion would still be serving with their unit in October 1916. As almost every division serving on the Western Front had been through the maelstrom of the Somme Battle, very few would still retain their original complement of men. Second, very few platoons had ever been listed. It is true that many battalions had, on the eve of going to France, published their own muster rolls of men. However, these were usually broken down into company strength, 250 men, and not into the four platoons that make up a company.

In the end, the unit chosen for the series was the 10th Battalion of the East Yorkshire Regiment. The 10th Battalion was the first of four Kitchener units raised in Hull in 1914, to be collectively known as the Hull Pals. The battalion did not arrive on the Western Front until March 1916 and, although due to go over the top on 1 July as part of the Somme offensive, it was held back owing to the disastrous attack made by neighbouring units. This lucky escape was compounded when the whole brigade was removed from the line for refitting. They were to play only a minor role in the Somme Battle until late October. As a result the 10th Battalion was one of the very few Kitchener units to have remained largely intact throughout the Somme Battle. Furthermore, recent books on the Pals, most notably David Bilton's seminal record of the four battalions, called *The Hull Pals*, enabled the programme creators to collate, through his exacting research, the names of a group of men from 16 Platoon in D Company. As this unit re-entered the line in late October 1916, a closer fit to the criteria required for the men of the proposed trench seemed unlikely.

*

At around 7.30 p.m. on the evening of Sunday 30 August, 1914, the telephone rang in the home of a well-respected Hull business-man, Major William H. Carver. It was the Lord Lieutenant of the East Riding, Lord Nunburnholme, who had just returned from London where he had had a meeting with Lord Kitchener, the Secretary of State for War. In the light of the outbreak of war a new army would be needed, a civilian army made up of volunteers, and Lord Nunburnholme had been charged with rais-ing the first service battalion in his home city of Hull.

Major Carver was the obvious person to call. Not only was he a personal friend of Lord Nunburnholme but, with the advent of war, the forty-six-year-old had just been recommissioned into the army after serving seventeen years in the militia. 'Lord Nunburnholme asked me if I would start the battalion,' recalled Major Carver years later. 'It was a request that rather over-whelmed me at first.' He was told he was to be the 'commanding officer, adjutant, quartermaster – everything, in fact, until a com-mencement was made'. Anxious that his services should be used to the full, Carver readily agreed to start work the following day on building the new battalion, to be known as the 7th (Hull) Battalion, East Yorkshire Regiment, later to be re-christened as the 10th Battalion, East Yorkshire Regiment.

'My father, while he was never a regular soldier, was always a soldier at heart,' recalls Major Carver's 102-year-old daughter, Patricia Wilson. 'Many years earlier, he had been about to go into the army but then, just before the all-important interview, he had got measles and was very ill. When he eventually recovered, he chose instead to join his brother in the family importation business in Hull. Nevertheless, my father was quite sure that there would be a war, and when Lord Nunburnholme rang, he was more than keen to help, so much so that he walked out of his business and became a soldier. He got on very well with his brother and, of course, he understood perfectly.'

The following day in Hull, posters were printed and placed strategically around the city, inviting men of a commercial background, such as clerks, grocers, drapers, and artisans, to enlist. This targeted appeal to the middle classes was deliberate. In the first weeks of the war, recruitment to the army had been slow, and a debate began in the local press as to the reason. A letter signed 'Middle Class' was sent to the *Hull Daily Mail*, stating that men of that standing in society had refrained from enlisting for the simple reason that they wished to consort with men of a similar background. They did not want to be herded into a battalion in which they would be as one with men of a lower order. Such snobbery, as we would see it today, was not limited to the middle classes of Hull, but was typical of that generation of men across the highly stratified class system that was Britain in 1914. The 12th Battalion of the Gloucestershire regiment (the 'Bristol's Own') had similarly appealed for men of the mercantile and professional classes to form their battalion. The 12th Battalion of the York and Lancaster Regiment was also made up of the elite of Sheffield and was known as its 'City' battalion. Across the country, other battalions were being formed, each of 1,000 men, including battalions of civil servants, stockbrokers, artists, and even simply of former public-school boys.

O.H.M.S.

IT has been suggested to me that there are many men, such as Clerks and others, engaged in commercial business, who wish to serve their KING and COUNTRY, and would be willing to enlist in the New Army if they felt assured that they would be serving with their own friends, and not put into Battalions with unknown men as their companions.

EARL KITCHENER has sanctioned the raising of a Hull Battalion which would be composed of the classes mentioned, and in which a man could be certain that he would be among his own friends.

THE CONDITIONS OF SERVICE WILL BE THE SAME AS IN OTHER BATTALIONS IN THE REGULAR ARMY.

The New Battalion will be 1000 strong, and will be named the

7TH (HULL) BATTALION EAST YORKSHIRE REGIMENT.

Those who wish to serve in it will be enrolled, enlisted and clothed at the WENLOCK BARRACKS, HULL. Recruiting will commence from 10 a.m. on TUESDAY, 1st SEPTEMBER. For the present, Recruits joining will be billeted in their own homes.

I shall be glad to receive the names of ex-Officers who will help in the above work until the Officers have been appointed to the Battalion.

Major W. H. CARVER has been temporarily appointed Acting Adjutant for the Battalion at Wenlock Barracks.

GOD SAVE THE KING.

NUNBURNHOLME
LORD LIEUTENANT, E. YORKS.

The recruiting poster calling for those in 'commercial business' to enlist in one of the new Kitchener Battalions. This poster was distributed around Hull a day before Major Carver started recruiting at Wenlock Barracks on 1 September 1914.

In response to the letter the *Hull Daily Mail* felt compelled to comment. There was a simple and logical rationale, the paper argued: 'It must not be thought there is a desire for class distinction but, just as the docker will feel more at home amongst his every-day mates, so the wielder of the pen and drawing pencil will be better as friends together.'

Given the homogeneity of these battalions, it was felt that *esprit de corps* was almost guaranteed. No matter what the individual's social standing, there was a right battalion to fit, where men could enlist together from their places of work, knowing that they would not be split up or forced to mix with men from other classes. Nicknames reflecting the clientele of the unit quickly followed, and the 10th East Yorks became known as the Hull Commercials, while the second and third battalions raised subsequently in Hull were called the Tradesmen and the Sportsmen. The last of the four Hull Pals battalions to be formed was more of a hotchpotch of volunteers and wished on themselves the appropriate title of 'T'others'.

Just twenty-four hours after the posters had been printed, Major Carver left home for Wenlock Barracks, Anlaby Road, Hull. The date was Tuesday 1 September, 1914, and the first group of civilians waited outside the barracks to enlist in the British Army. 'I asked if I could go with him,' remembers Carver's daughter, 'and I can see them now: there were about twenty or thirty men waiting for him to arrive, so they could enlist. They were standing outside the door and I remember that my father was very pleased to see there were at least some men waiting to be signed up.'

In fact recruitment was so brisk that attestation forms ran out, forcing Major Carver to print more for fear of losing recruits if he waited for replacements to be sent. By the end of the first day, around seven hundred men had enlisted, not just from Hull, but from local towns such as Bridlington, Beverley, Withernsea and Hornsea. On the following day, Wednesday, Carver found he had enough recruits to form the battalion, enabling recruitment to stop and training to start.

Several retired army officers and NCOs volunteered their assistance, although, as Patricia Wilson recalls, her father had also 'roped in other members of the family, a nephew, two or three cousins, as well as friends, to supply the officers, including his nephew R. B. Carver, Gerry Wilson – a cousin – and John Harrison-Broadley, who was a neighbour and friend.' They were just the first of twenty thousand Hull men who came forward to enlist in the first six months of the war.

While the names of 16 Platoon, D Company, were known, it was important that the new volunteers of 2001 were oblivious to the fact that they would be following in the footsteps of actual men. According to BBC adverts placed in the local press, the programme was no more specific than that men from the Hull area were being encouraged to enlist as 10th Battalion volunteers. While avoiding any potential play acting, it was still important to maintain the link between the men of today and those of 1916. Our new volunteers would keep their own names, but, unknown to them, would adopt the rank and number of a man in the chosen battalion so, for example, Kitchener volunteer Private Smith,

10/1123 of the 10th Battalion, would be shadowed by our 2001 volunteer Private Jones 10/1123. Their destinies in the series would be inextricably linked. If Private Smith was killed in October 1916, then our Private Jones would be 'killed', although in Jones' case his death would simply be effected by a permanent removal from the trench. Giving expert advice and material support, and joining the volunteers as NCOs and officers to provide encouragement and practical assistance, would be a group of the Khaki Chums.

Notices were placed in the press and a feature was broadcast on 'Calendar', the regional television news report. Recruitment was restricted to those who lived in Hull or the East Riding of Yorkshire, disappointing the scores of willing volunteers who had applied from across Britain, after reading speculative reports on the programmes' content in the press.

The recruitment hall at Wenlock Barracks, used to sign up the original Hull Pals in August 1914, was used again, with volunteers requested to turn up and enlist on what was coincidentally the eighty-seventh anniversary of the outbreak of war, on Saturday 4 August, 2001. The recruitment hall was open between 10 a.m. and 2 p.m., during which time 156 men aged between nineteen and thirty-eight arrived. Details were written down, whilst a simple physical exercise was undertaken, as much to keep the volunteers occupied as for the producers to see who was hopelessly unfit.

Before further selection could be made, each volunteer was asked questions about his interest in the war and if any family member had served. Motivation was important in helping to weed out those, such as professional actors, who misunderstood the aim of the production as some sort of theatre rather than as a documentary. All the volunteers had to be able to get a minimum of four weeks off work, although all would be compensated for loss of earnings with a basic wage somewhat greater than the shilling-a-day earned by the Kitchener's men of 1914. Lastly, doctor's certificates were required from each recruit, clearing him medically not just for service at 'the front' but also for the strenuous training schedule the men would go through with serving army physical training instructors.

On 8 October forty-four volunteers arrived at Vimy Barracks, part of Catterick Army Camp, for three days of physical training with regular soldiers. The Khaki Chums, who were to take over training for seven days from 11 October, were keen that the army should not attempt to teach any drill, as this differed greatly from that practised in 1914. Quite apart from the fact that in World War One men marched in ranks of four, as opposed to three today, the purpose of marching itself has largely changed. In the First World War, marching was a way of getting a body of men from A to B. As transport improved through the century, so marching has become more a matter of ceremony, glossier even: arms swing higher, and there is a great deal more stamping of feet than was ever the case in 1914.

Rising early in the morning has not changed. Up at 5.30 a.m., the volunteers were split into five groups of nine. For the next three days, each group was given constant fitness tests in order to root out any faint-hearts as well as to give others the chance to opt out of the programme altogether on the basis that such training 'was not, on reflection, for them'. As might have been expected, the physical exercises revealed a significant disparity in fitness, the number of press-ups achieved in two minutes, for example, varying from around ten to sixty, but those sergeants who took control of training were genuinely impressed by the resolve of almost everyone to fight on, regardless of fitness. Running in army boots, wearing helmets and overalls, was very hard work although, in the end, only one person dropped out during the course. This volunteer had once served in the forces and found that his ability to subject himself to the will of an army sergeant had worn thin in the intervening years of civilian life.

As well as undertaking assault courses and steeplechases, the volunteers were given basic map reading, rifle drill and command tests to discover who might have the aptitude to lead. The tests, both physical and mental, were useful in bringing out the characters of the volunteers, and, although by the evening of the third day forty-three men were still in the running, picking those who should go was, in the end, easier than anticipated. On the morning of the fourth day, nineteen men were cut from the list, leaving a final twenty-four who were handed over to the Khaki Chums. The level of disappointment amongst those who had not been chosen was, however, appreciable, five volunteering to be reserves should they be needed.

The final twenty-four volunteers of 2001, unlike their forebears the Hull Commercials, came from a wide range of occupations. Some were from traditional jobs, a gardener, two printers, a taxi driver, a surveyor, a student, a fireman, a city councillor, a furniture restorer, as well as a sprinkling of 'new' occupations such as a telecommunications engineer, an IT engineer, and a graphic designer. Two were unemployed. Eleven were married, and thirteen were single.

The volunteers of 2001 were very different in physique from their counterparts of eighty-seven years ago. Since 1914, the average height of a British man has increased from around five foot five inches to five foot eleven inches. In the first month of the war, the minimum height for enlistment was five foot three, rapidly raised to five foot six in order to stem the flow of recruits. Only two of our twenty-four recruits would have had any problems enlisting with that new height, while the majority might well have been directed to the Guards Regiments, which tended to take men of greater height. Of those who volunteered in 1914, only thirty-four per cent were graded '1', as men of good to satisfactory health. Arthur Barraclough, one of thirteen children and a hairdresser before the war, weighed under eight stone and had flat feet when he enlisted in 1916 on his eighteenth birthday. The original volunteers of 1914 were often so undernourished that their average height and weight increased by as much as two inches and several pounds during the year's training before embarkation to France. As Field Marshal Sir William Robertson is reputed to have said about the British Army, 'We have always had compulsory service, the compulsion of hunger.' By contrast, very few of our volunteers were rejected for any physical disabilities other than perhaps being too well fed.

Of the twenty-four volunteers, fourteen were six foot or taller, and only six were between five foot four and five foot nine, the approximate heights one would have expected of the Kitchener volunteers of 1914. As one might anticipate, there were great variations in the physical attributes of the men of 2001. Chest size varied from 34 to 48 inches, shoe size, from six to twelve, waists varied from 29 to 42 inches. As far as weight was concerned, the heaviest volunteer weighed over twice the lightest, 16½ stone to a slight eight stone, although the average weight was around a trim 12 to 13 stone, underlining the fact that, as the army had found during physical training, many of the volunteers had kept themselves reasonably fit and well.

Lastly, the age of our men was on average significantly higher than that of the Kitchener volunteers. Their average age, 31.8 years, was more akin to that of the pre-war regular army that had gone to France in the first weeks of the war than those who enlisted in the heady months of September and October 1914.

Sadly, none of our volunteers had a relative in the 10th Battalion, although six had had a grandfather or great-uncle in the East Yorkshire Regiment. One of the volunteers, Steven Spivey, had two grandfathers, Arthur Spivey and Edward Jackson, who had served in the 8th and 7th Battalions of the East Yorkshire Regiment. Arthur was a Kitchener volunteer who had served at the front, but he had eventually been sent home, as his occupation as a skilled shipbuilder meant he was more needed in the yards than at the front. Edward Jackson had served in France until he was killed in the last week of the war, on 4 November 1918. Steven had no doubts about volunteering. 'I wanted to say thank you, as well as finding out just a little bit about what he had been through.'

Another volunteer, thirty-one-year-old Nick Skelton, equally had no doubts about enlisting. A maintenance surveyor from Hull, married with one child, he had relatives who had also served in the East Yorkshire Regiment at Gallipoli. A member of the Western Front Association, an organization devoted to the study of the First World War, he was keen to find out what life in a trench would be like. Although missing his wife and one-year-old child, his determination to stick the regime at Catterick and in France was based on a belief that failure would be paying scant respect to the men who had fought eighty-five years before.

The training at Catterick was overseen by Allen Prior, a Khaki Chum with a specialist knowledge of Army instruction during the Great War. He organized the teaching of the drill, the musketry and the bayonet. It was just as important to learn the personal administration side: how to look after yourself. The volunteers were shown how to put their puttees on, how best to fill their large packs with their kit, how to clean their cap badges, and then while they were doing that, they were given a lecture on the unit's history. Then they were shown the classics of soldier survival, such as how to soap their socks to prevent blisters, or how to strop a razorblade on a belt or on the palm of your hand to give an edge to it. Experience gained and research done by the Chums was handed on. As Allen Prior explained: 'There are all sorts of little things you can do to make life more comfortable but it does require you to be switched on all the time. When you are living in a trench you don't have the luxuries, everything takes a long time, which is why they will find their day fills up very quickly, because getting up, finding water to have a cup of tea, to wash, to shave takes up to five times as long as it would normally. You don't have water on tap, you have to find it, you've got to heat it, which means building a fire, which means finding fuel, which means lighting it.

'They may well be thinking, "What will we do during the other twelve hours of darkness?" They'll find out that a fire pit has to be dug, the fuel has to be found, you have to get it lit and kept alight. You have to send sentries out, you have to find places to sleep, scrapes in the trench wall to be dug, a latrine pit to dig, there is a lot of work involved. You've got to look after yourself, your rifle, your feet, and you've got to be all packed up again in the morning.'

Kitting out the volunteers was a mammoth undertaking and was achieved in a little over four weeks, start to finish. Specific measurements could not be taken until the final selection, and with such a great differential in sizes, the fitting of uniforms was never going to be more than approximate. They looked, on first wearing, like sacks of potatoes, until accurate measurements were taken, leaving some of the Khaki Chums, experts at reproducing authentic-looking uniforms, to tailor into the night to turn sacks into Hull Pals.

The Chums and their friends and relatives across the country also worked all hours to make everything from mess-tin covers to helmet liners and complete sets of 1914 pattern leather equipment. Shoulder titles had to be cast in brass, while the soldiers' boots were purchased en masse from former army stores, an Ipswich cobbler returning to the roots of his trade as he hammered hundreds of hobnails into the soles. A few items were found in military warehouses, including brand new Second World War army underpants that are almost identical to those worn in the Great War – and just as uncomfortable.

The volunteers were then introduced to the equipment that they would have to carry and that would, they hoped, sustain them in the trench. In their haversack, there would be one iron ration consisting of meat preserve, biscuit, cheese, groceries in tins and meat extract. Together with the uniform, the whole weight was considered in 1914 to be 62lb 5oz. But that was before the soldiers were issued with steel helmets, gas helmets; unlike their predecessors in 1916, the first soldiers to arrive in France wouldn't have been carrying wire cutters, hand grenades, general service shovels and extra ammunition. The bullets alone would weigh another 5lb.

In the end some items were delivered to Catterick literally a matter of hours before they were due to be issued; nevertheless, in the nick of time, each man was given every item of clothing, equipment, and weaponry that he would have been issued with in 1916.

Any headaches over supply helped put the inevitable teething problems during training into perspective. Discipline had to be maintained and the volunteers knew that the Chums were, with one exception, no more soldiers than they were. The exception was Captain Robert Yuill, a Light Infantry signalling officer currently serving with the Royal Green Jackets. In the trench, he would serve as a lieutenant. Otherwise, civilians in First World War uniforms were to lead other civilians, and in time on y respect for the Chums' knowledge of, and passion for, the details of the subject would earn obedience and allegiance.

When the uniforms were issued, the men were told to bag up

their own civilian clothes and leave them in a room from where they would be sent home, just as the army would expect a man to do. The texture of khaki uniforms is rough, and even without lice (the bane of a front line soldier's life) the uniforms are exceptionally itchy in comparison with modern clothes. The desire to change back into their civilian clothes at the end of the day was intense, and indeed the programme lost one volunteer unwilling to continue. But every twenty-first-century device was jettisoned. Even authentic-looking cigarettes, minus the filters, were brought into the camp. Apart from the modern barracks they slept in at Catterick and the food served in the mess hall, the men in every other respect returned to 1914.

In 1914, of course, this would be just the start of a long period of instruction. Basic pre-war military training took around seven weeks, although it took twelve months to fully train an infantryman. It took even longer to become a consummate professional, with proficiency pay awarded as skills were honed over time. During the war, most of Kitchener's New Army divisions, although by no means all, received at least a year's training. Training was cut according to the need for troops and how battle-ready the divisions were believed to be. After the disastrous offensive at Neuve Chapelle and the fighting around Ypres in April 1915, the 9th, 12th and 14th Kitchener Divisions found themselves in France within nine months of their formation. In the Battle of Loos in September, the 9th Division was pressed into service for the first time and suffered heavily, losing 5,480 men killed or wounded, nearly half the division's fighting strength.

The methodology of training men during the war remained remarkably unchanged, even if the content, in terms of tactics, gradually evolved. Basic training required the breaking of the new recruit's will so that in time he would obey orders automatically. To an extent, humiliation was used, soldiers being verbally assailed by a litany of derogatory remarks, although the men were never physically assaulted. Likewise, the constant repetition of drill reinforced obedience, as did the unending rotation of fatigues in which cleaning, scrubbing and polishing were of primary concern. Privates were not the only ones to receive such 'management'; officer cadets were put through their paces, too, as one volunteer in the Seaforth Highlanders, Norman Collins, described in a letter home in 1916. 'We are always scrubbing floors, forming fours etc, doing 160 paces per minute on the square, brushing boots every hour from 5 a.m. until 7.30 p.m. when we are free to write up notes until 9.30 p.m. We are called miscellaneous names by sergeants who know nothing, it is a dog's life and several cadets from the firing line want to go back to the front.'

At the outbreak of the war the British Expeditionary Force had left for France, leaving few serving soldiers at home to train the new Kitchener Army. In these circumstances, training was undertaken by retired NCOs and officers, many of whom had not been in the army since the Boer War. Drill and tactics were outmoded and it was only when wounded men returned from France, unfit for further front line service, that a new body of men became available to teach 1914 drill and to disseminate ideas and tactics learnt from the battlefield during 1915.

To an extent, 1915 was a year of muddle and adjustment. The British Army had had to adapt to the new industrial war at a time when, ironically, it was short of artillery shells, severely hampering offensive operations. Only the following year, after the catastrophe of the first day of the Somme Battle, were lessons learnt quickly, so that, as early as the middle of July 1916, attacks were being launched under the protective cover of darkness. At the end of the battle, the information gained from fighting was collated in a series of training manuals. For the first time the infantry section was broken down into four distinct parts – rifle bombers, Lewis gunners, bombers and riflemen – each with a clearly defined role. In action, these men would now advance in a diamond formation rather than in a line. These new training methods were introduced in England in early 1917 and were used during training at Catterick with the volunteers of 2001.

By mid-1916, new volunteers were given around six months' training before they were sent to France, usually as soon as they reached the minimum age (nineteen) to serve overseas. Andrew Bowie, a private in the Cameron Highlanders, received six months' training, as did Harry Patch of the Duke of Cornwall's Light Infantry; Arthur Barraclough, who arrived at the front in January 1917, had only four months. For those requiring technical instruction, such as Royal Engineer Arthur Halestrap, training could last much longer, in his case, as he was a signaller, upwards of fourteen months. Equally, should a particular skill be needed at the front, a man could find himself posted overseas almost immediately. One veteran recalls that he enlisted on 7 April 1915, disembarked at Rouen eleven days later and found himself in the

Ypres Salient in May, never having fired a rifle. His confession that he knew how to drive a motor vehicle ensured his rapid departure to France and to a staff car.

By 1918 when the shortage of soldiers became critical, the age at which a soldier could be sent to the front was cut to just eighteen years and six months. After the German offensive in March, boys were sent into the line often with as little as three months' training; the rest would have to be learnt by experience, most of which was hard, bloody and often short.

It was not the aim for the volunteers of 2001 to replicate wartime training. Nevertheless the Chums did what they could to recreate the feeling of camp life in 1914–16. In every army, subsuming the individual into the collective is one of the cornerstones to building a cohesive unit. Part of the methodology has always been the constant frustration and harassment of recruits, keeping them busy, always giving men just that little bit less time than they feel they need, engendering discipline through routine. In the short time available the Chums in charge of training did what they could not only to pass on practical advice that might help the volunteers 'catch up' with their forebears, but also to recreate those same routines. 'For Church Parade on Sunday,' explained one volunteer, 'all you need is your belt, so you've got to take all this webbing off; and then next thing you hear is "Right, battle order" and you put it all on again, and it's all set for you, so when you get your greatcoat on, you need to adjust the belt. And they're not just easily adjusted, you have to take the belt off to widen it if you've got a greatcoat on, but then if you've got your tunic on, you need it just a little bit smaller. It's just so annoying. Of course it's all "Come on, quick, quick, quick, you're on parade in two minutes, rush, rush, rush." What's our section motto? "Rush, rush, wait, wait, wait." They're always rushing you, and you rush like mad to get it all done, you get it all in the bag and you rush outside and then you're stood there for about twenty minutes, thinking, "I could have spent another ten minutes on my backpack."'

Initially sorting out the webbing caused the most problems. 'When we had to do the webbing, we were all panicking. Which bit goes where? It was a nightmare – what does this do? Where does this buckle go? And some of the states of the webbing when we came on parade was just diabolical. It's so funny when someone's getting a bollocking and you want to laugh but you can't.

'Getting dressed – you don't think about it now,' the volunteer commented later. 'You just do it, that's where we've become most competent. The rifles became second nature, you know just what to do, how to fill it, how to get it clean, how to strip it, how to put it back together. The webbing, that was the hardest part, everybody's was such a sham, straps round your neck and back-packs round your behind.'

Subjugating the individual will to the collective *esprit de corps* in one week was nigh impossible. However, the constant reinforcement of daily routines, drill, route marching and cleaning, made plausible soldiers that impressed even the regular army NCOs. The real test would be France and living outdoors, and there was little doubt amongst the regular NCOs that the men would fail. 'They will snap like twigs,' was their parting comment.

*

Typical of the Kitchener units that were springing up right across the country, the Hull Commercials initially had neither uniforms nor rifles. Only squad drill on the local fair ground and route marches were possible, all conducted in civilian clothes with only armbands to signify enlistment. The battalion was searched for anyone with previous military training, indeed for anyone who had the slightest knowledge of any drill whatsoever. In the end, 120 men with some experience were made NCOs in order to teach the rudiments of drill, which they themselves struggled hard to recall.

Everything was being done on an *ad hoc* basis, the officers and men returning to sleep at home or in local lodgings. The spirit of amateurism was alive, fostering some humorous incidents which were recorded for posterity – such as one 'historic' occasion noted in the battalion's War History, when, as the rain began to fall during a route march, one recruit carefully unfurled his umbrella.

The training of the Kitchener recruits was largely left to those who had formed the battalions, although, as Major Carver had never held a regular commission, it was only a matter of time before the War Office sent an ex-regular officer to take command. On 12 September the then fifty-two-year-old Lieutenant-Colonel Richardson arrived to take over. Major Carver stepped down to second-in-command, handing over, as he did so, the battalion's only horse – lent by Lord Nunburnholme in the first place – so that Lieutenant-Colonel Richardson could address the men. 'Gentlemen,' he is reputed to have begun. It was a reflection of the social standing of those under his command that during the war as many as a quarter of the battalion's original complement took commissions.

Throughout September and October, the battalion continued to train locally, practising skirmishing and outpost duty, as well as the usual drill and physical training. On 3 October the four Hull Pals battalions, numbering four thousand men in all, were marched around the city of Hull for the first time, to everyone's pride and delight.

Khaki uniforms and leather equipment arrived in stages from early November, just prior to a move to Hornsea on the east coast. Rumours of a German landing brought about the sudden move, although with no rifles to fire – indeed with next to no musketry training whatsoever – the battalion would have had little more than their enthusiasm with which to repel the enemy. On arrival at Hornsea the rumours turned out to be just gossip, and the men were moved off to huts in a newly built camp perched on a cliff top. Here, on a mid-winter's night, the men waded through ankle-deep mud, guided to their accommodation by nothing more than the fitful light of a hurricane lamp. To their consternation they discovered that the huts were neither fully constructed nor equipped, many missing both doors and windows. For the next few nights, sixty soldiers were required to sleep in huts designed for thirty, while the men's first meal was resourcefully cooked in the camp's new latrine buckets. Little wonder, perhaps, that Patricia Wilson's mother 'soon went to Hornsea, where she took a house for my father. He came home each night, bringing his servant, Griffiths, who cleaned my father's uniform and generally proved himself useful around the place.'

It was symptomatic of the time that, although the battalion had managed to collect a few outdated rifles, they had but a few rounds of small arms ammunition for use strictly against the enemy. This inaction had been the cause of some concern, and Colonel Richardson sent a telegram to the War Office outlining his dissatisfaction. A reply from the War Office read 'Reference your . . . Report on efficiency of rifles', to which the Colonel made the celebrated reply: 'Reference your telegram . . . Rifles will certainly go off, doubtful which end.'

The lack of any fire-power was partially resolved in the closing days of 1914, as Major Carver recalled: 'We had no ammunition to expend upon the ranges, so with the help of Lord Nunburnholme some money was collected and ammunition bought, and on Christmas Day, 1914, the men had their first experience of trying to get a bull's eye.'

Throughout December 1914 the battalion remained on coastal duty. They endlessly patrolled the shoreline and learnt to dig trenches on the cliff tops, the results of which efforts were soon lost owing to the erosion of the shore by the sea. On 16 December there was a moment of considerable excitement when the troops clearly heard the German naval bombardment of the east coast towns of Scarborough, Whitby and Hartlepool: three cruisers opened fire on the towns without warning, causing much damage and a thousand casualties.

By early in the New Year training was stepped up as specialists such as signallers, machine gunners and stretcher bearers were selected. Company commanders were asked to recommend those NCOs capable of higher rank, while all those who had only been 'acting' NCOs now had their rank confirmed. Even so, in an attempt to ensure there was no lingering nepotism in the battalion, Colonel Richardson asserted that the qualifications to become an NCO demanded character, determination and good mental powers: 'The CO will recommend no-one who does not give proof of possessing the above, no matter how many employers, fathers, or grandmothers try to pull the strings.'

The 10th Battalion had clearly retained some of its parochialism. It was important that the men were imbued with the right attitudes, for within months the first of the New Army divisions would be heading for France, and Richardson expected his battalion to be among them. To get the men to the peak of fitness, route marches of between fifteen and twenty-five miles in full pack were common. There was even one march of thirty-two miles, resulting in 126 falling out en route, to the annoyance of Richardson, who pointed out that in 1910 the 1st Battalion of the Regiment had marched thirty-nine miles in one day with only one man failing to get back to barracks. It was soon noted that sick parades grew when a long march was planned, with those given M&D (medicine and duty) missing the route march as the battalion had already departed. To combat this, NCOs were left to await the medical officer's decision, swiftly gathering up those returned to duty and marching them rapidly out of barracks to catch up with the battalion on the road.

Despite the occasional grumbles, morale remained exceptionally high. In June the battalion marched from Hornsea to Ripon camp for advanced brigade and, for the first time, large-scale divisional training.

The four battalions of the Hull Pals had been designated the 92nd Infantry Brigade, the first of three consecutively numbered brigades in 31st Division. The other brigades included men from across Yorkshire and Lancashire, including battalions of the West Yorkshire Regiment, the York and Lancaster Regiment and the 11th East Lancashire Regiment, better known to posterity as the Accrington Pals. As a division, their collective future would be inextricably linked.

In early November 1915 the division was sent to Salisbury Plain for final training before posting overseas. Just before leaving they were addressed by Colonel Richardson who announced that, because of his age, there was little chance of his joining them in France. He was handing over temporary command once more to Major Carver. His training methods had been severe and, as the War History notes, 'apparently ruthless'. However, it was clear that Richardson had a great affection for the men under his command and in his final speech he proudly noted that in thirteen months of hard training there had been no desertions and only one court martial, stating that any man would be honoured and proud to command the battalion. He finished: 'Well, goodbye, gentlemen, and the best of luck.'

At Salisbury the battalion were finally able to rid themselves of their outdated rifles, being issued with the standard infantry weapon of the period, the Short Magazine Lee Enfield. Over the following weeks the battalion trained extensively on the plain, digging and occupying trenches, and relieving other units in the line, marching past Stonehenge on the way up to the 'front'. They also completed the final part of their General Musketry Course, while 'preparations were carried out with feverish energy', according to the War History. They were about to leave England for active service overseas, not to France, as all had expected, but to Port Said and Egypt. They would not reach the front line on the Somme until March 1916, when, as part of a division, they were to take part in the major new offensive planned for 1 July 1916.

CHAPTER TWO

THE TRENCH 1916 AND 2001

'The Germans had some wonderful dugouts but ours were a proper washout. There were plenty of times you went into the firing line and there were no dugouts at all and it was a case of digging a hole inside of a trench, so you could just sit inside if it were wet or cold.' Arthur Barraclough's memories are not exceptional. Talk to any surviving veteran who served on the Somme, and as like as not, he will tell you that German trench systems were far superior to his own. Their dugouts, he often marvels, were forty feet deep, with proper beds, gramophones, grandfather clocks, even wallpapered walls 'Our dugouts, compared to theirs, were like pig-sties,' noted one veteran. In places, perhaps too many places for Allied liking, this was true. The Germans had arrived on the Somme in late September 1914 and had begun to dig, and dig deep. They took the advantageous positions, which in reality meant the high ground, spending the next eighteen months constructing a massive underground world of deep trenches, interconnecting tunnels and dugouts. One veteran, Fred Francis of the Border Regiment, recalls the sensation when an enemy dugout was briefly visited. 'We went on a patrol one night and as we didn't get any prisoners the CO in charge said "We'll go back now." On the way two of our party got separated from us; they were too far away to the left, and when they got back they crawled through the barbed wire and let themselves down into the dugout. But to their amazement they'd let themselves down into the German dugouts and all the way through there was electric light. Anyway, they got out as quick as they could and got back to our lousy trenches.'

The Germans had built dugouts to last. They had no intention of going anywhere and had no desire to pursue expansionism in northern France, but merely to preserve the pre-war status quo by keeping the gains made during the Franco-Prussian War of 1870. As Germany was also fighting simultaneously against Russia, a holding strategy in the west was the best policy. If the Allies were ever going to shift them out of northern France, it was expected that they would have to expend great efforts on breaking heavily fortified and defended lines, where, at a couple of minutes' notice, the Germans could bring forward any number of reserves from underground to man the front line or support trenches.

In order to help the French shorten the breadth of frontage they had to hold, the British agreed to take over some of the line held by their Allies north of the River Somme. The French stayed south of the river so that when the time came the Allies could symbolically fight side by side. But when the British arrived in July and August 1915, that fight would still be a year away.

There had been skirmishing on the Somme. Mines blown under the German lines at La Boisselle, known collectively as the Glory Hole, are testament to limited, though occasional, violent action by the French in early 1915. But in essence the area was a quiet sector, allowing the Germans to complete their elaborate defensive preparations. These positions were finished when the British launched their preliminary week-long bombardment on 24 June 1916 to smash the German lines and leave, as was commonly said, 'not a rat alive'. When the British attacked on 1 July 1916, the rows of advancing infantry were largely broken owing to the intense machine gun fire from German soldiers who were anything but dead. The shrapnel shells had made a mess of the German trenches above ground, but most enemy soldiers had remained deep underground, safe, though driven half-mad by the unending noise. The first-day objective, the village of Serre, where the 10th Battalion East Yorks were due to attack, was not taken during the entire five-month offensive. It was given up without a shot being fired when the Germans retreated to the Hindenburg Line in February 1917.

The British trench system was less developed than the German, but this was not because they were technically less able, far from it. Drawings made by the Royal Engineers showed how scientific the whole business of trench construction became as the war dragged on. From the first scrapes made by the original members of the British Expeditionary Force in September and October 1914, through the isolated outposts which gradually

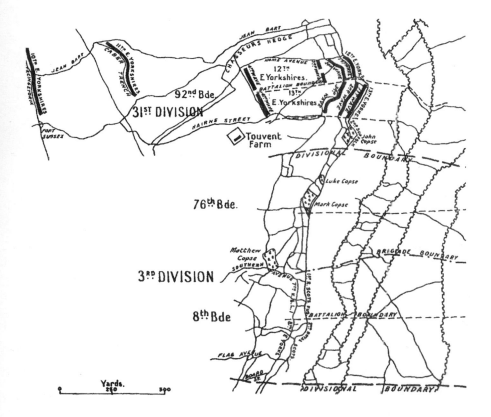

Opposing trench lines around the village of Serre prior to
the Hull Pals' attack, November 1916.

began to link together in the winter and spring months of 1914/15, to the complex interconnecting lines of trenches as seen on the Somme in 1916, the British trench system had evolved with great speed and imagination.

The difference in construction came not with relative abilities but with relative mentalities. While the Germans had dug deep anticipating the long haul, the French and, to a degree by implication of their alliance, the British grudgingly accepted 'war to the hilt'. French ground that could be held by the Allies should not be forfeited to the enemy or allowed to remain unoccupied. This led to the Allies taking positions that were geographically anything but strategic but had a psychological importance. The salients in front of Ypres and Verdun were held despite their position, where the enemy on the heights could shell the Allies on three sides. Trenches, too, were dug in compromising situations, enabling the Germans to look right down on to Allied positions. Such warfare by the French in particular was only slowly and reluctantly given up.

Conducting 'war to the hilt' meant that British and French troops were to all intents and purposes on an offensive footing at all times. Therefore the thinking went that there was never any reason to build dugouts similar to the Germans', as the next offensive would smash open the lines enabling a general advance to begin. Deep, cosy dugouts might encourage the British Tommy to become idle, and lose the spirit of the offensive. In the British manual of trench warfare published in 1917, this view that trenches were only a temporary position was maintained and fostered. Chapter One made the army's position crystal clear with the book's first heading, '1. TRENCH FIGHTING ONLY A PHASE OF WARFARE.' While acknowledging that trench construction had become highly technical, 'It must, nevertheless, be clearly understood that trench fighting is only a phase of operations, and that instruction in this subject, essential as it is, is only one branch of training troops. To gain a decisive success the enemy must be driven out of his defences and his armies crushed in the open.' The war could not be won by staying put. 'The aim of trench fighting is, therefore, to create a favourable situation for field operations, which the troops must be capable of turning to account.' Trenches were needed as a launch pad to further operations, a necessary evil leading to what would be a decisive war in the open.

The Germans and the Allies had had a war in the open, as widely conceived in their respective battle plans. The most famous, the German Schlieffen Plan, envisaged a rapid advance into France, through Belgium, ending in the encirclement of Paris and of the French armies, effectively ending the war within weeks. The French plan was a huge offensive, recapturing land lost in the war of 1870, at the same time delivering a massive defeat to the German army apparently on the basis of the élan of French soldiers and little else. The British, for their part, had an understanding that they would fight on the left flank of the French army in any European conflagration involving the likely enemy, Germany, although, improbable though it seems, some veterans recalled later that they were not entirely sure whom they were to fight, or indeed that they cared too much. They were all, however, ready.

In mid-August 1914, when the British Army arrived in Belgium, they had advanced by train and then on foot and had met the German army just outside the comfortable town of Mons. As a prelude to the battle, British cavalry had engaged their German counterparts in the open in a brief scrap in which the British sword had clashed with the German lance in a scene far more reminiscent of battles of one hundred years earlier. The following day, the units of the British Expeditionary Force fought a fierce engagement with advancing German soldiers on the edge of the town on either side of a canal. Sheer weight of enemy numbers forced the BEF to begin a famous retreat south, out of Belgium and into France, over the rivers Aisne and Marne to the east of Paris. This two hundred mile march was contested all the way, with cavalry units holding back to fight sharp engagements so as to give their comrades on foot the chance to get away. Only when the German forces swung away from taking Paris to follow the BEF south, did their lines of communication and supply become over-extended. A rapidly mobilized French army was driven from Paris in hastily requisitioned taxis, and attacked the Germans in their right flank. The audacious attack took the Germans by surprise and threatened to cut off their advancing forces, forcing them to retreat, firstly across the River Marne, and then the River Aisne, where they halted on the ridge above, known as the Chemin des Dames. Their plan to win a war quickly in the west had gone horribly awry, forcing the German First and Second Armies to dig in, creating simple earthworks in order to hold the heights. All sides were exhausted from participating in a rolling battle that had lasted for weeks.

Serious attempts to dislodge the Germans from the high ground continued until 18 September but it was soon realized that frontal assaults on a well-dug-in enemy were wasteful and that a flanking manoeuvre northwest might prove more fruitful. The Germans responded by moving troops to stop any attempt to get round the back, searching at the same time for a chance to out-flank the Allies. So began a series of moves that became known as the Race to the Sea, as both sides headed through northern France and back into Belgium, eventually ending up literally on the beach of a little town called Nieuport. With the French digging in to the south, a line had been created from the Belgium coast, all the way to the Swiss Alps, some 475 miles in all, along which millions of men would now face each other across a strip of barren, increas-ingly shell-pocked terrain – no man's land. The Race to the Sea had ended in October and was, in effect, the last mobile phase of the war until the late summer of 1918, when a combination of new British tactics and German exhaustion finally led to a decisive breach in the opposing lines.

In soldiers' parlance 'digging in' was a euphemism for not winning the war quickly. The early expectation of a war that would be 'over by Christmas' was not going to be fulfilled in 1914, although festive greetings sent to the soldiers at the front offered best wishes for a 'Victorious 1915', of which there seemed little doubt.

In 1914 it was easier to defend a position than it was to take it. As machine gun and rifle fire swept the open ground, frontal assaults proved futile and costly. All sides took the winter months off to take stock of the situation and devise new tactics to win the war. In the meantime, the men would have to dig in and learn how to live a new, static life. A whole culture, effectively 'trench life', grew out of the mud of Flanders and France, in which set routines and duties would be performed daily by soldiers of the line. In future, fresh battalions or new drafts sent out to the front would have to learn this life, often being sent to quiet sectors of the line to be initiated into trench life by the 'old sweats' of regular or territorial battalions.

To give an idea of what the front line was like, in Britain trenches were dug, such as The Loos Trenches built along the Lytham Road in Blackpool. These were constructed and opened to the public, with guides chosen from convalescing or discharged soldiers, helping to raise war funds. Today, former trench lines are open for public scrutiny both in the grass slopes at Newfoundland Park and, lined with concrete sandbags, at Vimy Ridge. At Sanctuary Wood near Ypres, the trenches wend their way through a wood, where muddy puddles collecting on the floor give a hint, but only a hint, of what might have been. They may follow the lines as they existed during the war, and give a true impression of how far away or how close opposing trench systems were, but in reality none reflects what life in the line was like, not least because there was great variation across the Western Front, depending on the army occupying the trenches and the terrain in which they were built.

Water was perhaps the defining factor in the location and depth of trench construction. The geology of the land, if ignored or misunderstood, could make trenches a total misery for the men forced to live waist deep in liquid mud. In time, the Royal

Engineers provided a small staff of officers who criss-crossed the battlefields carrying detailed geological maps of each region. They were responsible for determining, to an extent, the best location for trenches, but more specifically where the ground was best suited for the digging of dugouts.

The Western Front wended its way across low-lying fenland near the coast of Belgium to the mountains in the French-held Vosges. In the British sector there were primarily two types of geology, the clay soils in Flanders, and the rolling landscape of the Somme region with its chalky ground, overlaid with a surface of crumbly flint-filled soil. In each area, the particular geology would determine how porous the ground was, how quick the run-off, and therefore the height of the corresponding water table. In short, the height of the water table would determine whether trench construction would be below ground level as on the Somme, or above ground level as around Ypres, making for two entirely different types of trench system. Around Ypres and Ploegsteert it was only possible to dig down a foot or two before hitting the water table. In place of trenches, breastworks were built above ground made of literally millions of sandbags filled with earth, sand or clay. On the Somme, the ground proved far easier to dig. In the chalk, the trenches were sunk to a depth of around nine or ten feet, revetted with wood and corrugated iron.

Digging the trenches of France and Flanders were the Pioneer battalions, fighting men who were supremely fit: civilians who before the war had been miners or road-menders. Behind the lines the work was undertaken by medically downgraded former combatants whose wounds precluded further direct participation in the fighting. These men later formed the Labour Corps, their efforts being supplemented by working parties of infantrymen out on 'rest' and units of Chinese coolies. Construction took place at night, and the speed at which men dug depended on the type of soil they were attacking, the hardness of the ground, the height of the water table and the likelihood and fear of being caught in the open by shell or machine gun fire.

Despite differences in the terrain, there were basic features to any trench. Each trench had a parados at the back and a parapet at the front, usually made of sandbags and earth. Early on in the war the bottom of the trench was lined simply with wooden planks, but by mid-1915 these had been replaced by a floor of inter-connecting duckboards built above a sump which carried the water and liquid mud away. Every duckboard was built with an 'A' frame, so that the two joists that ran the length of the duckboard narrowed slightly at the end to fit between the joists of the board in front. Each duckboard had slats of wood hammered into place across the frame, while later on, chicken wire was sometimes stretched over the surface of the frame for extra grip. Two or three feet above the duckboards, facing the enemy, was the firestep. This earthen ledge, when stood upon, allowed the soldier a view over the top of the parapet and therefore a position from which to repel an enemy. The firestep was also a useful place to rest or sleep, and it kept men out of the way of soldiers passing by. Both sides of the trench were carefully revetted to stop the walls either crumbling or collapsing, while in the walls themselves 'funk holes' were dug, simple scoops out of the side in which men could sleep or get under cover from the rain.

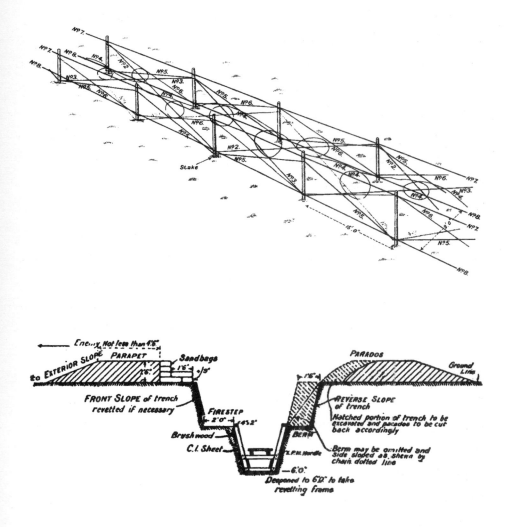

Top, the approved method of putting up wire
entanglements in front of a trench. In theory, thirty men
were required to erect a complex mesh such as this.
Below, cross-section of a trench.

The front line trench (or firing line) was the point of contact with the enemy and might be as little as thirty yards or as much as a mile from his, although on average the distance was perhaps two or three hundred yards; this usually depended on the terrain and the ferocity of the fighting. In front of the trench were barbed-wire defences two or three metres deep, with wire held in place either by wooden posts or, by 1916, with steel pickets that corkscrewed into the ground. Beyond the wire was no man's land, which was not entirely unmanned, for saps were dug out from the firing line into which a machine gun crew would be sent. Their job was to act as an early warning system for the men behind should an attack be made and to be a first line of defence. Listening posts were also established into which two men were placed to listen for enemy activity in no man's land or below ground, where tunnellers would attempt to detonate explosives under the firing line.

The sophistication of trench construction grew as the war progressed, and front lines became linked to a series of trenches that ran roughly parallel to the front line. These were known as the support and reserve lines, and were three or four in number, again depending on the location and the level of local activity. Connecting all these lines were narrow, one-way communication trenches, little more than three or four feet across, snaking their way forward. There was no need for a firestep here, but usually built into the sides of the trench were the officers' dugouts and a first aid post. Dugouts varied in depth according to which trench-line they were in. Perhaps contrary to expectations, the deeper dugouts were to be found in the second and third lines, and were

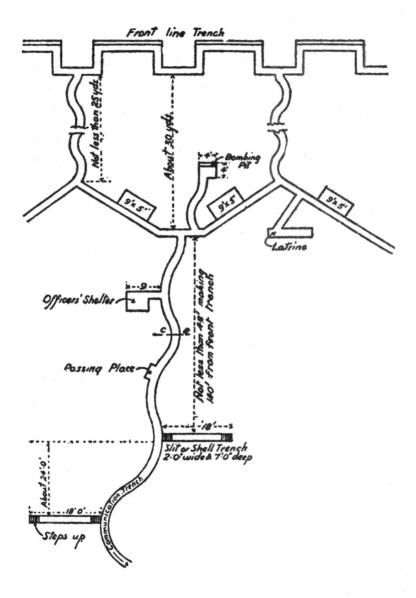

A typical section of the front line, with support and
communication trenches.

generally proof against all but heavy shells. Built into the forward side of the trench, they had their doorways facing the rear, to eliminate the chance that a shell might pitch into the trench and directly into the dugout, killing all inside. These dugouts could be twenty to thirty feet deep and as plush as the occupying battalion wished to make them, with bunk beds, tables and chairs a general requirement. Closer to the firing line, dugouts were shallower, with a short flight of steps at best and with fewer amenities. The reasoning was logical. Men sheltering in deep dugouts were likely to be caught underground during a sudden raid or attack. Furthermore, the enemy expended less time using heavy shells to bombard the front line as these were needed to hit the reserve trenches and roads, along which all supplies to the front line were brought. Equally, where opposing trenches were close, the heavy artillery, firing perhaps over three or four miles, had nearly as much chance of their shells falling short on to their own men as on to the enemy. For this reason, lighter shells and trench mortars were used on the front line as they were more accurate and could be fired at short notice if troop movements into the front line were spotted. Covered in earth and sandbags, the dugouts could withstand the effects of shrapnel and the impact of light shells with some degree of success, even against direct hits.

Dugouts were not the main protection against accurate shellfire; this was the trench design itself. All the combatants built their lines in such a way as to protect as many men as possible from shells bursting in the trench; this was done by a system of traverses. From the air, the trench had the appearance of a series of dog-legs, each protecting the men on one side of a traverse, the fire-bay, from a shell bursting on the next. Similarly, should the enemy attack the flank and gain access to one end of a trench, or indeed should an aircraft attempt to strafe the line, there was protection against a machine gun simply wiping out a long line of men for as far as the gunner could see. In this regard, German and British trenches were of similar appearance, although the French, not renowned amongst the British soldiers for their trench building, preferred a series of gentle zig-zags in their line, reducing considerably the amount of manual labour needed to build the trench, and the amount of material needed subsequently to maintain its shape. The trenches taken over by the British on the Somme in the summer of 1915 were of French construction, including those held by the Hull Pals at Serre. While much was done to renovate these to British standards, from the air most maintained their French-built appearance.

Just where the 2001 trench should be dug was problematic, and there was some discussion as to whether a trench should be dug in Britain, or whether the feeling of authenticity should be maintained by digging abroad. To utilize a trench in Britain would have been relatively easy; they already exist in Essex and in Yorkshire, built to a high standard by enthusiasts, and used on an irregular basis.

The decision to construct a trench in France was made for two principal reasons. The more important was authenticity. The volunteers needed to feel that they were crossing over to the continent; that they were not only in a foreign country, but that they were in France. Surrounded by the evidence of the losses incurred by all sides in the war, of the cemeteries and the memorials to the missing, the men, it was hoped, would show the greatest respect possible to their grandfathers by sticking to the task in hand. Second, given how strenuous their life in the line would be, it was deemed advisable to take them a long distance from their families and friends, far enough for there to be little possibility of their upping sticks and merely walking home, making a telephone call or catching a bus. The sense of separation, from wives, girlfriends and children, would heighten their awareness of just how much the men at the front missed their loved ones, when leave was so infrequent.

Finding a location in France for the trench was uncharted territory. In late October and early November 1916, the Hull Pals had been in the line near the village of Serre, on the northern edge of the main Somme Battlefield. This village had been so heavily fought over, the ground so pitted by shellfire, that any thought of building a trench there was deemed too insensitive. Indeed, the idea of placing the trench anywhere near a site of action was at first felt inappropriate. Furthermore, the location had to be far enough away from a village to keep disturbance to a minimum, secure enough to ensure the safety of all concerned, lonely enough to give the location credibility – high-level power lines or modern houses would certainly detract from the atmosphere – and inaccessible enough that it would not attract sightseers from miles around.

Only one site proved to be outstanding. It lay on the southern edge of the village of Flesquières near Cambrai, in a shallow valley, hidden from all main roads with the exception of one that lay the best part of one mile away. The field was of very poor quality and had remained fallow for many years, although surrounded by land of good agricultural value. The site sloped downwards between two farm tracks and was approximately 200m in length and 100m in width. The only village that could be seen lay two miles to the southwest, but a copse lay in between and for the most part cut out any views of what, in any case, looked much as a village might have appeared in 1916. As the prevailing wind blew away from the village, there should be few problems with sound.

As in 1916, our volunteers would not be expected to remain in the front line for the twelve days they would spend in France; indeed, the War Diary of the 10th Battalion frequently mentions the men going into rest, and this diary the producers intended to follow as closely as possible. A rest billet was needed and a perfect location was found barely a mile away. It was a stone out-building, and it was perfect to the extent that it had been used in 1917 as a billet by the men of the 9th Scottish Division. Outside, a cobbled courtyard added to the authenticity of the location, as indeed did the shrapnel-scarred walls. Inside the building, the original nineteenth-century horse boxes were still intact, as well as the high-level sleeping quarters for the stable boys. Apart from one large room for the men to sleep in, there was an extra room at the end of the building in which it was proposed that the NCOs slept, while at the other end, a two-storey pigeon loft provided both an Orderly Office on the ground floor and an officers' billet upstairs. One added detail was a well in the centre of the courtyard, at which men of the 9th Scottish Division were filmed and photographed during their occupation 84 years before.

Local contacts and knowledge of the area had proved absolutely crucial in finding the right site quickly, although, as in Britain, public opinion had to be won over. French people were rightly concerned about the aims of the project, and were not helped by lurid press reports that ran with titles such as 'Jeu de Massacre' ('Game of Massacre'), and even insisted prostitutes would be supplied to the men in the line. But once on board, local people were fantastic in their response to the whole project. Farmers brought over original barbed-wire pickets (which, even today, are commonly used as fence posts), and elephant iron, original metal roof supports that often form part of a pig-sty or lie redundant in farmyards. Even the local museum provided original braziers used to cook with in the reserve trenches.

There was only one problem left: the site had a First World War trench running from one corner of the field to the other. The trench was part of the Hindenburg Support line, built by the Germans in late 1916 and occupied after they retreated from the Somme in February 1917. The position was later overrun by the British during the fighting that took place around Flesquières in November 1917. Unlike that on the Somme, the fighting over this part of the battlefield was relatively light, but was it justified to dig through a trench with the risk, albeit low, of discovering a body?

There is no getting away from the sad fact that the whole of northern France and much of Belgium is a battlefield. The First and Second World War armies ranged right across the region, whereas Britain has had the good fortune to avoid invasion for the best part of a thousand years. Our battlefields, such as at Hastings, Bosworth or Naseby, are tiny and self-contained; battles were fought on a few hundred acres of land. This is simply not the case in northern France, and yet road-widening schemes and the construction of factories and warehousing continue unabated. Recently the proposed building of a BMW factory near Arras uncovered over twenty bodies of men from the Lincolnshire Regiment. As it happened the site was abandoned, although that had nothing to do with finding dead soldiers' remains, and the land stays earmarked for development. To a degree, wherever the trench was dug was potentially a battle site, so it was agreed to dig at Flesquières, with the proviso that the French Archaeological Institute was on hand to oversee the careful removal of any remains, should they be discovered. In the end nothing was found except a litany of battlefield artefacts.

The equipment found was fascinating. There were German water bottles, helmets, a few rounds of German ammunition, and several stick grenades. As the British had taken and occupied the line, much Allied material was also uncovered. The soles of two British boots came out of the ground, one of which still had studs underneath. There were mess tins, which, when washed, were seen to be imprinted with the words Canadian Aluminium Goods Supply Co Ltd 1914. There were the remains of a woollen glove, and knives, forks and spoons. A wick from a little field cooker or Tilley lamp (hurricane lamp) was unearthed, there were bottles of various makes including one of Yorkshire Relish, made by the Goodall Backhouse Company, and there were endless rounds of .303 bullets, live shells, coils of barbed wire, the eyepiece from a gas helmet, and telephone cable. Also found were barbed-wire pickets, as well as petrol tins, many with holes punched in them by the soldiers to make them into braziers.

Further down the slope, it became apparent that the field had been used later as a British artillery position. The digger bucket, as it cut through the ground, uncovered many brass transport bungs that had been attached to the shells when they had first arrived in France, as well as the empty cans for shell fuses. The battery position, at the bottom of the slope, had been perfectly sited to fire over the ridge towards the next German line.

The best find of all was a small piece of trench sign, 15 inches by 10 inches, on the bottom right-hand corner of which was the sign of the 47th Division – a white daisy, with eight pointed petals and a blue boss on a hollow blue square. It was just possible to make out what looked like the remains of the letters I C, and then a couple of other words, possibly 'Officer in Charge'.

Before digging the trench, a survey was made of the ground. Soundings were taken to a depth of six feet with any unidentifiable objects flagged for later examination. One large concrete feature that might have been a bunker turned out on closer inspection to be no more than rubble buried many years ago by a builder. However, at least 25 live shells, two gas shells and several hand grenades were discovered and sprayed red as a warning before they were taken away and destroyed.

The construction of the trench system took approximately twenty-eight days from start to finish. Deadlines were very tight. Members of the Khaki Chums were due to enter the line on 16 October, giving them three days to muddy up the trench, in effect making the dugouts, firestep, and duckboards appear lived in and used. This was important, as the First War veteran Arthur Halestrap was due to visit and give his verdict. Several of the Khaki Chums had never met a veteran of the war and meeting him in a trench, with the Chums in full uniform, would be a moment of great poignancy.

The trench system in which the Hull Pals had served in October 1916 had been an old French line originally dug in 1915. This trench had been 'anglicized' but maintained the zig-zag pattern of the French trenches rather than the British ones, typified by their fire-bays. Within the trench of 2001 the British style of construction was followed in the making of funk holes in the front line for the men to sleep in, a dugout for the officers and a store for ammunition. Latrines were also dug, with little discernible change from those used in 1916, while a long communication trench (in all 140 metres in length) was constructed leading back to a support line.

The trench was as authentic as possible, built to a proper depth, with a parapet, firestep and dugouts, original photographs being used to cross-reference many details. The trench proper, its walls and floor, were constructed according to the Royal Engineers' manuals of 1916, and ran eighty metres from end to end. It included sumps under the duckboards, and the proper revetting of the internal sides of the trench. In front of the firing line, pickets were screwed into the ground with barbed wire passed through loops to act as a defence against attack.

Owing to health and safety requirements, some rules had to be followed once the men had entered the line. The bayonets were real. However, while in the war men normally had bayonets fixed throughout their period in the front line, this time the men would fix bayonets only at controlled times such as at Stand To when, at dawn and at dusk, soldiers manned the firestep ready to repulse any attack. Tired and disorientated men were likely to impale themselves or each other had the bayonets remained fixed at all times. The rifles were live firing and loaded with blank ammunition, which is harmless except at very close range. There were, nevertheless, strict rules about not carrying weapons back into the trench proper unless the safety catches were on.

The shell explosions, while little more dangerous than a thunder flash used by the army, still had to be controlled. Safe areas were marked on maps held by all crew members, while areas of danger were designated, ensuring entry by express permission only. During bombardments (the explosions were made by blowing up a mixture of peat and cork), the appearance of random shelling masked the fact that the location of every charge was known and closely monitored; detonation was carried out at a safe distance from the men at all times.

The net result of all the sweat and tears, and even a little blood, was a trench the like of which had not been built since the First World War ended in 1918.

CHAPTER THREE

GOING UP THE LINE

There are a thousand and one different places one can stand on
the former Somme Battlefields and believe that no conflict ever
took place on the pleasant fields that gently roll and fold away into
the distance. Small villages dot the landscape, surrounded by little
copses and medium-sized woods of mature growth. But move a
hundred yards to the left and a small War Cemetery, with its
chalk-white headstones, will stand out stark against the pervading
green of the land; a hundred yards to the right and a monument
to the dead will come into view; and then look at the ground,
break a clump of soil, flick away a stone and then look closely. As
the eye gets attuned to man-made shapes, a shrapnel ball may
appear, then perhaps a bullet, then a sliver of shell case. There is
a good chance, too, that as you view what you have found, a dead
body or part of a dead body lies only a few yards away, while closer

still there may be live shells, a hand grenade or two, perhaps a trench mortar, all buried together in the earth.

And deeper somewhere beneath your feet there is an entire underground city that occasionally comes to light, a labyrinth of subterranean passages and dugouts built by the Germans and the Allies during their three years occupying the area. They form part of the three thousand miles of tunnels dug across the old Western Front, making them the largest man-made structure since the building of the Great Wall of China. The vast majority of these tunnels remain unexplored; they hint at their presence only occasionally. Road-widening schemes cut through some, tractors ploughing a field sometimes fall into others. Recently, a farmer's wife, emerging from the rear of her house as she had done for decades, fell straight through the ground into a German-built dugout. The dugout, which would have slept a hundred men or more, was found to run right across the back yard and under her house. Covered up in 1918, its existence was lost until the roof timbers finally gave way after eighty years. Many more dugouts are known to farmers who understandably prefer to remain tight-lipped about their existence in quarries and sunken lanes. Most are in a dangerous state of repair. However, their sheer scale is an unspoken testimony to the enormity of the struggle that took place in northern France during the years 1914–18.

The efforts expended to dig this subterranean world accurately reflect those made to dig the trenches just a few feet above. These trenches are all but gone, but the ground is still riven with evidence that war once moonscaped the lush countryside. On the Somme, the biggest man-made feature is the massive Lochnagar

Crater at La Boisselle, or La Grande Mine as it is sign posted by the French. Blown on 1 July 1916 by 60,000lb of ammonal explosive, it has survived simply because the hole was too great to fill in. When farmers finally sought to return the land to pasture, a British man, Richard Dunning, bought the crater to remain as a permanent memorial to those of all nationalities who fell during the fighting. Every year on 1 July, the anniversary of the first day of the offensive, a ceremony is held at precisely 7.30 a.m. to commemorate the first advance. The service is now attended by up to a thousand people, a thousand times more than attended in 1976, when one lone priest stood on the site.

The Somme Battlefield in 2001 is remarkably similar to that of 1916, unlike the infamous French battlefield of Verdun. Such was the damage at Verdun that after the war the French Government felt it had little option but to forest the entire area, but in what had been a primarily British sector, the farmers of the Somme were allowed to return to their land and rebuild the villages on precisely the same spot where their homes had once existed. Woods, such as High Wood and Delville Wood, have regrown to exactly the same size and dimensions as those of 1916. Even the small copses, of which there are many, have regrown as they were. Wedge Wood, a copse near the village of Guillemont, retains that precise wedge-like shape that gave it its name, despite being completely shattered during August and September 1916. Similarly, a photographic panorama taken from the ridge opposite the Schwaben Redoubt, near Thiepval, reveals little change. Taken in the days before the bombardment on 1 July, it shows the fields appearing serene, with little if any damage. Thiepval Wood, on the right of the picture, is only slightly more full than it is now.

The front line on 1 July extended along the battlefront in a deformed 'L' from the villages in the north, Gommecourt, Serre, Beaumont Hamel, Thiepval, Ovillers, La Boisselle, around the elbow of the 'L' to Fricourt, Mametz and Montauban. All have been rebuilt on the same sites where they were smashed out of existence between July and November 1916.

Dissecting the battlefield is an old Roman road, ten miles in length, running straight as a die (save for two recently constructed roundabouts) between Bapaume, which was held by Germans during the battle, and Albert, held by the British. At Albert there is the famous basilica, built as a rival to Lourdes, when for a brief period Albert's cultural and religious ambitions outstripped subsequent reality. The basilica was badly damaged in 1915 and 1916, when most British soldiers, at one time or another, saw its golden Madonna holding aloft Baby Jesus, tilted at 120 degrees overlooking the town square. It was a popular saying amongst British soldiers that the war would end when the statue fell, which indeed it did in 1918 when the building was largely destroyed. It has since been lovingly rebuilt, the recently re-gilded Madonna standing once again upright on top of the tower. So famous was the basilica, so significant its presence, that pieces often found their way back to England. One surviving veteran still sleeps next to a wooden crucifix found amongst the rubble of the basilica in 1916 and stuffed into a British limber for later retrieval.

To the north of Albert, around Newfoundland Park and Beaumont Hamel, is found the most complete fragment of

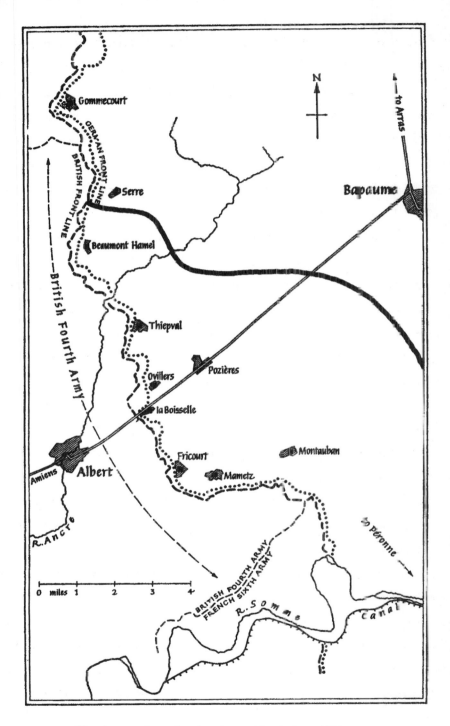

The Somme front showing the position in June 1916 (two broken lines, left) and on 18 November 1916 (solid line, right).

battlefield. Near here the war cameraman Geoffrey Malins filmed part of his record of the opening salvos of the battle. In a sunken road, the jumping-off trench for the 1st Lancashire Fusiliers, he filmed men waiting to go over the top. Within half an hour of his film, most of the men were killed or wounded. After this sequence, he scrambled back to a hastily constructed vantage point in front of the village, from where he filmed the massive Hawthorn Ridge mine explosion. Moments later he captured one of the few genuine shots of men attacking along the ridge towards the crater. The sunken road, the crater and the ridge all remain, almost unchanged from that day to this, and it is possible, with very little effort, to align oneself precisely with where the cameraman stood.

Examine the area even closer and there are any number of smaller details to be seen. At the crossroads at Bazentin Le Grand, there is a crucifix that survived the battle, although Jesus's body is scarred by shrapnel. His right foot is missing and there is a hole under one arm. At Le Sars, on a small track, there is a concrete memorial erected by the Germans in 1916. The plinth has survived many attempts to dismantle it. Just north of the Ulster Tower, there is the remnant of a German machine gun post, which inflicted horrific casualties on the Ulstermen attacking from Thiepval Wood on 1 July, while at Beaumont Hamel there is a tiny piece of stained glass in the church window brought back by a German soldier in the mid 1970s. The glass is the only surviving fragment of the original church that was erased from the face of the earth.

Elsewhere near Carnoy there are signs of mine explosions,

blown both by the French in 1915 and the British in 1916, as well as further craters in the eastern corner of High Wood. More subtly, there is evidence in the fields of long-filled-in trenches, the markings for which appear ghostly in the chalk downland during winter. There are the undulating patterns of gun pits and dugouts that can be seen in the ground, along the sides of protective ridges or sunken roads. On the Thiepval ridge there is the slight rise in the ground where the Leipzig Redoubt once stood, a strongpoint that cost hundreds of lives both in its defending and in its taking.

This evidence has meant that the landscape has proved to be a blessing to the avid consumer of First World War memoirs, who is able to follow very closely the footsteps of an author of eighty-five years ago. When George Ashurst, a 1st Lancashire Fusilier, recalls the events in the Sunken Road at Beaumont Hamel, when Stormont Gibbs recalls standing with a working party at the Crucifix at Bazentin Le Grand, when Frank Richards talks of the windmill on the high ground opposite High Wood, when Siegfried Sassoon makes his mad dash from Quadrangle Wood towards a German trench, west of Mametz Wood, it is possible for the visitor to stand on, or within a few yards of, the same spot.

On the surface of the ground there is much evidence of war. Each year, after ploughing, a new iron harvest is turned over of bullets, hand grenades, shrapnel balls, shell casings, rusting bayonets; they all work their way to the surface over time. A heavy rainstorm washes away the dust and dirt, revealing artefacts that would otherwise be missed. There is nothing that cannot be found on the Somme, from water bottles to helmets, from cap badges to rifles; it is the detritus of war that despite eighty years of battlefield clearance refuses to go away once and for all. And of course there are the bodies of the soldiers who simply disappeared in battle. At the impressive Thiepval Memorial to the missing, some 73,500 names crowd the white walls, British and Commonwealth soldiers for whom there is no known grave. Since its completion in 1932 a few men have been found and buried, with their identities inscribed on new headstones. However, even though bodies are found every year (around 150 have been found across the Western Front in the last two years), most remain 'known unto God'; time has rotted away identification to man. Occasionally a soldier is named. Recently the body of Private George Nugent of the Northumberland Fusiliers was found and reburied, as was that of a young Canadian soldier, David Carlson, but more commonly only the regimental identification or rank can be discerned. Last September, two more British soldiers were found during the building of a ring road. Neither could be identified, save that one had served with the King's Own Shropshire Light Infantry, and the other had been an NCO in a cavalry regiment.

The whole battlefield is, in effect, a cemetery, with so many men blown to pieces, yet it doesn't feel morbid or forbidding. On the contrary, the area feels peaceful and welcoming. Battlefield tourism has grown hugely and has become an integral part of the local economy. Many people, after their first visit, begin annual pilgrimages not only to remember the dead, but to enjoy the gentle landscape of the region. New restaurants have opened up to cater for the increased demand, as have hotels. Visitors' centres at key sites such as Delville Wood, the Ulster Tower and

Newfoundland Park have been opened, and another is proposed near the Thiepval Memorial. There are museums at Albert and Péronne, as well as many private collections held by local farmers and café owners.

Until recently, the veterans came in their numbers too. On the seventieth anniversary of the battle in July 1986, some forty to fifty old soldiers returned to France. They sat in cafés and chatted, they laid wreaths at memorials and they soaked up the sunny weather. For the eightieth anniversary in 1996, fourteen veterans returned to the battlefields of their youth. Many veterans were intrigued to know which of them would make the very final trip to France; there was almost a competition. The winner will soon be known. In 2001, the eighty-fifth anniversary, only two Great War veterans felt physically able to make the pilgrimage.

After arriving on the Somme in March 1916, the Hull Pals had undergone extensive training for their part in the July offensive. The men had practised bayonet fighting and musketry, and had kept fit with long route marches. Iron rations and steel helmets had been issued, while there had been extensive instruction in bombing, mining, and in combating the effects of gas attacks. They had undertaken several spells in the line and had suffered only minor casualties, Private Horsfield being the battalion's first fatality on 29 March, when a German shell exploded close by.

Prior to the July attack, virtually the whole battalion had been used on working parties, digging new trenches and repairing roads, as well as carrying coils of barbed wire, barbed-wire pickets and duckboards up to the line. At other times they unloaded convoys of lorries overburdened with trench supplies, making large dumps by the side of the road for working parties to carry forward. In early June the battalion suffered over twenty killed when the Germans launched a violent barrage on the Pals' trenches in retaliation for a trench raid; however, preparations continued unabated. It was only shortly before the offensive began that the news reached the battalion that they might not in fact take part in the general assault. Instead, their job would be to hold the trenches opposite the village of Serre during the preliminary bombardment, aimed at cutting the German wire and softening up the strong defences. On the night before the assault on the village by the 93rd and 94th Brigades, the 10th Battalion East Yorks would leave the line and wait in support to reinforce the attack if required. In the event, the assault by the two brigades was a bloody disaster, several of the battalions such as the Accrington Pals, the Sheffield City Battalion and the Bradford Pals losing over five hundred men each, well over two-thirds of their complement. Very few of the attackers ever reached the German trenches, and although a small party of men did penetrate as far as the village of Serre itself, all were killed or captured. At times companies of the 10th East Yorks were put on standby to renew the attack but in the end all subsequent forays were abandoned and on 2 July the battalion was withdrawn from the line, having suffered in excess of a hundred casualties from shellfire. On 3 July the men were in rest, opening letters and parcels sent from England that had collected during their time in the line, when a sudden order came to be ready in 'Battle order in ten minutes'. Scrambling to grab their kit, the men were forced to discard the precious parcels of assorted foodstuffs before they moved off, carrying extra ammunition, Lewis Gun parts, bombs and signalling equipment. Tempers were frayed as the men marched throughout the afternoon, and failed to improve when the reason for their sudden departure was made known. The order filtered down from the CO through each company and platoon that the men should adopt a cheery smile, as they were about to pass an army photographer and cameraman standing by the side of the road. They were to be momentary extras in the film *The Battle of the Somme*, being shot in France for public consumption at home. Fortunately the film was silent, for the abuse hurled at the cameraman was noted by all present, but not recorded verbatim. A still taken at the time was widely used later as an example of the excitement gripping the soldiers as they went forward for the attack on 1 July and was captioned 'Gallant East Yorkshires smiling as they go into action!' The date shot, the direction taken and the attitude of the Hull Pals was contrary to the caption in every way.

The BBC volunteers embarked for France on 18 October 2001 and billeted for the first night in a barn close to the line. In the morning they were taken to Thiepval where they laid a wreath to men killed on the Somme who have no known grave. The Last Post was played during what turned out to be an unexpectedly moving ceremony. At the end the men, like most visitors, looked for names of the dead that matched their own; most were successful.

In the afternoon there was a route march in full battle order. 'They gave you extra things to carry,' explains one volunteer. 'I had the wire cutters. You do feel like a packhorse and you slowly start losing your height. The only rest you get is when you stop and you bend over just to take the weight off your back, because if you sit down you've got to get a mate to get you back up, it's that heavy. The worst thing is just standing around in it. It's not so bad marching, because you are constantly moving and you can shift around.

'When we were marching back to the billet it was pitch black, and we were going along a farm track and it was all rutted, and wet. The wind was blowing under your helmet and all you heard were people falling over rocks, and the clink of bayonets and the like. Walking on uneven ground, it were terrible. You just follow each other, you see one person go one way and you think, well, that must be a good route I'll follow him, and if he stumbles you go with him. From above it would look like a little snake, all following the same sort of path.'

With everything prepared the men set off for the trenches. 'On the way into the line for the first time, we came to a crossroads and it was really muddy and there was a great big steep piece of mud and a big puddle and I thought, "Well, somebody is going to get that," and I put my foot down and it slipped and went straight into the puddle and bloody hell my foot was soaked before I even got there.'

The BBC had prepared a reception. A fierce bombardment would be underway as the men approached the line, the noise of which could be heard some distance away. Flares known as Very

The Tommy's increasing burden; by 1915 they often felt
like pack animals.

lights shot into the sky and machine guns rattled. It was exactly as when the 10th East Yorks had approached the line in 1916.

'We were nervous going into the line for the first time; there was the adrenalin, of course, and we didn't know what to expect, and as soon as we started moving into the trench there were shouts of "Come on quick, quick, keep close", and the bombs started going off all round us – bloody hell – bits flying all over the place, pinging off your helmet, gas and smoke; it was exciting and you could just imagine how it must have been. As we walked on, we were being buffeted by the explosions and the ground was shaking a little; I think they got the effect they wanted because we were all frightened to death.

'If anyone stumbles, we were told to leave him, and there's this chap, and he's lying there with all his pack, and he wasn't sure if he could get back up in full battle order. I was carrying some equipment for someone else, and I think my studs got caught in the wire netting on the duckboards and I slipped over and banged my arm, and then people were already past me. And then the next thing you know, you're in the line and you're getting on the firestep. You've lost all your bearings, you haven't got a clue where you are, and at the time it's chaos.'

'You can't create mortal fear, but there was fear,' explains Taff Gillingham of the Khaki Chums, now a sergeant in charge of a section. 'They were all geared up for action and I went to see Lieutenant Rob Yuill and said, "These guys are scared," and he looked at them and told me that their glazed looks were the same as the thousand-yard stares he'd seen amongst his men in Northern Ireland. These men had no idea what they were about

to face, just like their forefathers. You can create those same feelings and emotions. They are the same people and they think and
feel the same way. There were four or five incidents a day that I
saw which I had read about in memoirs by soldiers written eighty
years ago, and there they are, acted out in front of you by lads who
have never read those books.'

In 1916, the Hull Pals entered the line, but the War Diary notes
that one man, Private Walter Robinson, a twenty-four-year-old
teacher from Hull, had already been killed by shellfire. His
counterpart in 2001 was Lance Gadd.

'As soon as we got in they did a roll call, just to check that
everyone's in and we were shocked that one had gone already, I
couldn't believe it. Lance had gone through Catterick and he was
suffering from his feet really bad, just like I was, because I went to
see the medical officer with him; and we were talking there, and
he was a really nice kid, and he'd come all the way out here just to
be sent home again. Why? Poor bugger, he'd suffered with his feet
badly but he'd cracked on and given it his best shot, so I just felt
sorry for him because it was his first night and he didn't even have
the chance to see what it was like. Maybe if it was his second
night, perhaps fair enough, but first night, just coming into the
trench!'

Just as in 1916, sentries were immediately posted, and working
parties formed. The first night in the line, the men were constantly on the go, improving and repairing and extending the
trench. Work varied; during the week a crater was blown in no
man's land. Army regulations of the time expected the men to
seize the hole as soon as it was created, denying the Germans

access to a position closer to the British line. At night, attempts would be made to sap out to the crater.

'It was a relief working all night, to keep warm, to keep moving; stand still and it was freezing. Digging the saps out to the crater was difficult and you really sweated, even in the cold of night. It was really hard constantly digging for five hours; that surprised me. You had to keep your head down all the time, and it did your back in. Some of the big, stocky lads who you'd think could go on for ever got really knackered, but the little Jack Russells who were digging away were able to keep going. Working in the chalk makes you really thirsty as well, the dust and that: such a dry atmosphere, chipping away at chalk.'

Working all night kept body warmth up, but, despite the relatively mild weather for October, the clear skies ensured temperatures fell to around freezing during the early hours.

For all the volunteers, the first days were the hardest. 'That first morning after going in the trench was really bad. When we woke up we all thought, "I can't stick this for two weeks."'

CHAPTER FOUR

THE BRITISH ARMY ON THE WESTERN FRONT

The British Army in France and Flanders wasn't one army at all, but five. As the number of soldiers on active service grew exponentially, so did the number of armies, from one, in December 1914, to five by October 1916. The armies constituted part of what was known as the British Expeditionary Force (BEF), and in 1916 its commander-in-chief was the controversial figure of Field Marshal Douglas Haig. Haig commanded a BEF numbering some one and a half million men in the field at any given time, while, under him, five generals each commanded an army of between two and three hundred thousand men. Within each of these armies there were further subdivisions. Each army consisted of a number of army corps, with each corps being made up of at least three or four divisions totalling around 50,000 men. Correspondingly, in every division there were approximately

12,000 infantrymen, divided equally between three brigades, the brigade containing four battalions, each of 1,000 men.

The ordinary soldier had little knowledge of, and probably even less interest in, how many men formed a brigade, or what rank of officer led a corps. The British press might have claimed that Tommy Atkins was fighting tooth and nail for violated Belgium, occupied northern France, or for freedom itself, but in the day-to-day reality of life at the front, he was fighting for his mates, which meant first and foremost the men in his section.

The section, which numbered fifteen men, was the smallest unit to which the other ranks belonged and in effect the ordinary soldier's world revolved around it. He ate with his section, socialized with his section, answered roll call with his section, attacked with his section and if he died, then he probably died with his section, too. Four sections, each led by a non-commissioned officer (NCO), made up a platoon of sixty men led by a junior officer. Any 'other rank' would almost certainly have good friends within this close-knit unit, and, if casualties had been low, might well have known everyone's name. He paraded with his platoon and, as with his section, would have socialized widely within it. Four platoons made up a company, numbering 250 men and usually led by a captain. This was the parent unit as far as the other ranks were concerned, as companies could work as self-contained units. For example, B Company and D Company might be ordered into the firing line as A and C Companies were sent to the support trenches. When veteran Ted Francis first arrived in the line, it was not the first fatality in the *battalion* that caused the initial ripple of fear to pass through the men. 'The great sensation was the first man in the *company* to be killed. It kind of sobered us up and in another day or two three more were killed or wounded and it came to our minds this was no outing, this was real.'

The company was the largest unit with which a man personally consorted and while he would not know everyone, most faces would be familiar by the end of training, even if names were not.

The battalion – four companies led by a lieutenant-colonel – was the other ranks' pride and joy, and usually the unit to which each man paid his overall rather than his individual allegiance. There was great pride among the Kitchener volunteers in the fact that X and Y had joined up together in the Accrington Pals or the Bristol's Own Battalions, but equal pride in the fact that their units had their own officially designated positions within the British Army as the 11th East Lancashire and 12th Gloucestershire Regiments respectively. You might be fighting for your mates but you served with your battalion and your regiment.

Four battalions made up a brigade (4,000 men, until 1918 when it was reduced to three battalions). Little self-identification was bound up in the brigade, and it was mainly a unit for admini-strative convenience. For this reason many veterans when asked today will have forgotten which brigade their battalion belonged to. They are less likely to have forgotten their division, for this was the first military unit in the hierarchy of the army that worked pretty much independently. A division moved from front to front as one, and went in and out of the line as one. Out at rest, the soldiers of the division ate at their own canteens, played their own sports, and were entertained by their own concert parties. Maintaining the honour of the division could be almost as important to soldiers as pride in their regiment, particularly when the division was renowned for its fighting prowess. Dotted around the landscape of the Western Front today, there are memorials to almost every division in the British Army. Of course, divisional pride was 'learnt' by some veterans after the war, upon reading histories that highlighted the success of the 20th, 36th, or 51st Divisions, to name just three, although others, like Andrew Bowie, knew all too well their place in the British Army. 'We were the First Division of the British Army and we thought we were the king pins, a cut above the rest. 1st Camerons, 1st Black Watch, 1st Munsters and 1st Leinsters, that was the 1st Brigade of the 1st Division of the British Army and you had a bit of conceit about you. Later I joined the 9th Division. We were shock troops and we were always on the move and there was never a dull moment. Wherever the Germans seemed like they would break through they would send for a shock division, like the 9th or 51st Divisions. You are very proud of your division and of your regiment, but I wouldn't compare them.'

Regimental, battalion and divisional pride was instilled in every soldier during training and was not forgotten. After the war, battalion and divisional War Histories were published almost in tandem with the erection of battalion and divisional memorials. Few brigade histories were published and I know of no existing memorials to corps bar the one built at Le Cateau.

When a man enlisted as a Kitchener volunteer he could join the regiment of his choosing, such as the Northumberland Fusiliers, Cameron Highlanders, or East Yorkshire Regiment, although recruiting sergeants often tried to spread the influx of volunteers around. One man who went to enlist in the London Regiment was offered three choices instead, one of which, the Robin Hood Rifles (a battalion in the Sherwood Foresters, officially the Notts and Derby Regiment), sounded very romantic; and so his future was set. Others held out for their original chosen regiment. Some joined regiments far away from home so as to receive a free and, possibly, their first ever train ride. Others who enlisted under-age wisely opted to put distance between themselves and home for fear their parents might come after them.

Joe Yarwood was aged nineteen and just old enough to enlist in 1914. 'The war promised young people an adventure, going abroad and living a totally different life. We had that excited feeling, that things were happening. Of course we weren't thinking of the danger, we thought that we were going abroad to an exciting life, a change of life and that was important.'

The excitement amongst young boys to enlist was palpable in 1914, although, as the war dragged on, casualties increased and the number of recruits faltered. To encourage more volunteers, the Derby Scheme was introduced in 1915 to allow men to enlist but return to their jobs until they were actually needed. Andrew Bowie, for example, enlisted as an eighteen-year-old in February 1916 but was not called up until three months later in May. A month earlier, in January 1916, the Government had introduced conscription, ensuring a regular and predictable supply of men to the army. Being made a conscript, and *forced* to fight for one's country, was something of an embarrassment, and many sought to enlist as volunteers just days before call-up papers arrived on the doormat. For others, such as Harry Patch, the stigma of conscription itself was of no importance. 'I didn't want to join up. I came from a very sheltered family, the youngest of three brothers. I didn't want to go but it was a case of had to, and there you are. Army life didn't appeal to me at all and when I found what a rough and tumble it could be, I didn't like it one little bit. I had no inclination to fight anybody. I mean why should I go out and kill somebody I never knew, and for what reason?'

Once in the army, volunteer and conscript alike often found the regime far harder than expected. The day began at 5.30 or 6.00 a.m. and lights out at night was at 9.30 or 10.00 p.m. In between, the whole day was regulated by bugle calls, reveille, meal times, lights out, even the arrival of mail. Food was typically bread, jam and tea for breakfast, with lunch perhaps consisting of meat, potatoes and bread, and then jam, cheese, bread and butter in the evening.

The pay was a shilling a day for the lowliest private, and for that the army had free rein to work the men all day; drilling, route marches, cleaning, musketry were all part of the job and were practised *ad infinitum* or until they became second nature, whichever proved the quicker. Some soldiers took to soldiering, and loved their careers, others were more than a little reluctant. Either way, many, like Arthur Barraclough, had no time for over-zealous disciplinarians. 'There was a lot of tough, bullying stuff in England and it doesn't work. But there was only one fella that I hated in the army and that was the Regimental Sergeant Major. He was a so-and-so, a big ginger-headed fella. I think he was a regular, but he was the drill sergeant, and he had you drilling, and if you got half a step out he would be bawling, "Step out, come

The Derby Scheme, named after the Director General of
Recruiting, was introduced in October 1915 to allow men to
continue their civilian work until required by the army.
It had only a limited success, and conscription was
introduced early the following year.

back tonight." You had to go out after you'd come off parade, full pack, 90lb, and he'd run you round the parade ground. The men used to say "If he ever gets out to France, he'll never come away again." He was terrible, if you blinked he'd put you on what they called the peg, that is, put on a charge.

'I got sent to Clipstone. There was the usual physical training, running and jumping, then there was drilling and firing courses using live ammunition and, of course, the bayonet fighting. They put dummies up on long strings, then you charged them and body-stabbed them, then stabbed under the chin, it seemed daft really, then the stomach, and then turn round, boot end in the tummy and all that sort of thing. There were route marches, fifteen to twenty miles every Thursday. You marched with full pack, and after every hour fell out on the road and sat on your pack, and then you'd get up when the whistle blew and off again. You got pretty fit.

'For your bed, you got a straw pillow, and a straw palliasse to sleep on and three double blankets on top. Every morning the orderly officer would walk round slowly and everything had to be all wrapped up a certain way and kept dead straight, and if it wasn't, you were pegged, which meant that night you would have to go on parade again for another three-quarters of an hour. When you'd been out all day, you needed to sleep all night.'

When the reluctant Harry Patch was called up he went to Tolland Barracks in Somerset and then to a place near Exmouth where he did a few weeks' basic training. 'This was in the winter of 1916/17 and we used to go down to the sand dunes to do physical training and it was perishing cold. Square bashing, left

ABOVE LEFT AND ABOVE: Arthur Barraclough in 1916, aged 18, about to embark for France; and aged 104.

FAR LEFT AND LEFT: Andrew Bowie (seated) with friends; and in November 2001.

LEFT AND ABOVE: Arthur Halestrap aged 20, serving in the Army of Occupation in Germany, 1919; and enjoying a visit to Delville Wood on the Somme, October 2001.

LEFT: Harry Patch aged 103.

OPPOSITE: A recently rediscovered archive of the 10th Battalion, East Yorkshire Regiment – the Hull Pals: (*top*) six men enlisting on the first day of recruitment; (*middle*) the Hull Commercials on parade at Wenlock Barracks, September 1914, and (*bottom*) Major Carver marching at the head of the Hull Commercials.

All Wilberforce House: Hull City Museums and Art Galleries

ABOVE: Men of D Company, the Hull Commercials, 1 July 1916. This propaganda photo in fact shows them marching away from the trenches after the fighting, not towards the line as the caption at the time suggested. IWM Q713

BELOW: The Lewis Gun section of the 10th Battalion marching near Doullens during the Somme Battle. IWM Q724

Very lights burst in the night sky near the Somme village of Beaumont Hamel, 2 July 1916.
IWM Q757

ABOVE LEFT: A Lewis Gun team cleaning their equipment in the front line. They all have cigarettes in their mouths, although, interestingly, none is lit. IWM Q8460

ABOVE: Officers of the York and Lancaster · Regiment consult a map in the front line trenches near Cambrai, 6 February 1916. IWM Q8402

LEFT: Cameron Highlanders eating near the Somme village of Contalmaison, September 1916. Andrew Bowie joined these men at the front eight weeks later. IWM Q4133

ABOVE: Officers enjoying the comfort of a German dugout captured at Beaumont Hamel, November 1916. On the right, war correspondent Basil Clarke. IWM Q1532

TOP RIGHT: Exhausted stretcher bearers grab a little sleep near Arras, 29 August 1918. IWM 7014

RIGHT: A soldier emerges from a dugout in a front line trench. Mary Evans Picture Library

Men set off towards the line under cover of failing light. IWM Q2755

OPPOSITE

TOP: The exhausted survivors of D Company 11th Royal Fusiliers after the successful assault on Thiepval, September 1916. The men were fast asleep two minutes before and two minutes after this picture was taken.

CENTRE LEFT: An elderly French lady pours coffee for British troops at an *estaminet* near Armentières, May 1916. IWM Q635

CENTRE RIGHT: Men of the 9th Scottish Division at a well in the village of Flesquières. This same courtyard and the buildings were used as a billet for the volunteers in 2001. IWM Q6325

BOTTOM LEFT: 'Chatting' – soldiers hunting for lice in their shirt seams. IWM CO1403

BOTTOM RIGHT: The Somme, November 1916. A working party, wearing waterproof groundsheets and waders, awaits further orders. IWM Q4602

ABOVE: Clouds of toxic gas drift towards enemy trenches during the Somme Battle, July 1916. Popperfoto

FAR LEFT: Second-degree burns caused by mustard gas. Bleach ointment was used to treat minor burns.

LEFT: Three men pose for a photograph with their gas hoods on. In reality gas masks were claustrophobic and made breathing difficult.

and right turn, about turn. Then we went to Sutton Veny near Warminster. I was in the 33rd Reserve Battalion. I was eighteen and six months old at the time and our training was the usual left, right, turn by numbers. We did quite a bit of route marching around Salisbury Plain with full pack, an overcoat, your water bottle, bayonet and entrenching tool at the back. It wasn't very long before someone pinched a pair of my boots. That was one thing I learnt very quickly in the army; lock up everything.'

When orders finally arrived for embarkation for France, soldiers were given a short leave to see families and friends before setting off. When Cameron Highlander Andrew Bowie left, there was one final chance to say goodbye at Waverley Station in Edinburgh. 'The Military Police had said that no-one could leave the platform, but some rough fellows amongst our boys said, "We're coming out!" and the police stood aside. I was able to say goodbye to my relatives, but getting back on the train there were two big Highland boys, and they had nobody and tears were running down their faces.'

The Channel ports were the main point of departure for France, with troop ships sailing at night, usually with a destroyer as an escort to give protection against submarine attack. The French ports of Boulogne, Calais, Dieppe, Rouen and Le Havre were the principal destinations, the men disembarking to a friendly welcome from local people. Ted Francis recalled the general excitement. 'When we landed, you could see some of the men swelling up absolutely fit to burst with pride being cheered by the French, and mostly girls too. We thought it was great to be a soldier then – we'll show them, we'll push these

Germans back where they belong. It was just the thoughts of young men who didn't know any better.'

As a conscript, Harry Patch was sent with a draft to France in 1917. 'We had a week's embarkation leave; then in the second week of June, we were sent in an old paddle steamer from Folkestone to Boulogne. Then up the hill into camp. I wasn't carrying enough, so they gave me a fifteen-pound pack of bully beef to carry. On arrival we were separated and drafted to various regiments. I had a chum with me, who came from the same village; I went into the Duke of Cornwall's Light Infantry, and he was drafted to a regiment in Egypt, and we never met again.'

Such arbitrary decisions could save one man's life, and cost another his. Arthur Barraclough had one particular friend in the army, and all through training they had stuck together and pro-tected each other. 'His name was Harry Slater, and we were real pals. We joined up together in Bradford and we went right through to France and to the base camp. Anyway, they sent down for a batch and he happened to be in the batch what got sent up the line, and he got killed. If I'd been sent with him I'd as likely have been under the same bomb or shell. I lost a right good friend with him. I used to stick up for him. I could always scrap. I'd been brought up to fight, and if they put on him, they put on me.'

In difficult times, men like Harry Slater could find themselves being sent straight up the line and into action. During normal times, speed was not of the essence and instead men were often directed for final stiffening up at a base camp, the most notorious of which was Étaples, or 'Eat Apples' as it was popularly known, albeit with no particular affection. Andrew Bowie headed straight

THE TRENCH

for the camp, in November 1916, for his dose of army medicine. 'I spent about a week at Étaples, at the Bull Ring, a place where a lot of second-rate sergeant majors knocked steam out of you. You were there for fitness training, but it was over-fitness training really. Each morning we got up, had breakfast, and were given a couple of hard biscuits and a piece of cheese that was meant to last us the rest of the day. In the Bull Ring they would have you running round in circles and jumping over obstacles, and all the time these NCOs were roaring at you, swearing all the time. They tried to make you look ridiculous. We had to jump in and out of trenches, and if you didn't get out quick enough they would swear and make you do it again; if you weren't agile or athletic, you became a bit of a target. We weren't all built the same way. I played rugby and I was pretty good, but you could tell a lot of the men weren't up to it. Then, as you left the Bull Ring, if you were out of step or out of line, the instructors lined the road shouting at you, taking names. If you said anything to them, you were in trouble. Even if you looked at them, you could be up for dumb insolence. It only took a week in the Bull Ring and after that you weren't particular where you went. I think that was the idea.'

Once in France, the men were under the full weight of army discipline and military law. In all the excitement of landing in France, Arthur Halestrap had managed to lose his cap, leaning out of the window of the train as it trundled its way to the base camp. 'As we marched in as a squad, all of a sudden an order came, "Halt that squad! That man improperly dressed in a woollen cap, double up to me." That was me, and I had to double up to this Regimental Sergeant Major and he said, "Why do you come into my camp improperly dressed?" I told him about my accidental loss and he said, "Put this man on a charge for not looking after Government property." Then he said, "You'll know me before you've been here very long. About turn! Double back." Marching at twice the normal speed was the order for everyone who was moving outside of a tent or hut in the camp.

'The discipline was very strict indeed because we understood there had been trouble in an adjoining camp. As a result we had three parades every morning while we were there, 6 a.m., 7 a.m., and 8 a.m., to reinforce discipline and prevent us causing the same problems. When an additional parade was posted for 5 a.m. the next morning, I said to my pals, "I'm not going on that parade!" They told me I'd get into trouble, but I said, "If I do, it will be my own fault." So I stayed away from the first parade and when I went on to the next one the Instructor Sergeant, who was in his mid forties, with a long moustache, came up to me shaking nervously and said, "I'm sorry, my son, I . . . I . . . I had to report you, I don't know what they'll do." So I said, "Don't worry, Sergeant, I did it on my own initiative. Now I'll have to take the consequences." I was given three weeks' Number Two Field Punishment. I didn't realize that I was on active service and under different discipline to that at home. Every moment I was off duty or not under instruction I had to empty the latrine buckets, pour away the liquid and then take the solids to the furnace to be burned.'

Going up the line for the first time was something of a relief for Andrew Bowie, sick of the regime at his base camp; for others it was a great source of trepidation. No-one quite knew what to expect, even though, by the middle of the war, soldiers had a pretty good idea of how the trenches looked from pictures published in the newspapers back home. Even so, the distant rumble of gunfire was a constant reminder that death was ahead for some and injury for many of the rest. Trains took the men as far as a railhead, then, after a night or two in billets, the order to move closer to the line might arrive, at which time the first physical evidence of war would be apparent: shell holes in fields, a damaged village. Apprehension rose, as Arthur Barraclough remembers. 'There were people who'd never done owt in public life, sometimes office jobs, and they've read all this stuff in the paper about what goes on in war, and they come and they are frightened to death, especially when they get to France, that's when the trouble starts. And they see fellas coming down wounded and others going up the line, and it puts wind up them of course, and they think, "Oh, I hope I'm not going to that place." First time up the line, everybody was a bit nervous, and you couldn't help your knees knocking.'

As he was a signaller, Arthur Halestrap's first time up the line was not into the trenches but was a move from Division to Brigade Headquarters. Unlike the infantry he was not going to march, but instead join a convoy of horse-drawn transport. The convoy's night-time progress was steady and uneventful until the early hours of the morning when they reached a crossroads. 'All of a sudden a Very light lit up the place, an eerie sort of light, and, as it fell down, the darkness came again; then another Very light, and another one, and inevitably the shelling began. The fire was very accurate and in no time there was carnage and carcasses all over the place. The wagon to which I was attached was stopped because the leading horse on the team got its left legs in the mud on the side of the road and it couldn't move, and the lead horse on the other side was pawing the air and screaming. All the horses were screaming, and there's nothing worse than screaming horses, they are terrifying. The situation was immediately seen by an NCO in charge there, and he ordered some of the men to get on the back of the wagon to push and others to get on the wheels to wind them. I was sent to the front to get underneath the horse stuck in the mud. When the order came to move, I had to put my shoulder on to the front of this horse and heave. I heaved and everyone pushed on the wheels and we got the wagon going. That was my baptism of fire. It wasn't a nice one but strangely enough I wasn't frightened. I had a job to do. I look back upon this with amazement, but that's the truth. It was the result of the discipline instilled in us, to do the job that we were told to do regardless of anything else, and we did it.'

As with the transport, infantry would move up in the dark, often marching in platoons rather than as a whole battalion, to lessen the risk of heavy casualties should the unit be caught by a sudden salvo. As they marched, the noise from the front line would rise appreciably, and flashes on the horizon would be easily discernible. By contrast, noise among the troops would be kept to a minimum, raising the sense of anticipation to yet greater heights, as men looked at each other with nervous smiles, stomachs turning over endlessly. Then it was into the communication trench, anything up to a mile behind the front line, and an apparent matrix of trenches criss-crossing each other;

home-made trench boards stuck on earth walls indicated the name of a particular trench: Piccadilly Avenue, Dufferin Alley, Nairn Street, Broadway. With so many trenches, it often required a good guide to get the battalion into the correct position in the line, and on time.

The first sight of the firing line was not always inspiring, according to Arthur Halestrap who, by 1918, had been well weaned on press images of the front line. 'My first sight of a trench was of just two greasy clay walls with a parapet on the top, duckboards on the bottom and one or two bits of rubbish, with the people in it; it was not a very inviting place. The men were not looking very happy because it had been raining quite a lot. Some were sitting on the sides or standing, some were sleeping, others talking. There was a community atmosphere. I was greeted and welcomed, but there was no feeling of apprehension or fear, they were just sitting about wet, and none too jovial.'

Andrew Bowie had already been in France for two years by 1918. In July he was in the line when he saw a signalling corporal arrive, someone known to him. The man was an expert signaller and had been kept back to train others in Scotland. Now, in the final months of the war, he had been sent to France, and his excitement on finally reaching the front line was clear for all to see.

'He came up at night with the rations and joined our company. He'd been reading the papers at home about no man's land, and it was his ambition to see it. So we stood to the next morning and he asked, "Where's no man's land?" and one of the others said, "It's there! It's on the other side of that parapet." "Oh, is it? ' and he rushed forward to have a look. He got a bullet right through the head. He had only been out with us for less than twelve hours. And that was the end of him. He was one of my trainers, and was an expert reader of the Morse code.'

Andrew Bowie was well used to sudden death by this stage of the war, but for men new to the line, the first death was hard to take. When it occurred, everyone was keen to know what had happened, in order to avoid the same fate. 'The news flashed around in the first line of the trenches,' recalled one veteran. 'This fellow had been killed coming up a communication trench carrying food and water. Parts of the trench had been knocked away by shells and he was a bit careless, instead of bobbing down at one place he'd walked by and a sniper had got him in the head straight away. We saw nothing, of course, but it kind of put a doubt in our minds about this soldier business. Here we was in the real thing, and people were getting killed and we could hardly take it all in.'

New drafts quickly learnt the rules of survival. During the day only the most foolhardy soldier would risk a quick peep over the top into no man's land. Stuck in a hole for days on end, the temptation was always there to look and many soldiers did take a chance and got away with it. The danger was looking over at the same spot twice, for success was unlikely to be repeated once a sniper had registered the position. Most soldiers were prudent and used a trench periscope to look into no man's land. These periscopes varied greatly in design but in principle worked by reflective mirrors including some that could be clipped onto the end of the bayonet and held aloft. Some periscopes could be concertina'd, others looked like thin walking sticks with two small shutters that could be opened at either end of the cane. The most widely used and best known was the box periscope and as snipers delighted in shooting those spotted, most were camouflaged by being wrapped in sandbags or sacking, helping to break up the box's straight lines and making it blend in with the parapet.

Looking through the periscope, a man generally saw little except barbed wire, earth and rubbish thrown into no man's land. A man could serve in the line for months on end and not see a German, and when he did, it might be just a brief glimpse. It was sometimes hard, perhaps, to maintain the offensive spirit without a reason to hate. Like two cocks in a fighting pit, it was necessary to goad the enemy as often as possible, as the manual of trench warfare underlines: 'A good system of sniping and observation is of the utmost importance in trench warfare. Usually every battalion has a special detachment of trained snipers working under a selected officer or non-commissioned officer. Their duties are to keep the enemy's lines under constant observation, note any changes in the line and any new work undertaken by the enemy, keep the enemy's snipers in check, and to inflict casualties on the enemy whenever the opportunity offers.'

If anyone saw the enemy with any regularity it would be the sniper and, on either side, he rarely needed a second look. 'The Jerries were crack shots,' remembers Arthur Barraclough. 'You might have a quick peep over the top, just for a moment, but you wouldn't if you'd any sense at all. We lost fellas during the daytime just because they forgot and were careless for a moment. You didn't do anything foolish unless you hadn't been out before and you didnt't know nowt. But you did things without thinking sometimes, putting your hand up, just forgetting for a minute, just scratching your head, if you're on the firestep especially, you'd have a bullet through the palm of your hand.'

There were no definitive rules as to how a sniper should conceal himself, or where he should hide, although locations to the rear of the firing line or behind specially constructed positions known as Loopholes were suggested, as was the correct camouflage. Wherever snipers lay, their job was to kill outright, and their deliberate and steady aim made them feared. It was quite possible for a battalion to come out of a quiet part of the lines after three or four days and to have lost four or five men to snipers, and none to shell.

A sniper, too, was vulnerable, as soldiers would spend a great deal of effort to work out by triangulation just where he was hidden, before several fired simultaneously at the designated spot. After a battalion 'sniper had himself got sniped', Arthur Barraclough was given the job. 'I'm a bloody fair shot so they've put me on this stunt. You dug your own trench just big enough so that you could fit in, and lift your rifle. So the Germans couldn't see me or catch me from the side, I used to build up my position, use any old bricks or owt like that, and then you just lay down, quietly, and waited for somebody to strike a light, or fire a shot. Sometimes I used to get a brick and throw it away from me just to attract somebody to have a shot, and I'd be ready with my rifle. But I never caught anybody napping as far as I know. I didn't like the job, it were a lousy job lying there if it were wet and cold.'

In a war in which machine guns could wipe out dozens of men, and artillery fire hundreds, it seems strange that few snipers feel particularly comfortable talking about their job, and those that do rarely admit to shooting anybody. It was a ruthless job by its very nature and few snipers, if caught, lived to tell the tale.

In such instances of cold-blooded killing, or in the frenzy of battle, men could be brought to hate the enemy, and to hate with a passion. There were many occasions in the war where no quarter was asked for and none given, and even prisoners could be killed before the red-mist that afflicted so many men in battle cleared. But the term 'hate' was at times a misnomer. The fostering of the morning and the evening 'hate', when artillery on both sides blazed away at reserve trenches and crossroads, was as much as anything to remind the other that they were there.

For newcomers to the front just as for seasoned campaigners, there were moments when war could be seen as a tragedy afflicting all. 'Disturbing thoughts' entered the mind, as Norman Cliff, a Grenadier Guardsman, discovered. 'Behind the opposite parapet was a German sentry standing in mud as I was; feeling cold as I did; perhaps scanning the bright company of stars, as I was; thinking what folly war was . . . Fritz, old boy, what blind insane forces have thrown you and me into this ghastly dilemma?'

Fraternal thoughts did, on very rare occasions, lead to fraternal meetings. The Christmas Truce of 1914 is the most famous case of fraternization between British and German troops during that war, and perhaps any war. It was made all the more extraordinary by photographs that showed soldiers standing side-by-side and even exchanging gifts, as well as many detailed letters marvelling at the event. The temporary armistice lasted a few days at most, and the war started again in earnest. Yet that meeting of infantry-men was symptomatic of a mutual respect that periodically pervaded the ranks during the war, and led to many exchanges between the two sides. In the main, fraternization took the form of passing audible messages across no man's land: 'Morning, Tommy', 'Morning, Fritz', or clapping or cheering in response to a song sung by the enemy. Signs were occasionally displayed; one asked, 'We're Saxons and you're Anglo Saxons, what are we fighting for?' Another German posted a board asserting 'Gott mit Uns' (God with Us) only to be informed by the Tommies in the opposing trench that, 'We've got mittens too'. In a similar vein, Andrew Bowie recalled the Germans shouting 'Deutschland, Deutschland über Alles', only to receive the jocular riposte, 'Deutschland, Deutschland über Arseholes.'

Where opposing trenches were very close it was possible to fraternize with gifts. In 1915, Smiler Marshall, then serving with the Essex Yeomanry, was in a bombing sap opposite the Bavarians. 'Their sap and our sap was about eighteen yards apart and between was an old communication trench which was full of barbed wire and jam tins, that would rattle if anyone approached. One day, the Germans sent a stick grenade flying over, to which they had tied a couple of cigarettes. After a bit I went to the bomb, and my mates were saying, "For God's sake don't touch it." They thought the bomb would go off and blow me up. But I went and smoked one of the cigarettes and it was all right, so we actually sent back the same stick bomb with a whole packet attached. I hope they enjoyed them.'

CHAPTER FIVE

TRENCH ROUTINE

In his introduction to the reprint of Sydney Rogerson's classic war memoir *Twelve Days*, the eminent historian John Terraine cites a startling statistic sent to him by an anonymous survivor of an unknown regular battalion. After the war, this survivor calculated that out of the 1,553 days the conflict lasted, his battalion had been in 'general and active conflict with the enemy' for only twenty days. Three weeks' actual fighting in four years: if his calculations were correct, then it can only be assumed that on the majority of the other 1,533 days his battalion was involved in nothing more than normal trench duties or out at rest behind the line. Surprising figure as this is, it does not mean that because this man was not in 'active conflict' with the enemy he wasn't often in mortal danger. During his service, the anonymous writer calculated that his battalion was totally replenished eight times over by

No. A 40/125/5788
(If replying, please quote above No.)

ARMY FORM B. 104—82.

R. G. A Record Office,
Dover
May 22 1918

22 MAY 1918

Madam

It is my painful duty to inform you that a report has been received from the War Office notifying the death of :—

(No.) *166711* (Rank) *Gunner*

(Name) *Alfred Ford*

(Regiment) *V/VI Heavy Trench Battery R.G.A.*
which occurred *with the B.E.F. France*
on the *9th May 1918*

The report is to the effect that he *was*
" *Killed in Action* "

By His Majesty's command I am to forward the enclosed message of sympathy from Their Gracious Majesties the King and Queen. I am at the same time to express the regret of the Army Council at the soldier's death in his Country's service.

I am to add that any information that may be received as to the soldier's burial will be communicated to you in due course. A separate leaflet dealing more fully with this subject is enclosed.

I am,

Madam

Your obedient Servant,

Officer in charge of Records R.G.A.

18307. Wt. 15148/M 1365. 375m. 2/17. R. & L., Ltd.

P.T.O

The official notice of death. This soldier is now buried in
Cabaret-Rouge British Cemetery, near Souchez.

drafts from home. A fifth had been killed and nearly half wounded, many of whom would have been wounded more than once. This man's survival, whoever he was, should be considered lucky in the extreme.

Although 13.6 per cent of men who enlisted during the war actually died, this figure rises to as much as twenty-five per cent for front line battalions including, for example, the 10th East Yorks. When one takes into account the fact that for every one man killed, at least another two were wounded, then it is true to say that out of any battalion of a thousand front line infantrymen who went to France and Flanders in 1914 and 1915, very few would survive unscathed. The author Frank Richards, who served with the 1st Royal Welch Fusiliers, estimated that at the war's conclusion he was the only man of his battalion (other than one or two men with the unit's transport) to have come through the war uninjured. It is a sad fact that the rate of attrition finally caught up with most front line men at some time or other – but over a period of years, not necessarily weeks or even months.

Just how long a man spent in the trenches varied widely over the course of the war, depending, for example, on whether his division was considered adept at simply holding the line or at launching an assault on the enemy's positions. Nevertheless, useful estimates of time spent at the front have been made by veterans, and include a set of figures collated by the author and soldier Charles Carrington. From his diary for 1916, Carrington calculated that he had been in the front line for sixty-five days, and thirty-six in support, making a total of 101 days under fire, with a further 120 days in reserve, where he would have remained in danger from shelling. During the year, Carrington was in action four times, venturing six times into no man's land on patrols and working parties. Such statistics help debunk the popular notion that soldiers rarely left the front line during the First World War or, alternatively, that it was action all the time.

Going over the top, one of several defining moments of the First World War, was, in fact, a rare experience. A front line soldier might never take part in a general advance if his stay at the front happened to coincide with an extended lull between offensives, while most of the Kitchener battalions that took part in the assault on 1 July 1916 had never gone over the top despite being in France for many months, and in some cases a year. It was when battle was joined that it became possible to attack two or three times in a very short period. The 15th Hampshires and 12th Gloucesters both attacked twice in quick succession in September 1916, while by contrast the 10th East Yorks, as has been seen, did not go over the top during the entire Somme Battle.

Life in the line was generally a time of unrelieved boredom punctuated by occasional heart-stopping moments of action. As many veterans acknowledge, they were eighty per cent bored stiff, nineteen per cent frozen stiff and one per cent scared stiff. Even when a division was sent into the trenches, only a minority of men would be in the firing line at any one time. Carrington estimated that a division held about four miles of trenches 'as the bullet flies', the division's three brigades lying side by side in the line, each with two battalions being 'up', one in close support and one in reserve. Of the battalions 'up', only two of the four companies would actually be in the front line trench, while two others were held back in close supporting positions. 'Each company,' says Carrington, 'had three platoons actually posted in the front line trenches, and one standing to arms as an "inlying picket" under cover, ready to act in any emergency at two or three minutes' notice. If this may be taken as typical .. the six front-line battalions at quiet times held the whole divisional front with about thirty-six platoon posts, and since a platoon could rarely put more than thirty men on duty, we may conclude that the divisional front was held by 1,000 of its, say, 10,000 infantrymen.' By Carrington's calculation, there would have been just one man holding every seven yards of trench although, given the dog-leg nature of the lines, and the fact that trenches were rarely 'bullet' straight but bent and twisted, the yardage patrolled by each man would have been significantly higher.

There was no hard and fast rule as to how many men should hold the line; common practice varied from division to division, and according to the perceived threat at the time. Generally speaking, strategies for holding the front line changed slowly, with a general move away from packing the firing line with troops. to defending in depth. The introduction of the Lewis Machine Gun in late 1914 had effectively subsumed the work of ten riflemen. as the 1917 British manual of trench warfare made clear. 'The extra power now placed in the hands of brigade and battalion commanders by the increase in the number of machine guns enables men to be economized in the front trenches and a larger force thus left for counter attack.' This reduction in numbers helped avoid heavy casualties during a bombardment and reduced the risk of a great number of men being captured should the front line be overrun. Writing home from the Somme in early November 1916, one officer of the 51st Division noted how 'The thing that strikes me most about the trenches is the small number of men holding the line. One can walk for a hundred yards along the front line trench and never see a soul except a single sentry.' Similarly, in British raids on the German trenches, it is surprising how often men recollect having to hunt for an enemy soldier in seemingly sleepy front line trenches.

The usual tour of duty is generally given as three to four days in the front line, the same in support and then again in the reserve, before the battalion was relieved to go into rest which, as we will see later, was far from anything of the sort. In 'normal' times, there would be a rotation of battalions in the line, which distributed the work of holding the trenches roughly evenly within the division. This rotation could be severely disrupted for several different reasons. The most mundane would be the weather. In wintry conditions, with water and mud coursing through the trenches, it is hard to imagine how any battalion could survive, let alone repel an attack. The front line was the critical point of contact with the enemy and no amount of encouragement, or rum to stiffen the resolve, would ever keep men fighting-fit. In such conditions, battalions' duties would be alternated, almost on a nightly basis. The second reason would be an imminent offensive. For those battalions taking part in an attack, on-going instruction behind the lines would ensure that, in the days prior to an advance, each unit would hold the line for short periods of time in order to facilitate training. Lastly, a crisis at the front might necessitate a battalion holding the line for far longer than expected, with two weeks not unexceptional, and with greater stays of up to a month or more recorded with pride in some battalion war diaries.

Unlike their German counterparts who tended to stay put, the British Tommy was switched with his unit from front to front with alarming regularity. This enforced 'tour' was exacerbated by injury, so that a returning soldier stood a good chance of being sent to a new battalion. Andrew Bowie served with the 1st, 5th, and 6th Cameron Highlanders during his war, Arthur Barraclough served with the 2/4th and later the 1/4th Duke of Wellington's, both men being shifted to new battalions as they returned from England. Likewise, divisions could be switched according to need, from the Somme, to Arras, to Ypres and back again in a short space of time. The fact that the Hull Pals happened to find themselves opposite the village of Serre for the attacks on both 1 July and 13 November was unusual and was in this instance by design rather than chance. The Hull Pals would be given a second chance to crack the German defence of the village.

Few soldiers saw the same trenches on more than two or three occasions, Carrington estimating that he moved his equipment eighty times during 1916, sixty-six times on a route march and another fourteen times by rail. It was therefore a matter of im-portance as well as normal routine that company commanders should carefully reconnoitre any trenches prior to the battalion moving forward. This preparatory visit usually took place the day before the battalion went up the line, a guide first taking the officer to the dugout of the company commander of the unit due for relief.

It was the incoming officer's job to make detailed notes on the state of the trenches and any work that might be required. The number of listening posts in no man's land had to be ascertained, with their exact position and condition. The extent and thickness of the wire in front of the trench would be noted, as would any gaps. Trench stores, machine gun posts, telephones, ammunition, bombs and latrines: all would come under the officer's remit during his visit. *The Trench Routine*, which was published by every division, lists some twenty-five different aspects of trench administration that had to be checked before an incoming officer was satisfied. The next day before the relief was finally complete, a detailed inventory of all the trench stores was made. Everything had to be seen and counted, for once the incoming officer had placed his initials against each item on the list, he became responsible for its continued presence and good condition, before he in turn handed it over to another officer in a subsequent relief.

Before moving up towards the trenches, the men allocated to front and support lines would eat an evening meal then leave their packs with the transport under the watchful eye of the quartermaster, the men taking only what they would need in their small haversacks. After a statutory roll call, they would set off just before darkness, but this did not mean they were free to amble into the line. On the contrary, the men were loaded up with an array of trench stores, including small arms ammunition, boxes of grenades, barbed wire, duckboards, sandbags, tins of water and rations for the following day.

Ideally, as the men were heavily laden, one line of men would move forward up one communication trench, as the soldiers being relieved began to pass down another. This did not always happen, and a silent pandemonium often resulted as two lines of heaving, overburdened men attempted to squeeze past each other in the narrow confines of the trench. On one occasion Andrew Bowie witnessed an extraordinary meeting in a communication trench: 'A battalion of the Durham Light Infantry were going out and we were going in and one of them shouted "Have you anyone in your lot, the Camerons, called Corporal so and so," and somebody said, "Yes, he's in the next part of the communication trench." "Well, tell him that his brother's here from Australia." His brother had come from Australia and they hadn't seen each other in seven years and in that semi-darkness they met. I didn't see it happen but I heard the voices.' More usually, though, when the opposing trenches were close together silence was crucial, for any suspicion that a relief was underway would alert the Germans to a hopelessly vulnerable target, offering every shell, bullet and bomb two men for the price of one. 'You daren't let anything tinkle like a cup or any of your equipment, you mustn't let the Germans hear that, because if they did detect it, that was an invitation,' recalls Harry Patch. 'We left and they came in and we'd have to pass each other. The trench was never empty. It was very difficult not to let your equipment rattle, especially carrying a bag of spare parts. You would tell them, "Keep your head down, don't look up". If you looked up to see where the German lines were, you were dead. There's a sniper ready every time, see a tin hat, bang.'

Once in the line, sentries were posted immediately, the

observation of no man's land being maintained throughout the night. A small number of men would be detailed to follow a sergeant, climbing out to occupy listening posts, which were sited roughly a third of the way across no man's land and gave advance warning of enemy patrols or raids. In the trench, sentries would remain on the firestep, the recommended proportion being one sentry for every three men in the line. At night, machine guns, on both sides, were fixed on pre-set targets, such as the parapet, enabling machine gunners to sweep the enemy line with accuracy during darkness. For this reason, all sentries were instructed to stand head and shoulders above the parapet, as a bullet in the shoulder was less dangerous than one in the head. Sentries stared into the darkness looking for any movement. After an hour, they would usually be relieved. Like the man on watch, the first relief was forbidden to sleep in the hour prior to taking over, and was expected to simply rest on the firestep; the second relief was able to sleep. Whether on sentry duty or not, it was incumbent on all men to be fully prepared to meet the enemy. Rifles were stood on the firestep with a round in the chamber, with the safety catch on, while bayonets remained fixed. Full webbing was worn all the time, and no article of clothing could be removed. Only in the reserve trenches were men allowed to remove their webbing, although the equipment had to be ready at a moment's notice. Here, too, bayonets could be unfixed during the day, but were refixed once again at night.

Being prepared to meet the enemy at any time, of course, made good sense. But that state of readiness also underpinned the army's general belief that trench warfare was only a phase of operations, and that the offensive spirit amongst its men should always be fostered. 'The chief problem to be faced in the ordinary routine of trench work,' noted the manual of trench warfare, 'is to ensure that the maximum amount of work is done daily toward the subjection and annoyance of the enemy and the improvement of the trenches, consistent with the necessity for every man to get a proper amount of rest and sleep.'

The best method of marrying the defensive with the offensive was the system of patrols. Out of the army's insistence that the British and not the Germans should dominate no man's land whenever possible, patrols were sent over the parapet, usually on the first night in the line. There were different types: listening patrols; fighting patrols; and consequently, depending on its role, different sizes too, from two to perhaps thirty men. Listening patrols might need to go very close to the German wire and the men were therefore lightly armed, so as not to clank or rattle as they approached, and in order to facilitate a quick exit back to the British lines if required. A fighting patrol would carry an array of weapons, not just rifles, knives and bombs, but homemade equip-ment for silent skirmishing, ranging from articles akin to knuckle-dusters with a spike attached, to trench clubs embedded with hobnails. As the name suggests, this patrol was looking for trouble as part of the will to dominate no man's land, as well as to grab a prisoner or two for interrogation.

Those who went out on patrols could be said to fall into two brackets, the tested and the untested. Officers new to the line were often 'encouraged' to take a patrol out under a competent NCO to gain experience and confidence. Hartlepool-born Norman

Collins, an officer in the Seaforth Highlanders, had only just arrived in France when he was sent over the top. The battalion was out of the line at the time and the officers had been enjoying a Hallowe'en drink, during which Norman had become a little worse for wear. At the party it was decided that he should go out on a patrol. 'Early next morning I had to go up to the front line with a sergeant to do a reconnaissance before it became light,' he explained. 'I got back to billets, a tent it was, and shortly afterwards I set off. I had to catch a very primitive vehicle – I can remember the smell of the exhaust was pretty awful – and go up to the line at Beaumont Hamel and do a reconnoitre, over the top, just to have a look round to see what I could see. Well, I was feeling a bit sick, especially with the fumes of the lorry exhaust. We went up the communication trench into the front line, up a short ladder and into no man's land. We crawled about but I'm afraid I wasn't really any use because I didn't really know what I was there for, having just got to France and never having been up before. I had a look round to see what I could see which wasn't much and then I had to get back to the regiment because by now it was daybreak and I had to report to the orderly room and the adjutant.'

Arthur Barraclough was a tried and trusted veteran of the line when he took part in patrols to find out if the Germans were digging under the British lines in order to lay a mine and blow them up. 'There was a sunken road nearby and at night our section had to go out and drop down into the sunken road and walk along, then climb up on the edge and lay flat on our bellies outside the barbed wire. It was a dangerous job, you hadn't to breathe hardly, listening with ears to the ground. Some of the men used to black up, but if a bomb's coming, what's a bit of muck going to do? I just used to pull my tin hat well down. Out at night, the men would be very careful not to cough, and if anybody wanted to sneeze they'd bury their head in the muck before they dared.'

The custom of rotating the jobs in no man's land varied greatly from battalion to battalion. In the 16th Royal Warwickshires, the most dangerous tasks were reserved for those with proven nerve and determination. Ted Francis was frequently chosen to take part in excursions into no man's land. 'Some jobs were risky like going over to their wire – great swirls of the stuff – and clipping it with wire cutters. We were only about six or seven yards from the sentry walking up and down the German trench. Once, we were heard, and every machine gun and bomb was on us and we had to duck down in the nearest shell hole. We had to stop there and not show ourselves for an hour before we could creep back to our own lines. On another occasion fifteen of us were sent out to grab a German sentry, keep him quiet and drag him over to our side for information. Three men who were very strong grabbed this young chap, no older than myself, eighteen or nineteen. He was absolutely petrified because he thought he was going to be shot, but we did have one man who knew a little German and put his fist over his mouth and said, "Be quiet, you're all right, we shan't shoot you, the war for you is ended", and those few words made him quiet and we dragged him off and in a few days the officers got a lot of information from him.'

Ted was a willing participant in such actions because it was a trade-off in risk. 'Doing the dangerous jobs had a purpose, as I

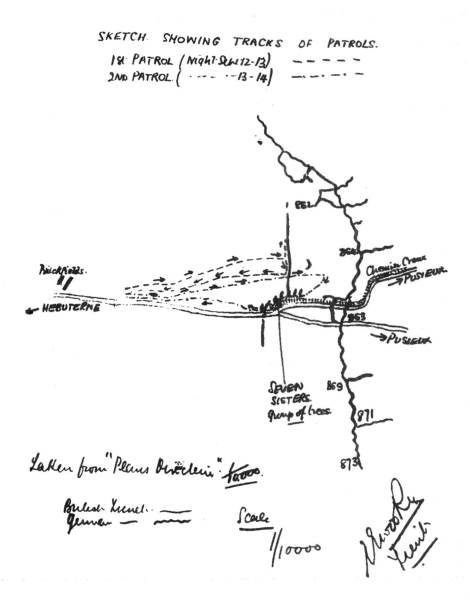

An officer's wartime sketch showing paths taken by patrols
into no man's land.

hoped that when anything very, very dangerous came along, such as an attack on the German line, I should be excused. A few officers, a few non-commissioned officers and some men were always left behind because very often you'd go into a terrible attack and when you came back most men had been killed or wounded, so some were kept back to carry on. One or two pals were very envious that I'd been excused a certain rough action and they tried to offer themselves for dangerous jobs, but the officers kept a list of those they trusted and practically the same men went out each time.'

These 'jobs' were usually led by a junior officer or a senior NCO, a briefing being given as to the aims and conduct of the mission. Before raids into the enemy lines, the men going would prepare, removing any badges that would denote their unit, while paybooks and personal items were left. Some men, although by no means all, chose to blacken their faces. Sentries would be fore-warned that a patrol or raid was going out, and a password was issued. Then, just before the 'off', compass bearings would be taken before going over the top through pre-cut lanes in the British wire. Bearings were vital. In the dark, it was easy to become disorientated, and it was perfectly possible to crawl stealthily back to one's own lines to discover with horror that the sentry's challenge was being made not in English but in German. For this reason the scope of patrols was generally conservative because of the necessity of keeping more or less to a straight line going out, so as to make the return relatively straightforward. Ted Francis was on one patrol when he 'was nearly shot by one of our own men because it was pitch black and I'd wandered a little off our company trench and towards the next regiment's trench. When they heard me coming they shouted "Halt! Who goes there?" and they'd got their fingers on their triggers. I said a few choice words. It was a near thing because when I got there one of them said, "By gad, I nearly shot you." '

The following is the hitherto unpublished report of one fighting patrol of seven men as written up by a junior officer of the 1/4th Royal Berkshire Regiment. It is dated 3 August 1915, and was written directly on his return to the trench:

Patrol went out at 9.15 p.m. from the sap on the right of Hoche Trench, armed with rifles with fixed bayonets and bombs. The object was to discover the movements of, and, if possible, to capture, an enemy patrol. The patrol went down the hedge which runs down at right angles to our trenches beginning 35 yards from the Sap Head. This hedge provides a good egress, but its further end, where it breaks into a succession of bushes, should be approached with care. The end of the hedge is about 250 yards from our trenches and probably about 180 from the German. The patrol was disposed in two parties, one 20 yards from the end of the hedge in the grass, the rest under cover in the rear. The idea was that the enemy might approach the hedge to discover the cause of the noise the previous night, and be encouraged to advance up the hedge, when the advanced party would have closed in behind them. No sign of the enemy was seen or heard for ¾ hour either near the hedge or in the region on either side. The patrol then moved across to the two poplar trees on the Bucquoy Road. These stand at the junction of the Road with a metalled track which runs away in a S E direction. None of the enemy were met with or seen, but there are numerous places where the grass is beaten down. The patrol returned up the Bucquoy Road at 11.30 p.m. This road is in better repair than most roads between trenches. The ground in front of our trenches appears normal, consisting of wild crops and rank grass growing to about 2½ feet high. G.K. Rose Lt.

Lt Rose's report appears comprehensive, although not all patrols were as diligent in doing their duty. In the dark, there was a great temptation to linger just beyond the British wire and sit tight in a shell hole until it was time to return. Andrew Bowie recalls one case that became a whispering point in his company. 'One captain, who had been the adjutant in Invergordon, came out to the battalion and went out on patrol as ordered from his part of the trench. Another patrol under a young lieutenant called Stephenson went out as well, and they were supposed to go along no man's land and meet and come back again. Stephenson came in and said he had not met the captain in no man's land, but the captain said he had gone right along there as ordered but hadn't seen Stephenson. The captain had told a deliberate lie, because the men who had been with the captain told the truth and said "He never did that, we were with him and we just went over into no man's land and we all sat down and came back in again into the trench, he never did his patrol!" That was very serious, of course, he could have been court martialled. The other men backed Stephenson, that he had gone along all right but nothing had been seen of the captain. He was a pure coward and the men had a nasty feeling about him.'

Those occupying saps and those chosen for patrols were not the only men forward of the front line trench at night; both sides worked feverishly on their own barbed-wire defences, repairing any damage caused by shelling, machine guns or cutting by hand. In the early days of the war, wire defences had been fairly simple, with stakes driven into the ground by wooden mallets, and wire wrapped around. As the war progressed, defences became highly sophisticated, with deep belts of wire protecting the British line, a minimum of ten yards in depth. Intricate matrices for wiring were developed to the extent that the 1917 manual of trench warfare devotes a full seventeen pages to diagrams. Drawings feature every size of screw picket, every method by which wire could be bound and carried, and every conceivable method of distributing it which, from the plans, could appear as attractive as any child's cat's-cradle made of string. The reality was very different. Barbed wire was feared by all soldiers, and from any point of view the mesh of wire entanglements was nothing but evil to look at, wicked to construct and lethal to get caught in.

'It were the lousiest job in the world, were the barbed-wire job,' recalls Arthur Barraclough. 'We went out in pitch dark on our bellies and white tape was handed out to the one at the front, and this white tape was let out wherever you went. No man's land was full of shell holes and in winter it got wet and anybody falling in, they'd had it. So the lance corporal took the tape, and about four men would go round the shell holes so that when the wiring party started you wouldn't topple in. Handling that stuff, barbed wire, it were terrible. The wire had inch-long needles and you daren't get clipped to it because you couldn't pull yourself off, it was like

'The lousiest job': clipping the barbed wire.

somebody grabbing hold of you. You'd have to go out with special
wire cutters trying to clip them off the barbed wire but there were
more than one lad shot, fastened on. Before the wire came out in
balls we used to have to put it through the loops of wire pickets,
and wrap the wire round it. We wore gloves, of course, just ordinary thick gloves, but you got some terrible awful scratches. If
you're frightened to death, that don't make any difference, you go
and do it just the same. It was a terrible job at night, it was a feared
job with the troops, but nobody ever refused as far as I know.'

Screw pickets had replaced mallets because of the noise that
hammering posts into the ground would unavoidably make. It was
true that as British soldiers mended their wire, there was every
chance the Germans were doing the same, and a sort of unspoken
armistice prevailed, as each side left the other unmolested to carry

on their work. The fear came when there was silence opposite. Andrew Bowie was detailed to join a working party of forty men that had been ordered to dig a new communication trench from the front line backwards. They had not been working long before the inevitable happened. 'We had this brave captain in charge, I felt sorry for him, he'd been told to do this job and he couldn't, because as soon as the Germans heard our spades they straffed us and we all lay down. You could hear the bullets whistle past your ear. The captain remained standing and was very annoyed and called us all "cowardly bastards" and everything else. He said, "Stand up and dig! Stand up and dig!" But as soon as the Germans heard the spades again, they opened up, and once again he shouted at us. He was standing when he was hit and badly wounded. I heard the shouts, "He's hit." The captain was carried down in a blanket and died a few hours later. It was a silly order, we should have dug a trench forwards, not back. The Germans were bound to hear us and spray the place. He hadn't the nerve to say no to the order; it was pride. He'd been told to do a job and he had set his mind to do it.'

The noise of forty spades hardly required a Very light to confirm visually what was plain to the ear; it was perfectly obvious that a working party was out in the open. When a Very light did explode, the temptation was always to fall to the floor, but the movement of one or several men caught the eye, as Arthur Barraclough explains. 'The rule was, if you got caught in no man's land by a Very light you had to stay dead still, you hadn't to move a muscle if you could help it, because the slightest movement showed up and a machine gun would get you straight off. Even if your hand was in the air, you stopped. Now Jerry would send up these lights every five minutes and brought things like daylight; I never saw anything as beautiful and as powerful. They were shooting them all along the line, all night long, every five minutes, going up and coming down. Everything had to be done in that small period before another went up. It took some doing to stand still when there were bullets flying about, but you had to, to save your life.'

Not all veterans recall Very lights as being beautiful Arthur Halestrap found they gave off a 'very eerie light indeed. I can almost say a frightening sort of light, because it was a light that was almost out of this world. As the light fell it was gradually getting dimmer and dimmer until it hit the ground and was extinguished. By the time one had gone to ground there was another one in the air, so it was a succession of these lights which in itself was rather disturbing, because once the first one was extinguished it was a relief, and then another one went up. It was a peculiar feeling and I've never felt like it in any other circumstances.'

A man did not have to be in no man's land to feel vulnerable to the power of a Very light. Sentries on the firestep were also uncomfortable, exposed as they were, head and shoulders above the parapet. As they awaited the return of a patrol, or peered into no man's land, the prolonged inactivity became exhausting. In such circumstances clear senses were needed. Hearing was obviously just as useful to a man as seeing, and orders forbade the wearing of mufflers or a cap, while loud talking was forbidden. The reduction in the number of front line soldiers was primarily a daytime rather than night-time measure, for in the darkness men who felt isolated were liable to become jumpy. The order that 'sufficient strength' be kept in the firing line was deemed necessary not just to repulse sudden raids but to soothe the nerves of sentries. In the dark a bush could resemble a German with evil intent; a single shot fired by a sentry could trigger a reply and counter-reply that could spread down the line within minutes, with even artillery getting in on the act. Such was the risk of a flight of fancy, so difficult the job of staring into darkness, that one officer and one NCO per company were always on duty to visit sentries, to keep them alert as well as to receive any reports.

Staying awake was a torment; eyes smarted and eyelids weighed so heavily that sleep was only ever moments away. A sentry asleep on duty risked court martial, and potentially a firing squad, although in the end only two men were shot for the offence during the war. In the battle to stay awake and avoid charges, soldiers went as far as sticking their bayonet under their chin, a pointed reminder, if ever there was one, not to nod off. 'At night you just stood there looking at nothing and you start imagining, you see things when they aren't there,' recalls Arthur Barraclough. 'The most terrible thing was to stop awake. We had an officer, a young officer, and he used to walk down the trench at night, and one night he said, "You were asleep, you know!" I said, "No, I wasn't, sir." He said, "I've just passed three others and they were all asleep." He could have had us shot, you wasn't supposed to fall asleep on guard out there, but I thought he was a real good sport. We used to stand in one place and stare at nothing. You do it automatically in the pitch black, with only these Very lights going up. You can fall asleep with every intention of keeping awake.'

Invariably, tired men plotted to steal valuable minutes from the next relief, by tricking him to take over early. Equally, there was every temptation to arrive on sentry duty just a few minutes late. 'On my hour on sentry, the corporal had relieved me late each time, and the last time he was ten minutes overdue, so he got told off – my mate Travis was next up, deliberately relieved him late and told him about it. The corporal said something back to him and got hit on the nose for saying it!' recalled one veteran many years later.

Supporting the sentries were the machine gunners. On entry into the line they would pick the most advantageous position for their gun, ready to spray no man's land if required. Harry Patch was a Lewis gunner. 'I was at Ypres during the summer nights; what it was like in the winter I hate to think. But even in the summer it was chilly too. About three to five in the morning it would get very cold and you'd do what you could to keep yourself warm and then if the sun came out you were all right. I just clapped my hands together, and moved as much as I could. You stand on the firestep and look out and if you saw anything you thought was a German working party you would report it to the officer and he would have a look with his field glasses, to see if anyone was showing a face or a hand. Even if he was a bit doubtful, a Very light might be sent up to see and if you thought it was anything, righto, give 'em a burst! You'd leave it up to the officer to decide; that was up to him. If he thought it was worth a burst, well, let them have it. If it was a bush, then the bush stayed there. You would never fire a magazine from the same position because the Germans would take a bearing on the gun, and firing again from that spot was asking for half-a-dozen whizzbangs. We'd always move, perhaps twenty, perhaps thirty yards either way in the trenches and have another go, and then perhaps, later on, you'd go back to the same part of the line again. We were all doing our duty just the same as the infantry, watching, watching, watching. Oh, the darkness played hell with you, with your eyesight.'

For a greater part of the First World War, the British soldier had become nocturnal. Trench life had necessitated the turning of daily routine on its head; the working day began after dark; rest and sleep some while after dawn. In the hours of darkness a whole world appeared to wake up, as hundreds of thousands of men from the Belgian coast to the Swiss Alps were employed in good housekeeping on a fantastic scale, as Andrew Bowie recalls. 'Many times you see pictures of the front line soldiers and they're just sitting on their bottoms doing nothing, and you think that's what their life is. Far from it, you worked like a slave, doing all the odd jobs. Once it was dark and you were on a working party, you had to work like blazes, carrying sleepers, carrying duckboards, everything needed to maintain a trench. It was no sitting down job, and during the day you rested. It was no joke being a private soldier in a line regiment at night, and if the weather was bad you just had to work through it.'

After a short period of rest and refitting, by the middle of July 1916 the 10th Battalion of the East Yorkshire Regiment was back in the line, albeit in a quiet sector near Neuve Chapelle. During the summer, the battalion did short six-day tours of the line, suffering intermittent casualties; a little more than a dozen men were killed between July and mid-October. But even if the battalion was avoiding the rest of the Somme Battle, they would have been far from idle. The modern-day Hull Pals, too, worked hard, beginning their time in the trench with forty hours' nonstop ferrying and carrying, maintenance and digging, followed by a march back to the billet, where they finally got their heads down in the afternoon when 'everybody was just out for the count.'

In 1916, the same exhausting routine was carried out all along the front. Those men in the front line were continuously occupied repairing and improving the parados and parapet, digging saps, replacing duckboards, filling sandbags and revetting trench walls. Depending on local conditions, it was often up to the men in the support or reserve line to send forward working parties to go out and patrol no man's land, or to improve and strengthen the barbed-wire defences, while further back, parties of men out at rest would bring food and trench stores up the line. Not all jobs were necessarily orthodox, as Andrew Bowie recalls. 'One job we got started with the "you, you, and you" business, about six of us. "There's a dead mule lying outside our parapet", we were told. "Go out and bury it." A dead thing like that always gave off a bit of a stench, and someone decided that it must be buried. That was the order but it was easier said than done. Well, we went out, and I don't know if you have ever handled a dead mule, but we couldn't move the blasted thing, so we took our spades and put mud on it, thinking that would hide it. But the next morning we looked out, and there was the poor beast still there with these pats of mud on it.'

There was one little advantage that the Allies never lost in the war and that came with the approaching dawn. As working parties began to pack up, there was always the chance that as the first shafts of light appeared over the back of the German trenches, the enemy might be caught in the open, suddenly silhouetted against the sky. By that time the British were ready, for half an hour before dawn the call came to Stand To. This meant an hour on the firestep, beginning thirty minutes before dawn and dusk, bayonet fixed, ready to repulse a surprise raid or attack. Dawn was considered the most propitious time to attack, for final preparations for any assault could be made in the night, unseen by the enemy, while the half-light afforded cover during the launch of an attack. In reality, both armies were aware that on either side of no man's land men were ready to repel the enemy, so each side effectively cancelled the other out. Instead, Stand To was usually a necessary period of boredom until Stand Down.

As the men stood on the firestep, an issue of rum was brought round to warm them up. After Stand Down they washed and shaved; this was followed by a general inspection of rifles and ammunition. 'We used to have an arms inspection every day,' says Harry Patch, 'and our revolvers and rifles were checked and if there was a round missing you had to say where it had gone and why you fired it. Ammunition was hard to bring into the front line so you had to account for almost every round. The officers were also very, very particular that the gun and the spare parts were kept scrupulously clean, otherwise you were put on a charge. A damaged round could jam the gun and so could a little bit of mud, and there was plenty of that around, so they were ensuring that we were ready if the Germans mounted an attack.'

Further inspections of gas helmets, feet, socks, iron rations, field dressings and trench stores were also undertaken before the men were dismissed by the company commander. Only then, after all these jobs were done, would breakfast be taken at around 9 a.m., two to four hours after Stand To, depending, of course, on the time of year.

After breakfast, sentries were posted – two hours on and four off – and parties would then be detailed to repair any damage to the trench, to improve the drainage and strengthen or repair any dugouts. Trench stores would also be cleaned up, with loose ammunition being bagged up and labelled. The military authorities placed a great emphasis on salvage and encouraged all ranks to 'take every opportunity of salvaging Government property', a dump being established at each battalion headquarters. The pressure to work was relentless. Apart from the army's general antipathy towards men taking life easy, there was an almost constant requirement to repair and maintain the trenches. In winter the rain and snow exacerbated the problem as parapets crumbled; likewise, in summer, there was a need to pre-empt the effects of autumn and winter weather. In the following note written by the officer commanding D Company of the 1/4th Royal Berkshire Regiment, the emphasis on maintenance is clear.

In going round the trenches lately the following are a few points that I notice want attention.

(1) Very few men working – every advantage must be taken of this fine weather to repair the trenches and no one must be idle – it is of the utmost importance to get the place straight

before more rain comes. Whole of your Coy [Company] must be at work – on fire and communication trenches.

(2)   Bombs in front line must be Coy charge and must be kept clean and the boxes closed. I think bombs are removed to go on listening post etc and not cleaned before being put back – this must be done.

(3)   Ammunition boxes must be kept clean and in their places and must be lying on their sides.

(4)   I seldom meet an officer on duty in the trenches.

(5)   Officers must supervise working parties and see the work is well done.

(6)   Too many rifles that are not perfectly clean.

(7)   Want of dry standing for sentries – just a piece of board is sufficient.

At midday, lunch would be served: bully-beef stew, bread and tea, after which the men not on sentry duty would settle down for an afternoon sleep, the only time of concerted rest in any twenty-four-hour period in the line. Sleep lasted three or four hours before tea was taken at 4.00 p.m. with a further inspection of equipment at 4.30 p.m. Preparations were then made for that night's work, men being detailed to their various jobs with the necessary tools being handed out from the stores. Work commenced half an hour after dusk, when the Western Front once more beavered away, repairing, as one veteran says, 'all the work we had done the previous night before Jerry decided to knock it down with his shelling'.

*

In the absence of any real enemy, the 2001 programme makers decided nonetheless to stage some destruction on the replica trench soon after the arrival of the volunteers. 'We built a dugout,' explained one modern-day Hull Pal, describing the hard work this had entailed. 'The corporal slept in it one night but the next day they knocked it down and burnt all the wood out, ripped it all out just to see the reaction; but we had it all back up again in an hour. You could see that they were surprised.'

But at least work kept the men warm during the night. Although the month of October turned out to be the warmest on record, in the two or three hours before dawn the temperature was still barely above freezing, as would be expected in late autumn. 'The first week my rib cage was constantly in and out, it was like a generator, constantly shivering,' commented one volunteer. 'The second week I wasn't so bad, to be fair. I don't know if it's these puttees that cut the circulation to your feet, but your toes are always cold, just rattling in your boots. My jaw aches from shivering and you are clenching your teeth all the time, sub-consciously, even in your sleep, and that's what wakes you up, the shivering.

'When you are there on the firestep and the mud and damp is crawling into you, and you are laying on your side and your bones are getting cold, do you really want to turn over and let the one side which is slightly warm get cold as well? You want to go to the toilet and it is four o'clock in the morning and you're dying for a piss, and yet you are prepared to hang on for hours lying in a foetal position until Stand To, instead of going through the effort of getting up. Every one degree that the sun rises in the morning so your spirits rise, too, although the temperature doesn't really have an effect until the afternoon.'

Just occasionally, sleep allowed the volunteers a brief respite from the arduous routine and conditions. 'The sun had come up and I was laid in the arch asleep,' remembered one. 'It was quite warm, and then all of a sudden the alarms went "Stand To", and it was back to reality. Just for a split second the sun was shining, the birds were singing, the sky was blue; I was thinking it was really nice, really ace, then, "Stand To, Stand To!" And I thought, "Oh, shit!"'

Overall, sleeping during the day, or when possible at night, was far harder than expected. On average, the volunteers reckoned they had been getting two to three hours a day since their arrival. As they could not remove their webbing, boots or any clothes in the front line, they were forced to sleep in any position that proved slightly less uncomfortable than another.

'You've got bruises from the ground you sleep on, you've got aches and pains all over from your webbing, you've got a constant shiver, and then you've got the puttees, and if you wind them too tight and you take them off you've got tramlines all round your legs. It's like you've got a line of trapped skin going all round your leg. It feels weird and you scratch like mad.

'Trying to sleep with these ammunition pouches is impossible, they dig into your hip bones. Sitting and lying on rocky ground, with chalk and flint in it, you can't seem to get the bed or your seat comfortable. You put wood on it but even the wood is uneven. You're laid out with your webbing on, with your water bottle one side and your bayonet on the other, you've got your entrenching tool at your back, and the cork comes out of the water bottle and wets your leg.'

But the unexpectedly mild weather, as well as ensuring that the volunteers' breaking-point was never reached, meant that no-one will be able to say, either way, whether the volunteers could have stuck the weather experienced by the soldiers of 10th Battalion East Yorks in 1916, when alternate frost and rain made life a misery in the front line.

CHAPTER SIX

MAINTAINING BODY AND SOUL

Because we'd had to dump our rations we ate anything we could find. We were digging biscuits out of the mud of the trench and washing them with water from petrol cans, and that's the way we managed until the corporal found a small sack of oatmeal on a railway track, and we lived on that for some considerable length of time. When you are hungry you'll use any means to make something edible that you find discarded by someone else.

ARTHUR HALESTRAP, AGED 103

In theory, the British Tommy was not badly fed, at least relatively. Ask a German family in the winter of 1917, when the Allied blockade and Germany's own economic mismanagement had almost exhausted the supply of food; ask a German stormtrooper who searched British dugouts and found not just food, but good quality provisions to eat, a feast compared with his own paltry rations.

Supplying food to the men in the firing line was of the utmost importance to every army commander, as there was nothing more injurious to morale and performance than hunger. Each army, French, German, American and British, was supposed to supply enough food to the line to ensure that the fighting troops ate at least four thousand calories a day. Energy was the key: tired, hungry troops cannot fight as efficiently as those who are well fed. When the Germans broke through in March 1918, overrunning British supplies, they were stunned to see the extent and variety of Allied foodstuffs. As they were ravenous, they stopped to eat what they could, and the momentum of the attack was lost.

Over four thousand calories per man might sound like a reasonable daily ration, but soldiers worked hard, and heavy manual labour, coupled with the rigours of living in an open trench, consumed body fat. It is part of the soldier's lot to grumble and gripe, and food was always high on the agenda for discussion. It was not the repetition of the same daily diet, although many swore they would never eat corned beef again; it was not the method of delivery, contaminated with muck; or whether the food was only lukewarm that was the cause of most anxiety. The primary concern was whether the food would arrive at all.

Hungry men like their food on time, and the minds of most soldiers will begin to turn to rations as the designated time for eating approaches. Moods brighten or darken accordingly, for food was well earned and any delay was frustrating. Eating was one of the few highlights; like meals served on a long-haul flight, the imminent arrival of food broke up the boredom; men could judge the passage of time with the meals, while the action of eating was in itself gratifying.

Hot or even warm food was welcomed most of all, although for the first year of the war men expected nothing better than a loaf of bread between four, bully beef and perhaps biscuits. By the end of 1915, company field kitchens had moved closer to the front and ration parties made their way up the line carrying large oval tins of food in what were known as dixies. If the communication trench was wide enough, these could be carried on farm-style yokes, a dixie on each shoulder, otherwise they were carried by hand or strapped to a soldier's back. Walking up with the company's hot rations was an onerous job, as the ration party carried not only the food but the hope and expectation of 250 men on their shoulders. Go the wrong way in a trench system and the food would arrive cold; stand on the end of a loose duckboard and the whole board might tip up, causing the man to fall and spill his precious cargo.

If the food was not hot, mules were used to carry sandbags full of bully beef, bread, sugar and tea close to the line. Mules, with smaller hooves, were more adept at walking in mud than horses, while Arthur Barraclough believed they 'were the best animals for carrying supplies because mules stood the shells'. Arthur left the line on several occasions to pick up the rations. 'These mules would come up both sides of the road, as far off the road as possible and then just dump the rations off. The platoon in the line had four sections. One section would be on watch at night, on the firestep, and one section would be out getting the rations in sandbags. Every night the Jerries knew what was happening. When we who were on rationing went out for supplies, Jerry knew those back areas and he always started shelling the road, that's why we always walked up one side, never on the road itself, before we got the rations back to the trench. Then we would have to go and lug these sandbags full of stuff, tins and what not, up to the line.'

The 'stuff' could vary. Breakfast in the front line was customarily bread, boiled bacon and tea, and served into the men's mess tins. Lunch was usually a stew, and in the evening bread, butter, and plum and apple jam was typical, with a cup of tea at midnight to warm the men up. Bread, biscuits and tins of bully beef were the basic fare, although they did not come without their constituent problems. 'We usually had to cut open the tin of bully with the jack knife, which was a helluva job, 'cause nine times out of ten that little key had disappeared from the side of the tin,' recalled one veteran. The biscuits were so hard that most soldiers had to soften them first by soaking them. For men with false teeth such biscuits often proved impossible to eat and instead were pressed into alternative service, as picture frames, perhaps, the soldier chiselling out the middle before pressing in the image of a loved one.

Another tinned food was Pork and Beans, haricot beans with not much more than greasy pork fat. If men were lucky they might receive a sought-after tin of Maconochie's, with its meat and vegetables, usually turnip and carrots, an irregular but very popular treat. 'If we wanted to heat a tin of Maconochie, we would make a stand of half a dozen candles and put the Maconochie on empty cans or anything we could find, put the tin bridging the gap, and those candles would soon heat up the food.'

Food was generally boring. 'In most sandbags, tea was tied in one corner, coffee in another, possibly rice tied in there, prunes too, which was standard issue,' remembers Arthur Halestrap. 'There were also tins of milk, and canned fruit, which we opened with our jack knife.'

The problems of getting food to the line were sometimes insurmountable, and men were left to go hungry, or were forced to rely on their emergency rations, which many ate without waiting for the officer's order. Equally, food, if it did arrive, could be peculiar. More than one veteran has recalled that, 'Instead of getting a loaf of bread they'd give us a roll of Dutch cheese, a thing as big as a football, painted red, and from which we used to cut chunks.' At other times, assorted 'extras' would make their way into the line, as Andrew Bowie recalls. 'When the rations were given out, they also handed out raisins, you could chew them. You could have cigarettes and raisins, but you could swap your cigarettes for extra raisins if you didn't smoke. You just got a handful and put them in your pocket and ate them like sweets.'

In the line, men usually had to rely on their own resources to make or 'drum up' a mug of tea that approached anything like the right temperature. Candles stuck together with jam provided enough heat for one small cup of tea. A rifle pull-through, immersed in whale oil and stuffed in a tin and lit, would heat water sufficiently in twenty-five minutes. But as light must not be shown for fear of attracting enemy fire, any flame had to be completely shielded.

Given the difficulties, men adapted remarkably well, dividing equally what little fare they had. Lewis gunner Harry Patch shared with his friends. 'We were a little group on our own, five of us, although we were part of C Company, part of the Regiment, of course. We took our orders from the officers, but when we were in the trenches we were just that little body alone, and we shared everything. I used to get a parcel from home occasionally, about every fortnight, and in that parcel there would be an ounce of tobacco, two packets of twenty cigarettes, some sweets, if the grocer could scrounge them, and a few cakes. Number Four on the Lewis Gun and I were pipe smokers so that ounce of tobacco was cut in half, half was mine and half was his. The forty cigarettes were divided amongst the other three, thirteen each and they used to take it in turns who should have the odd one. Cakes, chocolates, anything else, were all divided. If you had a pair of clean socks and a fellow had socks with holes in, he'd have the clean socks and threw the others away.'

You did not have to be special friends to pass food around. Arthur Halestrap was forever touched by one scene of sharing. 'I remember on one occasion we'd met up with a few infantrymen and we had this tin of Maconochie's. We were in a trench, in a dugout, and we found a means of heating this tin and we sat in a circle passing the food around, each taking a spoonful at a time and eating it. It was quite casual and normal, everyone taking his own share, that was all. Whenever we were together in those circumstances we were always very close to one another, one body

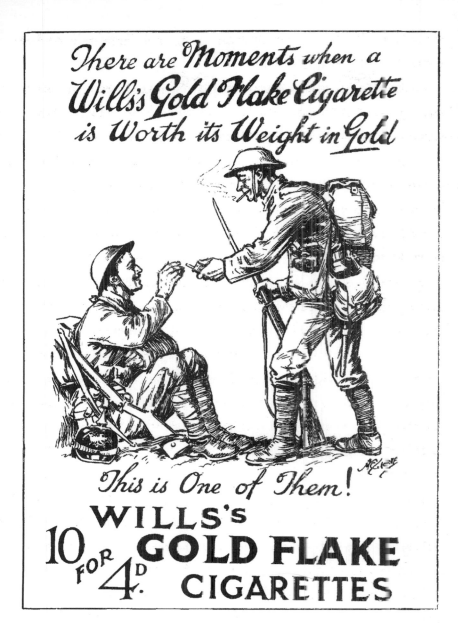

Cigarettes were very important as a source of comfort and a
boost to morale. As smoking was usually prohibited in the
front line, soldiers often held unlit cigarettes in their
mouths as placebos.

of brothers. We felt we depended on one another for our existence.'

If anything, thirst was a greater problem than hunger. Bully beef and biscuits were well known for making men thirsty but with water in short supply, the small tin of tea was rarely enough to satisfy men who, in civilian life, had liked to drink with their meals.

The supply of water to the army as a whole, and to the men in the line in particular, was a logistical nightmare. The old adage that it took half-a-dozen men behind the line to keep just one in it was true, for an enormous daily effort was required not just to supply soldiers with the weaponry of war, but to supply fighting men and their animals with enough food and water to survive.

Carrying provisions up to the front was almost always difficult in the autumn and winter months, and sometimes simply impossible. But inclement weather brought its blessings too. There was always the opportunity to chip away at ice, collect newly fallen snow, or siphon rainwater from a puddle, an activity less likely in summer, for any rainfall would quickly evaporate while the chalky ground of the Somme soon drained surface water.

To find enough water, the Royal Engineers were given the task of boring deep into the chalk to reach the water table, then pumping water to storage tanks. Elsewhere, water was drawn straight from the River Somme, purified and then pumped to water points, while extended pipelines were laid from wells to water depots near the town of Albert. On the battlefield, heavily sandbagged water butts were constructed, as were movable bowsers built on trolleys. Wooden water troughs were also made to fill water bottles and dixies, and canvas troughs carried water for horses and mules.

It was an enormous co-ordinated military effort supplemented by the soldiers' own use of village pumps and wells, and water drawn straight from springs, streams and rivers. Wells and rivers could be a risky source, as there was always the possibility of deliberate or accidental contamination. When men of the Royal Garrison Artillery filled their cooking dixies with water from one stream, they used only a sandbag to filter out anything untoward; it was hardly scientific.

Men filled their water bottles before going up the line, but this water was for emergencies only and could not be drunk unless with the express orders of an officer or *in extremis*. As Arthur Barraclough says, 'You had a water bottle, but in the ordinary way, you wouldn't use that unless it was the last gasp.' Instead, drinking water had to be brought to the line by men sent on nightly carrying parties. In the close confines of communication trenches, they would carry water in dixies, or more often in petrol cans, which retained their marking 'Highly Inflammable', although 'Highly Unpalatable' was more descriptive of the can's contents. A match dropped into the can was the best way to burn off any excess petrol, followed by a rinse, but in reality, it seemed to those who drank the offending water that nothing was done; the smell of Pratt's Motor Spirit or British Petroleum remained distinctive. One veteran who dropped a match into an empty can, after it had been used for water, found that a flame burnt for five minutes before being finally extinguished. As Harry Patch jokingly claimed, 'They said if you were there long enough you could tell the difference in taste whether that water came in a British Petroleum or a Shell can!'

The shortage of any sort of water for personal use was difficult for men to cope with. 'In the line, there was very little water to drink, never mind washing yourself or owt like that,' asserts Arthur Barraclough. 'You got so dirty, your face and hands got so filthy with digging. There wasn't much washing, not till you got out. You couldn't really shave in the front line.'

Shaving was, nevertheless, a daily requirement that usually meant saving the last dregs of tea. There was a good reason behind the order, health and hygiene apart: repetitive tasks helped maintain discipline and standards, but more importantly, when the Box Respirator, the new gas mask, was issued in late 1916, it was vital that the men's faces were clean to keep the mask's seal intact. Yet not all orders were as sensible. As a Company Signaller, Andrew Bowie received one or two absurd requests passed down from Divisional Headquarters. 'I was in a privileged position being close to the captain. Orders came through which said, "Although you are front line soldiers, you must bear in mind that you must keep very clean and respectable. Your boots must be kept clean of mud if possible, and you must shave every day", and, "as a Highland Regiment, you must wash your legs behind your knees", which was a joke. Later some posh officers came up and I was with the captain at the time, and they came to him and said, "We've come along the trenches and we have noticed that none of our orders have been obeyed; the men are looking muddy and unshaven. You haven't shaved, either." He said, "No, I won't. If my men can't get water to drink then I won't take water to shave."'

A present from home, including a depiction of the
censor's work.

Obedience engendered by thorough training ensured that most men carried out orders, whether they were under direct control or not. Arthur Halestrap went over the top in 1918, following up an advance made by the infantry. With no food or water, they hunted round until they managed to find a can of unpolluted water. 'We kept that for drinking and cooking purposes, but for washing we had an old German helmet in which we had some water which was petrol-tainted. We made sure the helmet was propped in such a way that we didn't lose the water and we used it for a whole week, because although we were on the move we washed and shaved using the same water. It was pretty juicy by the end. But the discipline was so great that we still cleaned ourselves every day.'

The volunteers of 2001 inevitably could not recreate all of the experience of trench life. The dirt, though, was still there. 'My shaving kit and cleaning kit is absolutely blasted, black,' exclaimed one. 'I could just maybe get one more shave out of it. My towel's black, filthy, and when the camera's coming round you try and hide it, you feel ashamed. I've stretched mine out for two weeks now, but how the hell did they stretch out their towels even longer?'

'You're trying to get a shave and all your shaving equipment is covered in dirt and dust, and your soap's knackered,' complained another volunteer. 'I threw mine away this morning, because I tried to wash my socks with it. You've got to use your soap for everything, getting a shave, a wash, washing your clothes, and when I washed my socks, lots of hair from my socks descended on my soap. Your brush doesn't dry out, so all your shaving gear is wet. The toothpowder, in fact, that was the bane of my life, two weeks trying to open a tin of toothpowder, it's a really tight fit aluminium tin; you can't do it with your hands, and when it's got a bit of water in, it all rusts round the edge, then you have to get your knife, and it takes ten minutes trying to get it open. Both parts are equal and, when we first got our kits, everybody opened this little circular tin to see what was inside and puff, both parts were full of powdered toothpowder, so as soon as we opened it, it went everywhere, so we lost half the tin straight away.'

As the days passed in the trench, some of the volunteers became more used to the conditions. Learning from experience was just how the original Hull Pals would have adapted to trench life, and the volunteers of 2001 were no different. 'When you're eating and there's explosions, all the muck goes everywhere. It's all swimming in the top of your tea, and it's all in your porridge, so either you flick it out with your spoon or you just mix it up and eat it. It's a nightmare to try and keep your mess tin clean, because we get very little water. In the end I cleaned mine with a tuft of grass, and it was fine.'

Other realities of trench life proved more difficult to get used to. 'There's no privacy at all with the latrines and that's been a problem,' admitted one. 'You go there and there's crap all round the seat and urine too, and it's really off-putting. When you go you've got to take all your kit off, take your tunic off, undo your braces. I just sneaked in, it was fairly early in the morning, you've got to go, you've been holding on all night, and you think 'I don't want to do this.'''

Such qualms would not have lasted long had the volunteers

stayed for months, says veteran Andrew Bowie. 'There was no privacy, well, you didn't think about privacy, and every man was the same. Nor was there toilet paper, you used your last love letter from your dearest friend, that's where all the good love letters went. You used to see them reading them for the last time before they came to a sticky end. If you had a sense of humour it helped a bit, you can imagine a lovely delicate lady doing her best to write a lovely letter, and that is how it ended.'

In the morning the latrine buckets had to be taken away, two heavy pails of excrement and urine lugged down the communication trench and emptied. This job was tackled by the latrine corporal (known popularly as the rear admiral), or if he was unavailable, by any man who had annoyed the sergeant during the previous twenty-four hours. A bag of chloride of lime was always on hand, the contents of which were liberally scattered around the latrines to act as a disinfectant. The latrines were situated in a part of the support trench that was dug away with little more than a pole or spar to sit on. There was precious little sanitation at all. 'It used to stink like hell,' recalled one veteran. This was especially true in the summer when thousands of bluebottle flies descended on the latrines. In the chalk of the Somme it was actually possible to locate the latrines by the blue hue that hung over them, while a large sudden swirl of flies would also alert the Germans to the toilet's use.

The modern volunteers were not slow in replicating their grandfathers' liking of the rum ration. 'That rum ration in the morning got the blood flowing again, and you could feel it burning down your throat. But I wouldn't say it was a life-saver or anything like that,' says one volunteer. 'I don't know if it's less strong than it once was; perhaps we are more used to alcohol nowadays. I will say this, though. No matter how mild the weather overall, in the morning it was bloody cold just before dawn. That rum was a nice treat to perk us up.'

The all-conquering, fifty-nine per cent proof rum ration of 1914 warmed the cockles of many a soldier's heart, both literally and metaphorically. It proved an invaluable tool in steeling the nerves of men about to go over the top, helping quell barely controllable fear. And day-to-day, on bitterly cold mornings, the news that the rum ration was on its way was heaven-sent to miserable men standing in ten inches of freezing water. As Andrew Bowie manned the front line trench during the war's harshest winter, his longing for that tot of rum was never greater. 'There was a chap from Inverness, one of the original territorial battalion, he was a fine fellow, and he'd come round with the rum and he used to sing a song "When the sands in the desert grow cold". As he went along the trench, he sang, and you knew he was coming, to give you this godsend, this drop of rum to keep you alive. You needed that rum. I was a teetotaller when I joined the army but I was glad of my tot. If you'd been standing in cold water all night, or been out working in the mud, you'd be glad, too. Rum won the war for us, because you felt you could not go on unless you had something to warm you up.'

The ration came in a large earthenware jar, with the letters SRD stamped on the side, which officially stood for Service Rations Department, and unofficially, to those in the line, as 'Seldom Reaches Destination'. According to some veterans who served for an extended period, the once viscous rum ration was gradually diluted. This may have been more to do with their increased tolerance, for the first-ever tot of rum given to a man invariably brought forth a startled glance, a gasp, followed by a fit of choking-and-coughing as the rum burnt its way down the throat. The rum was medicinal and had dramatic effects on men who were cold and tired, as witnessed by one Royal Fusilier officer, Richard Hawkins. 'I went round with the rum bottle every morning at dawn, and the tot was an eighth of a pint, and you could feel that rum going down into your boots, which were probably full of icy water, drying up the water and coming up to you and saying, "Now where's that ruddy Hun?" It saved lives! It was old navy rum, until supplies ran out; and then we got ordinary rum, by Jove, there was a difference.'

Given the potentially destructive effect rum could have on a man's senses, there were strict rules as to when and how it must be administered. Rum was issued during Stand To in the morning, and generally not in the evening, as men would become sleepy and therefore unfit for duty. It was deemed important that an officer should always be present and the rum, once given, had to be taken straight away. Just how much was given varied from company to company, with rum variously being measured into a glass, poured into a mess tin or offered on a large tablespoon. One veteran recalled the rum being put in his tea, another that he was offered the choice of rum or a glass of strong lemon squash.

Not all officers stuck to the letter of the law. For speed, some officers poured enough rum into one mess tin for half-a-dozen men or more to share amongst themselves. Other officers did not wait to see if the soldier drank his ration there and then, and there were some who preferred to delegate the responsibility. In Andrew Bowie's company, delegation was routine. 'No, the officer wasn't there. Instead he would say "Corporal so and so, you take charge of the rum." It was always given if possible to the man who was the teetotaller to carry it, to make sure it would be served in a proper way and not just given to pals. The officer would assume that the NCO was a responsible person and could be trusted, but that wasn't always the case because the NCO kept a little in his water bottle.'

Obviously, not all NCOs could be trusted. As with anything that had a premium value, there was always the chance that men would abuse their position and take more rum than was their share, secretly diluting the remainder. As one veteran, Smiler Marshall, sang with gusto, eighty years on:

> If the sergeant's pinched your rum, never mind, never mind
> If the sergeant's pinched your rum just swear and blind
> They're entitled to a tot, but they drink the blooming lot
> If the sergeant's pinched your rum, just never mind.

There was more than a hint of truth in the song, for as Andrew Bowie asserts, 'There was always a bit of argument about the rum jar, oh yes! You had a water bottle in your equipment and some of the NCOs always had them half full of rum, and if they had any chance to get the jar they would pinch the rum and put it in their water bottle, and the ordinary Tommy wouldn't get it. There was a lot of favouritism going on, too. Sergeant majors, nine out of ten would have a water bottle full of rum. They could make an excuse if they were found with it, they would say they'd kept it in reserve or something, which would be a lie. Yes, there was much friction. There was a corporal in our company called Skeet, and he was coming round with the rum jar and my friend Jock Ewart, he was rather a strong character, and he came to Ewart, this fella Skeet, and he handed him his rum and Jock said, "That's not a full ration." Skeet said that it was and Ewart insisted that it wasn't. "I want a full ration of rum." They were standing on the edge of a shell hole and Ewart lost his temper and gave Skeet a head butt right in the middle of the face, and knocked him into the shell hole. There was nothing said about it. Nobody would have told on Ewart, and even if it had gone to court everybody would have backed up Jock, because they knew what Skeet was doing. People would have said Skeet had slipped and fallen.'

For some men, the first issue of rum was their last, as they refused further issues, or passed their share on to a neighbour. Arthur Barraclough was never partial to his rum. 'There was a lance corporal in our group called Mike, a Scotsman, he was a big lad, nice fella and a good sort. We asked Mike if he liked rum and he said that he did, so four of us used to give him our ration into his water bottle, we all tipped it in carefully and he kept having a nip.' Passing on the ration was an act of kindness but it could have tragic consequences, and there was more than one occasion when a man with two or more tots in his stomach let bravado overcome sense and was sniped as he briefly rose above the height of the parapet to taunt the Germans.

Taken internally, rum was undoubtedly able to keep flagging

spirits on the right side of despair. Taken externally, rum had its uses too, according to Smiler Marshall, a veteran of more than three years' fighting in France. 'There were plenty of lads who'd give me their ration for one or two cigarettes and so my water bottle was always a third or a quarter full of this neat rum. When we were in the front line, the orderly officer and orderly sergeant used to come round twice during the night, once just before twelve, and once between five and six in the morning to see things were all right. When they'd gone past, I'd know they'd get a good distance along the front line to go. Then, as quick as lightning, I unwrapped my puttee and took my boot and sock off and I poured some rum into my hand, taking a little lick myself, then rubbed it into my toes for five minutes and then put my boot and puttee back on. When they went by next time I did the same to the other one and my feet were as good as anything. You are not allowed to take any clothes of any description off in the front line but I managed to do that for all three days we were there.'

As well as the physical demands for food and warmth, there was the endless desire to sleep. Men, forced to stay awake, standing on sentry duty, working on fatigue parties, craved rest so that their bodies and minds could recuperate. Living with sleep deprivation taught them to rely on very little rest, and to seize the smallest opportunity to sleep for as little as five or ten minutes at a time. A famous photograph taken by the official cameraman shows men of the 11th Royal Fusiliers sporting their trophies taken from German trenches after a successful attack. According to their officer, Lieutenant Richard Hawkins, the men in the picture were fast asleep two minutes before the official cameraman arrived and one minute after he left, such was their exhaustion. The adrenalin that pumped through the veins during an attack sapped men of all energy once the fighting was over, very different from the slow but incessant drain on the human battery expended during normal trench life. Either way, men learnt to sleep, a few minutes here, an hour there, surviving on an average of perhaps four or five hours a day. Even in the line where the noise of war continued almost unabated, men learnt to switch off, as Harry Patch recalls. 'Up to a point, you slept. I mean everyone when they want sleep will sleep. You may keep awake for hours on end but eventually you will drop off, you can't live without sleep, so you had a sleep of sorts, perhaps an hour, two hours, then you would wake up and wonder for a moment where the hell you were and what you were doing there.'

Those fortunate enough to sleep in dugouts had narrow wooden bunks six foot long, perhaps two foot wide, covered in chicken wire. Bunks were built two or three high, and might line both walls of a passageway, with just a small gap between to squeeze through. The smell was often beyond belief, and with rats as constant companions, the dugout was often less than appealing. Yet these shelters provided some modicum of safety from rain and shells, and as such they were rarely passed up by soldiers. For those men who had to sleep outside, there was the firestep or 'funk' holes cut into the trench walls. They sprawled out, oblivious to the equipment that dug into their backs and sides. In rainy weather they tried to keep dry by using groundsheets, which were rubber-coated on one side, to ward off the water, although as one soldier said, it was something of a Hobson's choice between remaining partially dry by lying on the groundsheet, thereby avoiding the rising damp from underneath, or sleeping under the sheet, and keeping off the drizzle from above but not the moisture below.

In summer men slept on groundsheets with nothing to cover them; in winter (between October and March) they were allowed to take their greatcoats up the line to use as blankets. The greatcoat was not waterproof, and a prolonged downpour left infantrymen soaked. In such situations, most elected to sleep upright, their helmets keeping the rain from trickling down the neck while the groundsheet was wrapped around the shoulders like a cloak. In cold weather, sleeping was a miserable experience, although Arthur Halestrap was luckier than most. Before enlisting, he had taken advice from former Boer War veterans on how to keep warm by always keeping as much of the cold ground temperature away from the spine as possible, although it was a technique that relied on having at least one blanket. 'I was always told to put the blanket underneath me and keep the uniform for putting over me, maximizing the amount of warm air between your greatcoat and your body, which is better for you. I'd have a woolly hat as well, and my tunic would cover my feet to keep my extremities warm. I learnt from my mistakes never to take my shoes off when it was frosty, though. I did on one occasion and my shoes were frozen when I came to put them on and I had to cuddle them under my arms to defrost them.'

So desperate was the need for sleep, so accustomed did men become to sleeping rough that, ironically, they found it difficult to readjust to soft beds. It was not uncommon for men to elect to

From a Sergeant of the Leicestershire Regt.,
British Expeditionary Force.

"I must let you know how grateful the fellows are to you for making such a warming and stimulating beverage as OXO. A patrol of us had to go out the other night in a great hurry to do some work. We got there and found that we had got a long job, and it was terribly cold. I am sure if it had not been for your famous OXO we should have been nearly frozen."

HOT

OXO

fortifies against chills

A cup of OXO and bread, or a few biscuits, enables one to carry on for hours, whether at the Front or at Home.

OXO Ltd., Thames House, London, E.C.

A soldier's 'endorsement' was a good marketing strategy aimed at families back home.

sleep on the floor when they returned home. It was more 'comfortable' there.

Sleep was a restorative; parcels from home were a high point. When rations arrived haphazardly at the line, there was nothing better than a parcel with delicious foodstuffs to reinvigorate dulled taste buds. Tinned or fresh fruit, Oxo cubes, cocoa powder, chocolate, a cooked chicken, a homemade cake, virtually anything could be sent if wrapped carefully enough. The army was well aware of the importance of contact with home, whether by parcel or by letter, and put enormous emphasis on a regular delivery; even British soldiers fighting in countries such as Italy could expect a parcel to be delivered within two weeks.

The Royal Engineers, with a staff of 250, had originally been given the responsibility for the delivery of letters and parcels reaching the front. However, as the numbers of servicemen in France grew, so an Army Postal Service was created, burgeoning to a staff of four thousand, responsible for sorting all mail in London by unit before shipping it to France. Once on the continent, the mail was sent on to the relevant railhead, according to the most up-to-date reports on unit location provided by General Headquarters, before being forwarded on the next supply column to the right division, and then onwards to the Field Post Offices. They in turn would ensure delivery to each unit's postal orderly, who would pass them on to the recipient.

The system was highly efficient (in both directions) and men out of the line in France or Belgium could normally expect to receive letters and parcels within two to three days of posting, and a week to ten days in the line. Mail was vitally important for morale, and prompt delivery, regardless of the volume of traffic, was one of the war's smaller triumphs. On each day the Army Postal Service handled many thousands of bags of mail and sixty thousand parcels, although at Christmas 1916 the letters and parcels filled a staggering 157,948 mail bags during the first week of December alone. One of those parcels was sent to Andrew Bowie. 'I got a gift from my aunt and uncle at Christmas including some shortbread and a haggis. The haggis had to be cooked, which was rather a problem, as one officer pointed out to me as he passed: "Hey, make sure you boil that for two hours." There were six of us looking with great admiration at the haggis being cooked on a stick fire, but I doubt whether it ever got two hours.'

As well as the parcels from home, hampers of food were sent out to the front from some of the leading stores of the day, such as Harrods, and Fortnum and Mason. While by no means the exclusive preserve of officers, the vast majority would clearly go to those who could best afford them, and were paid for by loved ones at home or drawn on the officer's own bank account. Hampers amidst carnage might seem wholly incongruous today and, even in 1916, some were taken aback at their presence on the battlefield. After one attack, 2nd Lieutenant Norman Collins took the pay-books of the dead to Brigade Headquarters. After passing body parts sticking out of the walls of the communication trench, he arrived at the steps of a deep dugout and, though dirty and dishevelled, proceeded downstairs. 'I stood there amazed by the luxury of the officers who were down there. I was asked very politely to have a cup of tea, and they handed me some cakes, which I ate. It was incredible. In front of me, I noticed some parcels and I saw that these lovely cakes came from a box labelled Fortnum and Mason, Piccadilly. It did seem strange that a short distance away you had the war going on and heavy shelling and in this dugout you were back in London.'

Officers were not always expected to pay up-front, despite the significant risk that any recipient might be dead before the parcel reached him. Lieutenant Richard Hawkins, fighting on the Somme, recalled how a fellow officer wrote to the tobacco firm Dunhill for a new pipe, a parcel being delivered to the dugout the day before an attack. The parcel contained not one but a whole selection of pipes with a note. 'We don't know what size or shape you prefer, so we are sending a dozen for you to choose from and when you've made your choice do please at your convenience return the remainder.' In this case the officer survived the attack but was killed shortly afterwards.

Harrison's Pomade, which purported to kill the lice that plagued soldiers, was another common request, as were socks, khaki handkerchiefs and tobacco. Cross-contamination was always a risk with items tightly packed together: one veteran remembered receiving a cocoa-covered chicken, while Harry Patch recalls one incident that proved especially frustrating. 'My brother was home on leave from France when he got married and I had a parcel from him with a piece of wedding cake and an ounce of tobacco. In transit both had got mixed up together and I couldn't use either.'

One or two items sent to the front were a little less mundane than tobacco or socks. In response to the war, firms across the country manufactured 'fail-safe' items that might just save the life of a loved one. Andrew Bowie had an older and very loving sister called Helen who was naturally concerned for Andrew's health. 'I had an uncle who happened to be an agent for bullet-proof vests, that looked similar to a thickly padded waistcoat. Now these vests would, in theory, stop a bullet, so my sister purchased one of these and sent it to me and I wore it under my tunic. There was a sergeant major, who was a rather cowardly type, and he knew about my bullet-proof vest and he used to say to me, "When you get killed, I'll have that vest." We were out on rest once towards the end of the war, and he said, "Come on, we'll try your vest out." So we draped it around a sandbag and went about fifty yards away and fired shots at it, and they went right through the vest, after which his eager claim dropped a bit. We were, though, firing from very close and it might still have given protection from a few hundred yards when a bullet's power was more spent.'

Along with the thousands of parcels came the millions of letters, a staggering twelve and a half million a week to all fronts by 1918, according to John Ellis in his book *Eye-Deep in Hell*. Letters from home were unrestricted in number and uncensored in content. Letters going the other way were, in theory, not rationed, although the time in which to write them often was. However, censorship was tight. All letters from France were subject to scrutiny by an officer, usually the platoon officer, who would laboriously plough through each one, striking out anything that hinted at a location, or the passing of a 'trade' secret. In general, officers found the contents of the letters boring or mildly amusing, not least for the extraordinary spelling contained therein; others found the letters' sentiments mildly embarrassing to read. With illiteracy rates still high in Great Britain and self-

An over-optimistic advert for the performance of a bullet–proof vest. Andrew Bowie found his less than satisfactory.

expression poor, many soldiers found simply saying anything of any consequence a great effort. Faced with the horror of their existence, writing down feelings would in any case cause their families distress and might undermine the soldier's own resolve to carry on. Instead, the chit-chat of the stiff upper lip was deemed more appropriate, with terms such as a 'fine show', or 'raring to go' meant quite earnestly. Others sent letters of remarkable frankness. 'Apart from the hardships of the trenches and weather, the continuous shelling for days on end is a great strain on the nerves and not a few break down completely (shell-shock they call it),' wrote one veteran.

There was no 'industry standard' as to what constituted a 'correct' remark. Soldiers who wrote home were occasionally pulled up for the mildest criticism of military authority. One veteran remembered how, after he wrote about the 'same old bully beef and biscuits', his officer asked why he couldn't say that he'd had 'delicious roast beef and baked potatoes' instead. The private, honest to a fault, merely retorted that he couldn't claim to have had what he'd never received. In contrast, another veteran believed he could get away with giving a full and frank description of his part in the first ever tank attack on the Somme, just eight days after the events. Writing on 23 September 1916, he concludes his letter, 'I think this is all I have to say at present (and quite enough too! From the censor's view I expect), so I will close.' The censor noted, 'Hear! Hear!!' at the foot of the page, although nothing was struck out in the seven-page letter. By early January, the same man felt confident enough to write the following in another letter: 'Thanks for that cutting from Sir Douglas Haig's despatch. It doesn't mention any names, but I don't think there is any harm now in mentioning that it was our Division with the 10th Queens well to the fore) which captured Flers.' Once again the censor saw no reason to strike out anything.

Those soldiers wishing to send personal and private information could use what was known as a 'Green' envelope. After enclosing a letter, the man in question could be confident that it would not be read by his officer but sent down the line, although the wording on the envelope that 'Correspondence in this envelope need not be censored Regimentally', meant there were no guarantees. Instead, 'Green' letters were liable to examination at the Base once the writer had endorsed the outside with his signature, guaranteeing that 'I certify on my honour that the contents of this envelope refer to nothing but private and family matters'.

These envelopes were popular with the men, although their availability was never unlimited, leading to a great deal of frustration amongst men worried, perhaps, about the fidelity of a loved one at home. Furthermore, the distribution of the envelopes was occasionally suspended to a whole company when a man had been found saying anything deemed militarily sensitive. An officer, too, could be disciplined for imprudent remarks in letters home, usually losing leave entitlement, perhaps for anything up to six months, by which time he might well be dead.

Restrictions on sending anything that could be construed as useful to the enemy was nevertheless a rule made to be bent. A lapel badge purchasable in Ypres and sent home clearly identified where that soldier was at the time of writing. Codes arranged by

1. Bethune
2. La Bassee
3. Loos.
4. Givenchy
5. Vimy Ridge
6. Arras
7. Mercatel
8. Gomiecourt
9. Signy
10. Le Sars

A soldier's code for disclosing his whereabouts when
writing home.

soldiers prior to their embarkation for France were another
favourite. One veteran wrote a list of town names, A for Arras, B
for Béthune, C for Cambrai; another used numbers so that,
through correspondence, his family could follow the progress of
their son. Andrew Bowie was also up to the latest tricks of the
trade. 'You could not say that you were fighting at Ypres, because
if you did then the officer would put a big black mark through it.
But people found a way to counter that. There would be an understanding with their people at home that the first letter in the first
paragraph would be a Y, "You are in our constant thoughts", the

next paragraph would start with a P, "Present days at the front are very trying" and the next paragraph would start with an R, "Received your letter with great thanks," and so on, and then E and then S – Ypres. So you would tell your friends at home that you were at Ypres. I think, in time, the army became aware of this trick and watched for it.' To avoid the scrutiny of the army altogether, a few tried their luck posting notes in civilian letterboxes. This was strictly against regulations, but some soldiers were lucky, noting their surprise that, as often as not, the letter got home.

'How important was mail? It was very important to receive letters from home, and you looked forward to receiving them,' says Andrew Bowie, 'even if you didn't acknowledge them all the time. Some men seemed to have a pad on their knee every time they came out of the trenches on rest, writing letters, but I never got down to writing lots of correspondence. You see I hadn't a wife or a sweetheart and I'd nothing to write about, except to my immediate family, and I'm sorry to say I hadn't much to tell.'

For those like Andrew Bowie who were not great correspondents, or for those wishing to send a quick message home, a field postcard proved very useful. These were pre-printed cards with phrases such as 'I am quite well' or 'I have received your letter dated_____ telegram dated_____ parcel dated_____,' the man deleting or dating the card as required. It kept men in touch with their families and offered a few the chance for pointed sarcasm, one veteran writing, 'I have received your parcel dated Never!'

The army's desire for secrecy was understandable but excessive. A ban on keeping diaries at the front was implemented early on in the war, followed in 1915 by another on keeping cameras.

NOTHING is to be written on this except the date and signature of the sender. Sentences not required may be erased. If anything else is added the post card will be destroyed.

I am quite well.

~~I have been admitted into hospital~~

~~sick~~ ~~and am going on well.~~

~~wounded~~ ~~and hope to be discharged soon.~~

I am being sent down to the base.

~~I have received your~~ ~~letter~~ ~~telegram~~ ~~parcel~~

~~Letter follows at first opportunity.~~

I have received no letter from you

~~lately.~~

for a long time.

Signature only.   W. J. Parkhouse.

Date *Sept 15th 1914*

[Postage must be prepaid on any letter or postcard addressed to the sender of this card.]

The field postcard used by soldiers throughout 1914–18.
W. F. Parkhouse survived the war.

Most soldiers did not think of keeping either or, knowing the rules, obeyed them. But in any army there were those who, regardless of laws, wished to record their war experiences, and many soldiers, of all ranks, took small pocket diaries and pocket cameras to France in which they jotted down or photographed daily events.

Despite the army's prohibition on keeping a record of front line life, diaries were specifically printed for use in France and sold, tempting would-be note takers. The 'Soldier's War Diary', published by Charles Letts & Co., London, contained 'Useful Information Invaluable to every Soldier at Home or at the Front', and was sold by various organizations including the YMCA, which was officially sanctioned to maintain canteens both at camps in England and on the continent. As well as providing space for daily notes, the diary provided advice and information on all manner of front line experiences, including cooking in the field, the penetration of rifle bullets, military abbreviations, comparisons between British and German guns, first aid, soldiers' slang, and a soldier's guide to French. In effect, it was not illegal to carry a diary, only to use it for its intended purpose.

Although the German Army saw no reason to restrict the private use of cameras in the line, the British Army thought differently. In 1914 a small number of men had taken their cameras to war, but these were banned in the New Year. For ease, speed of use and compactness, the popular camera taken to France was the Vest Pocket Kodak (VPK). A surprising number of these cameras were used across all fronts despite the fact that a court martial could face any miscreant caught with one. Most were used by officers who simply ignored the rule, and took their cameras anyway. They took photographs with happy abandon, and, at least in some battalions, senior officers were not just willing to turn a blind eye but actually posed for shots. Other ranks were less likely to use cameras, for reasons of cost if nothing else. Nevertheless, a few took cameras and photographed life in the front line and in reserve, one unconcernedly mentioning his photographic efforts in letters home.

One of the small details that can be discerned from pictures taken at the front or from letters home, is that smoking was a key requirement for a great number of soldiers. Cigarettes did as much to win the war as any tot of rum, but as their presence was general and unrestricted, the humble 'smoke' or 'Woodbine' has always been less celebrated.

The health risks of smoking would not be known for another fifty years, but during the war, not having a smoke was in every way just as vexatious to the spirit as having a smoke was dangerous to the lungs. Smoking kept men intact mentally, quelling fear and reducing stress. Pictures time and again show men with cigarettes balanced between their lips or tucked behind their ears. Chain-smoking amongst soldiers was common and the most truculent soldier could be brought on side by the simple restorative of a 'fag'. Cigarettes were one of the staple currencies of comradeship and were often the last request of a dying man, and the first of a wounded. Little wonder then that nurses commonly carried pockets full of cigarettes at hospitals close to the line, or that clergymen, such as the famous 'Woodbine Willie', did the same when they visited men in the trenches.

'To ease the pressure, we smoked, almost every man seemed to smoke,' recalled 2nd Lieutenant Norman Collins. 'Cigarettes were a great comfort and at the right time worked wonders. My favourite was a brand called Passing Cloud and I recall in many stressful circumstances lighting a cigarette, although out of view of the Germans. Most of the cigarettes were terrible and were hardly worth smoking. The cheap cigarette was the Woodbine, while the Players and Goldflake were quite good; sixpence for twenty or fivepence ha'penny for Players. I never inhaled so I can't say that I was a great addict but some men would take the end of a cigarette and relight it and even though it was saturated in tar and nicotine, they'd enjoy it. Smoking was all part of the camaraderie and, of course, it relieved stress, no doubt about it, it's a drug that relieved stress. You wouldn't sit smoking in the dark in a trench or you'd soon have a few whizzbangs come over. However, behind the lines the men used to gather together, light a cigarette and you could see the ends glowing in the dark.' A naked light could be easily seen half a mile away, and snipers were always on the lookout for any careless soldier who could not resist a quick draw on the end of a fag, the burning tip of which became an effective bull's eye. Harry Patch was a pipe smoker and found that he could smoke if he was careful. 'I used to turn the pipe upside-down so there was no glow from it at night. Just put my thumb over the tobacco. By day you could always get under a ground-sheet with a cigarette or pipe so no smoke went up, but the golden rule was always that you mustn't show any smoke, and at night you mustn't show a glimmer of light.'

The army provided cigarette rations to the men, usually fifty at a time, while all the army canteens that were strung along the Western Front also sold many varieties of cigarettes. Regiments would also provide cigarettes or tobacco for the men in the line as would the many charitable and welfare organizations set up in Britain during the war. There were a few 'lucky' regiments that were never short of cigarettes including one cavalry regiment that happened to have a member of the Gallagher Tobacco firm serving amongst its officers. His regiment at least would be guaranteed some of the most contented soldiers in the British Army.

CHAPTER SEVEN

THE HORRORS OF THE APOCALYPSE: MUD, RATS AND LICE

One of the war's horror stories – and there are many – is that of a man falling into a mud-filled shell hole, slowly sinking as his comrades passed by. They were unable to help owing to orders to keep moving, a decision which, taken out of context, appears callous. Experience however, shows there is a flip-side to every story.

One expedition mounted by the Khaki Chums involved constructing and living in a trench over Christmas. 'We decided that we would both dig our trench and re-fill it by hand when we left,' explains Taff Gillingham. 'On the last day the earth was like liquid glue, and as we back-filled the trench we found we were just shovelling sloppy mud. Eventually we managed to get the ground looking almost level, whereupon one Chum, Alf Godden, attempted to run across the surface from one side to the other and just sank straight in. It was hysterically funny at first and we were making jokes about leaving him and then you could see that as he was struggling he was noticeably getting lower and lower, the mud gradually going over his thighs. We started pulling and tugging but there was absolutely no way that he was going to come out that easily. When you read accounts of soldiers in the war just being left to die in the mud, you thought it totally heartless, but to get several men to dig one out is not cost-effective simply in military terms, especially if a whole battalion is held up going into the line. It took literally four or five of us digging down the side of our Chum to make any headway and although, after half an hour, the mud was cleared to his ankles, we still could not get him out. Even when his feet were exposed we couldn't break the suction until a shovel was put under each foot and he was actually levered out of the ground.'

The misery of winter life in the trenches epitomizes much of what the public at large believe about the war, that it was fought in impossible conditions, in which men all too frequently drowned or were stuck fast in the mud. Images of the battlefield at Ypres underline the view that there was something especially horrific about this war, different from any other war, before or since, and to an extent that view is true. But there was, of course, another side: a world of beauty, of flowers hanging precariously over the parapet, birds singing overhead, butterflies flitting down the trench. For men dozing in the afternoon of a hot July day there was a good chance of a suntan, sunburn and even sunstroke. Such beauty, even in a war, could fascinate a soldier, from the simple placing of a flower stem down the rifle barrel – when the sergeant wasn't looking – to careful drawings of flora and fauna. For

William Smallcombe, a lance corporal in the 12th Gloucesters, the hell of war could be temporarily sidelined as, on 24 August 1916, a day when temperatures reached a very comfortable 78 degrees Fahrenheit, he carefully drew in his pocketbook the butterflies and dragonflies he saw.

Blistering shellfire could not destroy such fine weather, despite what many veterans came to believe. At Ypres, in the late summer and early autumn of 1917, the rain seemed to pour day after day, turning the battlefield into a quagmire. The soldiers could not believe that it had nothing to do with the heavy shelling. As rain and shells fell concurrently, soldiers deduced that the metal passing through the low cloud must somehow induce precipitation. More than one veteran was to reiterate that belief, in interviews more than seventy years later.

What is without question is that the water was frequently there. It was common for men to wade in water ankle, knee, thigh and even chest deep. Trench walls collapsed and life became so intolerable that on more than one occasion both British and German troops were forced out of their trenches and on to the parapets in full view of each other. Relieving men in the line became a serious problem when communication trenches became impassable, and some of the long periods of front line occupation mentioned in memoirs stem from the impossibility or the impracticality of relieving an effectively marooned battalion in the firing line.

When men did come out of the line, they had to stick rigidly to the duckboard tracks or risk getting stuck in the muc, as Ted Francis recalls: 'We were relieved at night, it was raining and pitch black. We had to walk seven miles back to safety, between the heavy shelling that caused huge holes in the ground. You'd got to walk back with your rifle and kit and you'd got to be very careful, for when two shell holes nearly met, it left you about a foot or a yard to walk on safe ground, and many a poor fellow met his death there. We were all so tired, absolutely exhausted after six or seven days at it, and all we'd got to do was walk out, but one fellow slipped, carrying his rifle and kit, into a shell hole three parts full of water, and his shouts to the people passing, well who could refuse him? And the inevitable happened. Holding on to the muzzle of his rifle this man held out the butt to the man stuck, who pulled so hard he pulled the other fellow in and instead of one death there were two deaths. After that there was a very, very strict order that on no account must we help any of our comrades, whether wounded or stuck in a shell hole.'

Rescue, even if it came, brought no guarantee of success. Men who were not drowned were often stuck fast for many hours, even days, and as a consequence were off their heads when dug out. There were cases where rescued men actually left their clothes in the mud, such was the suction, while one man of the Royal Scots who was finally rescued is casually recorded as having died of exhaustion.

Mud got everywhere. 'We were filthy but you didn't take any notice of that. If you fell down and you got covered in mud, so be it,' recalled one veteran. Dried-on mud would be scraped off uniforms when men came out of the line. Of far more concern to the army were the effects that standing in mud and water had on the men's feet, and the resulting condition known as 'trench foot'.

For the volunteers of 2001, the marching alone soon caused an array of painful foot problems. 'Some days I've been marching great,' explained one volunteer, 'then I've put a fresh pair of socks on and my feet have been killing me, all in different places. If you haven't got your socks on just right you're in for trouble. Sometimes the top of my foot's been hurting, then the front, I couldn't work it out. I've had two really bad blisters on each heel and the other day when I took a plaster off for the first time to have a good look at my feet, all my skin came off the back of my heel, there was all blood and pus coming out of it, really painful; and if you've got bad feet, you can't soldier.'

Although this last insight was not lost on the High Command during the war, prior experience of foot problems had not produced solutions. Soldiers had suffered from the same debilitating complaint during the Crimean War sixty years before. It resulted from continuous exposure to wet and cold conditions which caused a reduction in blood circulation. Feet became swollen and typically red in colour and very tender, the sufferer feeling a terrible burning pain. The foot literally rotted, and eighty-seven per cent of cases required treatment at a base hospital. In the worst cases gangrene could take hold, resulting in the amputation of one or both feet. Even with a less serious case a soldier could be disabled for weeks. To combat the wet, trench-waders and boots were provided when the weather was very bad, although the haphazard way in which they were issued annoyed Andrew Bowie 'Some brainy fellow at headquarters decided we ought to be protected by rubber boots, thigh boots. Well, thigh boots and a kilt don't blend very well. The stupid thing was that each platoon got six pairs of rubber boots; what good was that to a platoon of thirty or forty men? We were supposed to carry the boots into the front line and put them on there. How on earth are you going to keep on exchanging rubber boots in all that mud? Impossible. Besides, that was against the rules in any case: you weren't allowed to take off your boots in the front line, you weren't allowed to discard anything, you had to be fully dressed, ready for the enemy.'

'In places you were sometimes up to your ankles in mud and other times up to your knees; sticky, black, more like treacle than mud,' recalls Arthur Barraclough. 'If you got bad feet, you were more or less put on a charge for it. You were supposed to look after them, but sometimes you did, sometimes you didn't. When we came out of trenches we were put under canvas, and at that time it were winter. First thing you did when you got inside the tent was to take your boots off. With treading about in water for a week, your feet froze with your boots. By the time we took us boots off, we couldn't get them on next morning, they were frozen hard. So what they did was, they sent one of the first aid men with some whale oil to stop us getting trench foot. We all sat down and he came round and rubbed the whale oil in. That oil saved our feet!'

A daily foot inspection became crucial to maintaining the combat effectiveness of the men in the line, although, as men were not supposed to remove any clothing, the inspections had to be done by strict rotation. Trench foot had become such a serious problem that, if feet were not looked after properly, a commanding officer could face disciplinary action and, in theory at least, even demotion. 'It should be a point of honour and pride for a platoon commander to be able to say no member of his platoon developed "Trench Feet" during the brigade's tour of duty,' was the encouragement in Standing Orders, but in winter weather this was impossible. Instead, officers reported that men had contracted 'sore feet' rather than trench foot so as to avoid sanctions. Great effort was made to combat the problem. Each man was to carry three pairs of socks, one to wear and two in their kit. (136.4 million socks were supplied during the war.) Boots were to be loosely laced and the puttees not too tight, to avoid circulatory problems. When wet socks were removed, feet were to be cleaned, dried and rubbed thoroughly. Nails had to be cut in a straight line and not too close to the toe. Typically men were detailed in twos to look after one another's feet while the whale oil that was rubbed into the soles acted as protection against the effects of standing in cold water. Remarkable improvements resulted. In 1915, thirty-eight per thousand men were treated for foot ailments; by 1918 this had been cut to fewer than four per thousand.

Standing in cold mud and water during the winter of 1916–17 eventually took its toll on Andrew Bowie's feet. He had only been at the front eight weeks when 'An irritation started around the ankles. I'd been standing in water for so long, the dirt had got in under the pores, and then I began to get swelling in both ankles and in the end I couldn't walk, it got so bad. I couldn't go on and eventually I had to go into hospital. The doctors took the decision that they were going to amputate the left leg below the knee to stop the poison running up the leg. But the next morning, when they came to look at it, the whole thing had burst open, it was like a big ball in front of my ankle, and they thought they'd give me another chance. I was sent back to England to Manchester Infirmary where they eventually cleaned it up.'

One creature seemingly unperturbed by the presence of dirty water was the hated rat. Rats, black or brown, were universally loathed by almost all soldiers in the line, not least because they grew fat on the rotting bodies of men, burrowing their way into the dead and using the cavities under the rib-cage as a home. Quickly attracted to anywhere where there was easy and abundant food, rats became corpulent, 'as big as bloomin' cats', their sheer size making them an easy target for soldiers, who took especial pleasure in their killing. If nothing else, it was recreational.

Out of the line ratting was a popular pastime. A good starting point was a hedgerow, with plenty of rats' holes. All the holes would be bunged with cordite except one. When the cordite was lit the rats poured out, and mass slaughter reigned, as spades and shovels flew in all directions.

In the line, 'If things were nice and quiet, and nothing much doing, I used to put a bit of cheese on the end of the bayonet, prop it on to the side of the firestep and just sit with my finger on the trigger. A rat would come along and start to eat the cheese and I just pressed the trigger and the bullet killed the rat outright. Otherwise we used to just try and carry something handy and hit as many as we could,' recalled Walter Green, a private in the Durham Light Infantry.

Another veteran, Smiler Marshall, joined in the fun. 'We used to throw our Maconochie tins, bully-beef tins or any mouldy bread over the parapet and that encouraged the rats. They used to come and sit there and look at you and more or less ask for food.

In this instance, you were allowed all the ammunition you wanted and as the big blooming rats run along the parapet, you could amuse yourself shooting them, because the bullets were going over no man's land to the German lines, so it didn't matter.'

There was always an abundance of rats, for one breeding couple could be responsible for hundreds of offspring in one year. Even in flooded conditions their noses would poke above the water as they swam through the trenches, their urine infecting the water with Weil's disease. Rats were bold and sought out food with amazing ingenuity. They attacked food kept in packs or kit bags, gnawing their way in and eating the contents despite the best efforts of the men to protect their precious supplies. As Arthur Barraclough recalls: 'We'd got down into this dugout and I saw a nail sticking out of the roof. Now because somebody said it was running with rats, I thought, "Well, I'll hang my rations up there." When I came to get my rations down in the morning I found a rat had climbed up from nowhere and tore a damn big hole in and pinched my biscuits, my emergency biscuits. How the hell that rat had got to swing on that roof and bite a lump out of my haversack, and it's tough stuff is them haversacks, I just don't know.'

In dugouts, rats made their homes in the walls, their eyes flashing in the candlelight. The moment the candles were extinguished the rats would topple the wax-ends from their perches and eat them. Men sleeping in dugouts could not get rid of their omnipresence and tried instead to ignore them, throwing blankets over their heads in order to sleep as rodents scampered over their prone figures. Failure to sleep under a blanket could result in one crossing a soldier's face, or worse still, the hind legs slipping into a sleeper's gaping mouth.

Soldiers from farms had less loathing than most, although one of the few veterans not overly concerned with them was city-born Andrew Bowie. 'I used to cover my face at night with my tunic. I could feel their feet running across the top of my forehead but it never made me shudder, and they would bolt as soon as you got up. I never found them a menace, nor did I feel any uneasiness about them. At one place underground the rats used to come out at night, the same rats, night after night, you got to know them, one without a tail, one with black marks on it. They used to come out looking for food, and go up and sniff the fellas living on the lower bunks. If I saw a rat I didn't do anything to it; some men liked to try and stick a bayonet into them. Rats – they were comrades in disaster, same as we were.'

'You should remember that roaming round the destroyed villages were not just rats but cats, dogs, mice; you name it, we had it,' says Harry Patch. 'Stray cats would come into the line, and a stray dog occasionally, and, as a rule, they'd be as vicious as hell. After the war I worked with a builder who had a terrier that had been born in the trenches. If you were in the same room as the dog, the only way you could get out was if you had a saw in your hand and you showed him the teeth. He was fierce. It was the way they had to live, they all had to get what they could from what was dead or abandoned.'

The exceptional toleration shown by Andrew Bowie towards rats did not extend to lice. No-one harboured lice out of choice; the perfect squatters, they appeared one day out of the blue and steadfastly refused to leave. 'You'd see the damn things crawling, they were all down the seams of your trousers, seams of your vests, your shirt, everywhere, in your hair, under your arms, wherever there was hair, there was lice,' remembers Harry Patch. One veteran estimated that it took approximately twelve days to become infested, although, as lice can survive away from the body for a short time, they could be picked up much more quickly from infested straw, blankets or clothes.

For old soldiers who had served in the Boer War, the appearance of lice in the Great War was no surprise. For young lads new to the line, the discovery of personal lice in a shirt or in underpants was often a cause for acute embarrassment. Brief, shameful secrecy followed before word got out that everybody was in the same boat and so began a collective and perennial battle against an enemy as implacable as any German soldier, indeed more so, for although the war came to an end in November 1918, the louse continued to fight on, remaining with many soldiers into the early days of the occupation of Germany.

The parasites were generally grey in colour, although their exact tone varied from white to grey to 'a sort of browny-white', according to Harry Patch. 'I never looked at the lice closely. I always thought they were whitish, but I was never so interested as to examine them,' states Arthur Barraclough. To experts, the female louse at 4mm was slightly bigger than her male counterpart at 3mm, laying five eggs at a time that took, on average, seven days to hatch, each louse living, if unmolested, for around eight weeks.

Soldiers were not curious about such facts. To them, a louse was a louse for it lived solely on human blood, feeding twice a day by sucking the blood through a puncture hole made in the skin, the bite making men itch almost uncontrollably, which as Arthur Barraclough saw, 'left the body terribly injured. The lice used to bite, making us scratch all the time, or forcing you to rub up against a wall. Some poor chaps were driven mad with it and were scratching so much with dirty fingernails that they caused blood poisoning that put them in hospital.'

To thrive, lice required warmth, humidity and shelter – which made the seams of soldiers' shirts and underwear the perfect habitat. When discarded shirts at a divisional bath were examined, fewer than five per cent were found to contain no lice at all, while over thirty per cent were found to contain between ten and thirty lice. At the upper end of the infestation scale, shirts were found festooned with the little creatures, with no fewer than seven per cent of shirts discovered to have between 130 and 350 lice. Regular baths, and the fumigation of lice-ridden clothes, helped combat the pest, although many veterans recall being quickly re-infested. The problem was that few soldiers had enough baths to make any sort of dent in their overall level of infestation and suffering. 'From the time I landed in France in June 1917 until I came away in September, I never had a bath, I never had any clean clothes. We used to turn our clothes inside out to get rid of the lousy lice but by next morning we were just as lousy as ever,' insists Harry Patch.

Baths, or commonly showers, came in a variety of shapes and sizes, the army utilizing anything that came to hand, including abandoned wash-houses and old brewery vats, the men climbing down ladders into the water. But even when filthy soldiers had the

FIGHTING FLEAS (?) IN FLANDERS

4TH DIVISION

FLIGHT OF FLEAS FROM FLANDERS

WITH BEST WISHES.

Xmas 1914.

opportunity for a wash, it was hardly a cleansing experience, as Arthur Barraclough remembers. 'The only bath you ever got were showers if you were out from the front line. We never got any really warm water, it was always half cold. You'd take your own towel and you'd dry yourself as best you could. It was better than nowt but sometimes there were that little water, it were hardly dropping through, you hardly got wet.'

'If you got a bath every two months you were lucky,' says Andrew Bowie. 'There would be a big tent, a big marquee and next to it an engine, the old roller type for flattening roads, that would boil water and send it through tubes not much thicker than my finger, with little nozzles. These nozzles, six of them, were located every five or six feet, in two rows under the marquee, and that was the bath. The hot water came from the engine outside and when you went in you took off all your clothes and they'd say "Soap up", and then you walked under this spray. But before you even got wet the voice would come "All out" and there you were, left all soapy and dirty. Talk about a bath, it was a farce. You have no idea how filthy we all were. And then when you got out of the shower they gave you what was called a clean shirt; it looked clean but it wasn't, it was still full of lice eggs.' As soon as Andrew was on the march again, his body warmth provided the perfect temperature for the eggs to hatch.

Ordinary soldiers, and not the army, fought on a daily basis to keep the level of infestation under control. 'We were walking with lice when we got out of the line,' recalls Arthur Barraclough. 'But there might be a "Lucky Canteen" and we'd buy a taper, which was a long waxy string, and you could light it and it wouldn't make too big a blaze to make holes in your shirt. You'd take your shirt off and just run it down quick, down every seam. That was one of the favourite ways of getting rid of them. You'd be surprised what came out but you had no hope of getting rid of them all – I'm itching just talking about it.'

'We would scratch them and try and get them out of the seams, or if they were crawling on bare flesh just knock them off,' remembered one veteran. 'Alternatively we might get a short end of candle and burn the lice out, after which I'd get a little hand brush or toothbrush and scrape them all out because they were dead.'

As with killing rats, there was always a certain satisfaction in despatching lice; some men even liked to fry them in a tin lid heated over a candle. Others found satisfaction in cracking them between thumbnails. Whatever the method, such activity, known as 'chatting', was often social, with three or four men gathered round a fire killing as they talked; hence 'having a chat' with friends took on a double meaning.

A less primitive method of killing came with the introduction of anti-lice paste known as Harrison's Pomade, although its effectiveness seems open to debate. According to Harry Patch, 'They used to send us Harrison's Pomade, which we used to rub in. It was supposed to kill them, but I think they thrived on it! Harrison's Pomade, it used to feed them!'

Andrew Bowie recalls that after the Pomade was rubbed on to the skin, the lice would gradually climb up the seams and 'out of your tunic where you could catch them at the top. I don't know if that was the idea but that's just what happened.

'I remember an amusing incident occurring during Church Parade. We never knew when Sunday was until they said "Church Parade today. What are you?" And you could have half a dozen religions in one minute trying to avoid the Parade. This particular day was the Presbyterian service, and the men were lined up and I was towards the back. There were about fifty men in front of me and the hymn was very appropriate, it was "Fight the good fight with all thy might," and all I could see were these fellows, who'd been rubbing in their Pomade, picking off the lice from around their necks as they sang.

'But you didn't really combat the lice; it was the lice that did the combating. You couldn't avoid them. Having lice was like breathing, it was just accepted.'

Not all men were resigned to permanent infestation. Arthur Halestrap found one cure out of adversity. 'I was nearly eaten by lice at one time and I said to the corporal one day, "Whatever do I do about these lice?" "Oh," he said, "that's quite easy. Light a candle and run it up the seams of your shirt and that will kill them." It did kill the lice, but I also burnt the stitches and my shirt-sleeves fell to pieces, which made me very unpopular with the quartermaster. So I wrote home to Mum, and Mum wrote back and said, "Silly boy, you've got some Lifebuoy soap haven't you? Well, I'll send you some more." Lifebuoy soap in those days was a very strong disinfectant soap, so I rubbed it up the seams and had no further trouble, and that's how I kept myself free of body lice.'

There are mixed feelings about the conditions in which veterans had to live. As soldiers look back on the rats, lice and glutinous mud, there is satisfaction, something almost akin to pride, that they survived such a terrible test of their resolve. And then there is an anger too, often deep-seated, that they were made to feel less than animals.

CHAPTER EIGHT

OUT OF HARM'S WAY

After 1 July, the Hull Pals were moved north to the village of Robecq near Béthune, where the battalion trained and was refitted, new reinforcements arriving as a matter of course. 'The calm and quiet of Robecq in mid-summer proved the most potent tonic the Battalion ever experienced,' noted the battalion's War History, and was 'the prelude to the most restful and enjoyable week spent during the whole sojourn in France.' The hospitality of the villagers was noted, as was the peacefulness of their lives, which had remained largely untouched by war.

By the middle of July, the Hull Pals were billeted near Richebourg St Vaast, the scene of a violent but short-lived offensive by the British in 1915. The place was 'definitely quiet' now, as the War History notes, allowing the men to wander around the village and examine the devastation, including the remains of the church and its huge bell, which lay amongst the debris, the date of its casting, 1370, still clearly decipherable.

While there, the battalion's first concert party was born from amongst the ranks of A Company, which used the partially destroyed village school for its debut show. The performance, while not noted for its professionalism, was still rapturously received by men who were starved of alternative entertainment.

Out of the trenches, on rest, the Pals were occasionally able to visit the nearby towns of Merville and Béthune to 'make contact, at long intervals, with a world that seemed almost unreal – a world of shops and tablecloths, of little children and house-proud women.'

There were, in reality, two types of 'rest' in the First World War although they were never officially defined as such. The first wasn't 'rest' in any normal sense of the word, as any surviving veteran will recall, probably with a wry smile. The term, as it applied to a battalion, meant simply a removal from the trenches to a position very close to the line; it was in no way a move in order to recuperate physically or emotionally. Far from it: the sixteen-day cycle of front line, support, reserve and rest ensured that the men, when they were not occupying the actual trenches, were beavering away behind them, manhandling supplies up the line or alternatively clearing roads, preparing defences, or shifting ammunition. As many soldiers rightly claimed, they were worked more during this 'rest' than when they manned the firing line. In late October 1916, 2nd Lieutenant Norman Collins was 'resting' just a thousand yards from the German lines, as a continuous stream of shells passed over his head towards the enemy trenches, so loud in fact that he could hardly hear other men speak. 'Yesterday I was scraping or rather ladling mud off the road from 8 a.m. to 5 p.m. and it rained steadily all day and all this on a sandwich of cheese and bread. This was about a mile from the trenches and was our "rest". We were well splashed with mud from the traffic.'

When not working, Norman's men slept in an open field or in the ruins of a village, inside a barn that had 'more holes than roof'. Villages so close to the line were usually devoid of any civilian life, although a little further back many local people showed themselves tenacious in clinging to their land throughout the war, continuing to farm close to the battle zone. One veteran recalled how he had heard the bells pealing in a village church just as he was about to go over the top. He could not help thinking how incongruous the picture was, of villagers being called to Mass as he was due to go into action. Such civilians could pay heavily for the risks they took when there was a sudden shift in the line towards them.

Before the Somme Battle, a number of villages close to the front line were still in reasonably good condition, and were consumed by shellfire only as the lines moved and they became the new objective. Villages close to the German-held town of Bapaume remained largely untouched by British shells, the church in Grevillers receiving only one unlucky hit on the steeple until the battle's latter stages. Likewise, behind British lines, the church in the village of Mailly-Maillet survived, despite shelling, its wonderfully carved gothic façade well protected by sandbagging. Larger towns were always the subject of both heavy and desultory shelling, but here, too, civilians clung on. Arras 'was once a lovely large town, but now it is a shameful sight. Thousands of houses are knocked to atoms and almost every one bears some trace of shellfire,' wrote one soldier in a letter home in 1916. Even so, he noticed that 'a few civilians still live in cellars. The contents of the houses are all left. Oil paintings, lovely furniture and valuables of all kinds are strewn all over the place. Near this house (we are in a cellar) is a room used for a museum and there are hundreds of pieces of fine Egyptian pottery in splendid condition. There is also a lovely carved oak chest there, being knocked about. Some of the pottery has been used as commodes for soldiers who were here before.' With so many valuables lying around, perhaps it isn't so surprising that civilians would stay until life became impossible, or sneak back whenever they had the chance. In Arras, veteran Ben Clouting remembered a gendarme and an elderly Frenchman pushing past him into the house to remove loose floorboards over a cellar trapdoor. Moments later they reappeared, clutching several bottles of wine. 'I felt annoyed at missing out on such a hoard as I watched them fill their wagon with as much wine as the horse could pull. Finally the old man handed me the last four bottles and pushed off, leaving me to replace the floorboards!'

Billeting in a private house, even if it was badly damaged, was a luxury for other ranks or NCOs, who were able to rearrange the surviving furniture to suit. More commonly, men were billeted all together on abandoned farms, within a central courtyard, protected by walls on three or four sides. One man described the surroundings on a typical farm on the Somme. 'I'm sat down with boots and stockings off and with my overcoat on, in a barn with mud walls. The biggest part of one side of the barn is gone and that is the side where my bed is tonight. Wind and rain is having its own way tonight, but I don't think it will affect us because when three of us tuck in together we will put a waterproof sheet over us. Good lad! One of my bedmates has just pinched three sheaves of straw – so more comfort tonight. There is a devilish stink of pigs here and I'm hungry – therefore I think of eggs and bacon – only think!'

The second 'rest', as it applied to a division, was more akin to a break from action. In such circumstances an entire division would be removed from the line to a back area to recuperate and re-inforce, although there was little time to relax, or put the collective feet up. The army was never willing to let men think in-dependently for too long, never mind allow them to lounge about. They were to be kept fully occupied, working to a daily schedule that was submitted to higher authority for approval. As Harry Patch says bluntly, 'The only rest you were getting was a rest from the shells'. From early morning to late afternoon the men trained, in effect reverting to the military life they would have known back in Britain. 'Today we had saluting drill. Isn't that the British Army all over?' wrote one officer. Men slipped back into a normal routine, and few cared as long as they were as far away from the firing line as humanly possible. The extent of their joy at being removed from the line was to be equalled only by the general air of depression at news of their impending return.

A proper rest meant retiring from the line twenty or thirty

miles and perhaps all the way down to a base camp. A long march or possibly a train ride into the unspoilt French countryside, and almost immediately hollow-eyed men were transformed, the scenery helping to foster a general bonhomie; the men were safe, or at least they felt safe, and there was a great relief in being able to look hours, even days, ahead and not just minute to minute. Only a chance long-range shell or a rogue German aircraft could touch them now, although as the 10th Royal West Surreys found to their cost, a surprise attack could still be devastating. Sleeping unprotected in bell tents miles behind the lines, nearly forty men were killed and sixty more injured one night in August 1917 by a well-aimed bomb dropped by an enemy plane.

Sleeping in bell tents in the middle of the countryside in summer might sound the ideal tonic for nerve-shattered, battle-worn soldiers. But for men starved of civilian contact it was the equivalent of drawing the short straw. It was nice to see the trees and flowers; it was nicer still to be billeted on a busy farm, in a working village or preferably close to a small town.

Prior to the arrival of a battalion in a village, the unit's billeting officer and a sergeant went ahead to make arrangements. When a village was frequently used as a billet, a diagram of its layout was available, giving an indication of the size of each property. A whole battalion might well be distributed across sixty or seventy houses, sheds and barns. The sum paid for each man was small, and bargaining was tough, the price per other rank being whatever the billeting officer could get away with; the maximum was a franc per man, although prices could be as cheap as ten centimes if a barn had little or no straw. Once the rate was agreed, the officer

A village map used by a billeting officer on the Somme in 1916, and a billeting certificate; payment for the commune would follow later.

chalked up the number of men to be accommodated before moving on, taking with him the owner's name so that he could be paid. No-one was expected to house the men for free, although money did not change hands straight away but was claimed by the commune as a whole for later distribution.

In order to pay a village, a Billeting Certificate was made in triplicate, and signed and endorsed by the mayor with the commune's stamp. Once it was completed, the original copy was left with the mayor or an 'influential inhabitant', while the duplicate was sent at once to the officer in charge of requisitions at Army Headquarters for payment. The third copy was kept by the billeting officer.

Once a billet had been established, the men settled in. Most farms that were still occupied were run by an assortment of grandparents, middle-aged women and young children, with young or middle-aged men conspicuous by their absence. Young children were a delight for soldiers, many of whom lavished attention and affection on the youngsters. Norman Collins made great friends with one family on whom he was billeted in June 1917, and he was particularly fond of one child. 'There were no young men there, but it was full of their children. I have snapshots of one little girl, her name was Denise and she is riding on my shoulders and I should think she was about seven years of age. I also have pictures of my bearer, Simpson. He had been a farm boy and for recreation used to hoe the vegetables on the farm just because he wanted to do it, it was a relief for him. And I watched him on many occasions hoeing these vegetables and wondered what he was thinking about. When he returned, the farmer gave him a bottle or two of cider or wine, and he certainly deserved it.'

These weeks away from the line were cathartic for all concerned. Norman marvelled at the opportunity to sleep under white sheets, while anyone billeted on the farm could ride the horses, if they so wished. The farmer even gave the men honey and milk. 'I still remember the scent of the broad beans and it still brings back the memory of that period whenever I smell them growing today, a lovely sweet smell.' The friendship was heart-felt on all sides and when the battalion finally left, Norman noted that 'the people belonging to the farm shed about a bucketful of tears'.

Not all soldiers were enamoured with the farm life they saw. Many were often taken aback at the conditions on French farms: beyond the normal agricultural smells, there was often widespread filth on the floors. The toilets were often shockingly rudimentary, typically little more than a screen erected above a midden, while the use of domestic pets as working animals was a strange sight to some. Misunderstandings arose, and relations between soldiers and civilians were often strained. With more than two million soldiers encamped on a strip of northern France and Belgium for an unknown period of time, feelings were not always fraternal. Farmers complained that chickens were stolen, hedgerows damaged, cows milked and fruit scrumped, while for their part British soldiers could not help feeling that such anger was just a mite ungrateful. 'If there were two or three fowls running wild in the farmyard, they were ours.' recalled one veteran. 'Did we pay for them? What did we have to pay for them with? We used to catch them and wring their necks and give them to the cook. The farmers used to complain, but what was the use in complaining? We couldn't speak French.' Soldiers often recalled seeing a Frenchman berating a mounted British officer about some misdemeanour or other by men in the ranks. Most got short shrift, for the officers themselves were not above a bit of pilfering; one veteran recalled an occasion when 'local peasants armed with various agricultural implements were seen chasing the new Medical Officer and one other Lieutenant across muddy fields.' Both officers, as it turned out, were 'handicapped by struggling salmon stuffed down the front of their breeches.'

During periods of rest the rations tended to be more reliable in both delivery and quality. 'Out of the line, we would still get the same old bully beef, and plum and apple jam too, but we might get fresh vegetables, a few spuds, a bit of cabbage perhaps. If you were lucky you might get a swede out of a field somewhere, if the farmer hadn't harvested them,' recalled Harry Patch. Soldiers bartered with local farmers, using the international language of mime, strutting around a farmyard dropping lumps of chalk for eggs, or puffing from an imaginary pipe to buy some home–grown tobacco. Not all mime worked: one veteran recalled how an attempt to procure a 'shovel' ended with the farmer returning with his 'cheval'. It is entirely possible of course that this was the farmer's homespun idea of a joke or equally that he simply did not wish to 'comprennez'.

As the scope of the war grew, so did the need for the army to formalize the supply of 'extras', such as writing paper, pencils, chocolate, tobacco, matches and even tins of fruit. In early 1915, the Canteen and Mess Co-operative Society, the forerunner of the NAAFI, was founded and opened a branch in France. Canteens were rapidly established to supply comforts to the men, and by 1918, 295 were in operation. Religious bodies also stepped in, such as the Young Men's Christian Association (YMCA), which were allowed to set up marquees in France from mid-1915 onwards, selling hot drinks, biscuits, cakes, notepaper, and cigarettes. There was the Church Army canteen, and canteens run by the Church of Scotland, the Catholic Club and the Salvation Army, most being found at places of major troop concentrations such as at main rail junctions.

'They used to run little canteens where there was a fair number of troops,' remembers Arthur Barraclough. 'The Salvation was one of the best of the lot; they used to come and open tents and sell bits of stuff which troops needed, miles in front of anybody else, and they were very good indeed, were the Salvation Army; there were all sorts of churches opening tents up and down behind the line, but the Salvation Army were nearer the scrapping than anybody.'

One of the few places soldiers could go beyond immediate military authority and discipline was the *estaminet*. Here men could dine out on eggs and chips – there was no choice on the menu – and they could drink *vin blanc* ('plonk'), *vin rouge* or watery beer to their hearts' content, or until kicking-out time at 8.30 p.m. Very often a piano would be brought into service and, for a couple of hours at least, it was possible to forget there was a war on as raucous singing and drinking games just about drowned out the noise of distant shelling. In truth, *estaminets* were mostly little more than private houses turned into a cross between a café and a pub. In British sectors, some tailored themselves to appeal to the British Tommy. The *estaminet* in Suzanne, a village on the Somme, was called Café Cavel, after the famous British nurse executed in 1915 by the Germans for aiding the escape of Allied soldiers trapped behind enemy lines. This seems likely to have been a generous mark of solidarity rather than an astute commercial move, for the owner forgot the second 'l' in Cavell when he painted the name on the *estaminet*'s wall.

To the consternation of some Tommies, comprehension of the English language was not widespread amongst the *patrons* of *estaminets*, and most soldiers knew no French other than the odd words, '*Encore Madame!*' or more likely, '*Non compris*'. A few picked up abbreviations learnt from listening to other soldiers, such as '*Café avec*', meaning coffee with a cognac, although a few more might have wished they had known '*Vous me volez!*' ('You're robbing me!') too. For all the happy times to be had in these *estaminets*, there were those profiteering *patrons* whose high prices helped squeeze the hapless Tommy between a rock and a hard place. Not only was he underpaid by the army, but his counterparts such as the Australians and Canadians earned significantly more, the law of supply and demand pushing prices at times grotesquely high.

Another complaint levelled at civilians was the deliberate removal of handles from farm or village pumps. 'When you were on a march and it was hot weather and you needed a drink of water, they would take the bucket from the well so we couldn't get any water. They valued their water and they did not want the well to be dry after a regiment had passed through,' recalled one veteran, seemingly without much rancour. Harry Patch felt more indignant. 'The farmer had a pump in the farmyard that was used to draw fresh water from the well, but he'd taken the damned handle off so that we couldn't use it. I was a plumber in civilian life, so I got to work. I got a strip of wood, coupled it up to the piston that goes up and down inside the pump barrel, bored a hole and put a pin through. As long as that piston was working it drew water. When we left I took the handle in case we wanted one somewhere else, while one of our men put a round through the suction pipe so that the farmer couldn't use the damn pump after we'd left.'

The army knew that by keeping soldiers occupied, flare-ups with civilians would be kept to a minimum. Physical exercise and entertainment were the answer. In Scottish divisions the pipe band often gave concerts, and exhibitions of highland dancing were common. Football matches were popular, as was boxing. Cross-country runs and swimming races were encouraged, prizes being given to the winners. Sports, especially team games, bonded men together and were played at every level in the army from platoon to company, then onwards up the hierarchy to battalion, brigade and divisional levels. Officers were expected to join in too, particularly in horse riding and shooting contests. Amongst the ranks of the 4th Seaforth Highlanders, Norman Collins discovered the boxing brother of the famous pugilist Bombardier Billy Wells. 'While we were out on rest I asked if he would give me boxing lessons. He was about six foot four and I was five foot four, even so he taught me several different techniques to hold my own against bigger men.'

Commanding officers were conscious that men ought to have

fun, and as well as the regulation tug of war, there were amusing exercises such as wheelbarrow races, piggy-back fights and blindfold boxing contests. Other activities may have appeared funny, but races in full kit or while wearing gas masks must have been uncomfortable for those taking part, although the prize of a barrel of beer often encouraged continued application and perseverance.

The men were not devoid of recreational ideas themselves, although whether it was a visit to a local brothel or a game of House (Bingo as it is known today), both activities were controlled and regulated by the army authorities. Such activities might have been considered something of a gamble, for both cost money, although the chance of contracting a sexually transmitted disease was much higher than that of walking away with a pocket full of money after a game of House. House was the only gambling officially sanctioned, but with men unsure whether they would survive the following week, chancing their luck was a sport in which they were well versed, and a pack of cards was always on hand. For hardened gamblers, there was also Crown and Anchor. This was banned by the army, although illicit games occurred on a regular basis, enriching players or stripping them of every penny in equal time. The game was played on a foldable board or roll-away mat; speed was of the essence, for games often had to be abandoned at short notice. The board was divided into six squares in each of which there was one symbol – a diamond, crown, heart, club, anchor or spade. Bets were laid on one or more of the symbols appearing when two dice with the same insignia were thrown. It was a game of pure luck, though the banker rarely came off worst, many making little fortunes in the process. Not surprisingly, bankers were generally men who were able to look after themselves in disputes.

Another entertainment was the Army Cinema, a rare but much appreciated distraction. In early 1917, men of the 10th East Yorks were able to watch their own, albeit limited, participation in the film *The Battle of the Somme*, which had been seen in England by around half the population and had been doing the rounds in France from as early as the previous September. It was, and remains, the best attended film ever at British cinemas with over twenty million people paying to see it. More generally, feature films were shown, the best known casting one of the first stars of the silver screen, Charlie Chaplin, whose career had begun to take off as the war broke out. Elsewhere, famous faces from the stage were brought out to France to entertain, including the music-hall star Harry Lauder. His determination to help all he could was made more poignant after the loss in action of his only son, Captain John Lauder, in late 1916.

The greatest source of entertainment was derived from the soldiers themselves. The best known, and most professional were the divisional concert parties. These were often made up of pre-war professionals or men who had discovered a hitherto latent talent for making others laugh. Groups called themselves such names as 'The Duds' (belonging to the 17th Division, and 'The Crumps' (59th Division). Other names included 'The Whizz Bangs' and 'Very Lights'. The men in these parties were few in number and, as a small group, were unlikely to influence the course of the war, so they were often held back from the line to prepare concerts. Jokes, skits, and songs were the order of the day, and while most of the humour would now seem dated, the soldiers at the time loved it. Not all performances were unrelieved jollity. One monologue, simply called 'Spotty', told the story in verse of two friends enlisting together and of their scrapes at the front. When Spotty is killed in the last verse, his friend mourns his passing, an all too familiar feeling for many in the audience.

> *And his eyes they couldn't see me, they never will no more*
> *With his twisted mouth he whispered 'So long mate au revoir'*
> *There was no one quite the same to me for him and me were pals*
> *And if I could only have him with me you could keep your fancy*
>   *girls*
> *But whatever place he's gone to I don't ask nothing more*
> *Than to line up with him like that, so long, Spotty, au revoir.*

Smaller impromptu concert parties were given by battalion or even company wags who felt the urge to entertain while out of the line. These men invariably carried the tools of their trade with them. One veteran, who was later captured during the March offensive of 1918, was concerned about what the Germans might have thought had they bothered to investigate his knapsack, as it contained a woman's wig and make-up. He shouldn't have worried. When the 51st Division captured a notorious defensive position on the Somme, known as Y Ravine, they discovered, amongst the captured stick-grenades and rifles, several women's dresses and 'dancing slippers'.

Newspapers and books were occasionally read, although

standards in literacy varied greatly. 'Brighter' soldiers might stuff a small book into their haversacks, but in surviving letters from the front it is noticeable how few asked for reading material to be sent from home. It was possible for soldiers to pick up a book amongst houses destroyed by shellfire, but whether it was to read or to use as toilet paper would be debatable. Almost all, of course, would be written in French, although one man, a signaller in the Royal West Kents, found several English-language books in the library of Bécourt Château on the Somme. These he 'borrowed', including *The Adventures of Robinson Crusoe*, a finely bound copy he kept for many years until it was lost on a torpedoed merchant ship during the Second World War; the veteran thankfully survived. Of those papers and magazines available to soldiers, a small number were printed in France and Belgium, and were written by the soldiers themselves. The best known was *The Wipers Times*, produced under the ramparts of Ypres and therefore under fire, which bestowed automatic credibility with soldiers. However, by far and away the largest number of newspapers and magazines circulating round the front came from home. Continental editions of papers such as the *Daily Mirror* were sent to France, as were popular magazines such as *John Bull*, *Punch*, *The War Illustrated* and *The Bystander*; others arrived simply as internal wrapping or padding for parcels. The newspapers would be shared, the reports of great victories a source of amusement amongst soldiers who knew otherwise. Conversely, reports of a 'push' often annoyed soldiers who were quick to recognize that a paper had incorrectly awarded a genuine success to one division rather than another. Perhaps for this reason, men like Norman Collins

*Sketches
of Tommy's life*
Up the line. — Nº 5

The main duties in the Front Line in the daytime are watching the periscope, and looking up in the air « trench mortars », with a whistle ready to blow for a warning.

Using a periscope, from *Sketches of Tommy's Life*.

preferred local newspapers, in his case the *Hartlepool Mail* which was faithfully sent out to the front by his brother Bolton.

Requiring less literacy were the comic postcards that were published and sold to British troops. Many hardly needed an explanatory note or punch line at the bottom; if they were good enough, then soldiers instinctively knew what they meant or why they were funny. Army life was the butt of postcard humour on both sides of the line. One popular series, printed in four sets, was 'Sketches of Tommy's Life', produced, according to the envelopes they were sold in, to remind the soldier 'of the bright or funny side of the war'. Each series was sold in a packet of ten cards for one franc and fifty centimes and followed a soldier's experience amid the mishaps of war; they were grouped in chronological order: 'In Training'; 'At the Base'; 'Up the Line'; and finally 'Out at Rest'.

Needing no introduction to soldiers was the best known, and most loved, of all those who provided entertainment in adversity, the cartoonist Bruce Bairnsfather. His creation 'Old Bill' was nothing if not resilient: a stoic, slightly cynical soldier of the front line. His was a personality that all soldiers could relate to, regardless of rank, and his drawings are masterpieces of perception and empathy. There is not one veteran alive who does not have some recollection of Bairnsfather's work, most of which was widely published under the title 'Fragments From France' in *The Bystander*, a magazine that gave Bairnsfather almost instant fame. In the foreword to each edition, the editor was never less than effusive in his praise of the artist. 'Bairnsfather has seen the simple man caught in the vortex of a war of unaccustomed complexity, and shown . . . that human nature and humour survive in the heart of horrors. In it is the spirit of the British citizen soldier.'

Bruce Bairnsfather had gone to France in 1914, a twenty-seven-year-old lieutenant in the 1st Royal Warwickshire Regiment. As the battalion's machine gun officer, he served at the front during the first winter of the war and while there, sought to cope with the horror by sketching cartoons of the events around him. Bairnsfather drew, in part, for the amusement of his men, and his cartoons were handed round within the battalion until he was encouraged to send some artwork to *The Bystander* for publication. More cartoons followed and, when he came to the attention of the military authorities, he was at first censured for having 'degraded' the image of the British Tommy to the outside world. However, such was his obvious popularity that the War Office relented and he was made the war's first official cartoonist.

The man himself was shy and retiring. He didn't always shun publicity, but was never comfortable in front of his appreciative audiences. After the war Bairnsfather's fame waned, although he never lost the tag of being the creator of 'Old Bill' and never saw the money he deserved to make from his cartoons.

Humour, and that special brand of cynical, stoic humour peculiar to the British Tommy, proved a fillip to morale. No-one, least of all the enemy, could understand it, believes Arthur Halestrap. 'The men sang songs such as "Take me back to dear old Blighty" and "I want to go home" and the Germans thought we had had enough and that morale was low; nothing could have been further from the truth; they just did not understand the humour of the British soldier.'

One place that became famous for its conviviality as a rest house and club was Talbot House in the small town of Poperinge. Toc H, its abbreviation in signaller's code and the name by which it was and remains more popularly known, was a fine-looking building. Abandoned by its wealthy owner at the beginning of the war, it was re-opened in December 1915 by the Rev. Philip Clayton, or Tubby Clayton as he was universally called, owing to his rotund shape. Put in charge, Tubby built a place of refuge for exhausted men out on rest. Garnering the furnishings from everyone and everywhere, Tubby opened Toc H with the idea that all those who entered did so without their rank, all were equal, it was a club for Everyman. One of those who spent time at Toc H in the summer of 1917 was Harry Patch. 'You couldn't relax unless you had the chance to go down to Poperinge into Toc H, that's the only time you could forget the strains of war, just for a couple of hours. Tubby Clayton ran the place and was the life and soul of the party. He had a deep, almost bass voice, and he could sing a good song, and he could tell a good tale. He would sing any old chorus. I remember he sang the Ivor Novello song "Keep the Home Fires Burning". The only time I heard that song in Belgium was Tubby singing it in Toc H.

'There were games going on, and you could join in, or if you wanted to borrow a book you could, and the price of a book was your cap, which was returned to you when you brought it back. I believe Toc H, at one time, was a grain store, and all the grain had been stored in the upstairs room, and I take it the wheat was in the centre as the middle was a bit dodgy and so everyone used to sit all around the edge.

'This room at the top was his chapel, where Tubby upstairs became a different man to the Tubby downstairs. He tried to re-assure people in that room, to the best of his ability, that everything was all right. He knew damn well it wasn't. The altar was an old carpenter's bench he'd found somewhere, and he knew, as I think most of the people who went in that room knew, that there would be people there who were about to go up to the front line and would not be coming back.' By the end of the war, Harry was just one of 25,000 men to have passed through Toc H and Tubby's gentle hands.

Church organizations played a great part in helping soldiers both spiritually and practically, with some padres paying a terrible price for this involvement: around a hundred killed. Most mainstream denominations were represented, and attendance on Church Parade on Sunday was mandatory, regardless of whether men were Methodists, Baptists, Catholics, or Anglicans. Out on rest, drum-head services were the norm, with men paraded in such a way as to form three sides of a square (atheists were not exempt but were allowed to turn their backs on proceedings). To many soldiers, such services were nothing more than another duty, and they sang hymns, typically 'Onward Christian Soldiers' and 'Fight the Good Fight', for padres were kept on a short leash by the army for fear that too many sermons about 'loving thine enemy' might soften Tommy's willingness to kill. Those padres who were held in the greatest respect were those who ventured into the trenches, men like the Reverend G. A. Studdert Kennedy (Woodbine Willie) or the Reverend Harold Gibb, shot through the temple and blinded, while those who were never seen anywhere near the firing line were treated with ambivalence or even disdain. It was inevitable that the quality of padres varied greatly between those who truly connected with the men they offered communion to, and those who prayed solemnly that, come the next battle, God would help the men slay as many Germans as possible. It came as something of a surprise and an insult to discover that the Germans had thought they had God's allegiance, for on the belts of the Germans slain, wounded and captive were the unmistakable words 'GOTT MIT UNS' (God with us). It was clear whose side the good Lord was on: the British Service buttons, on which the words 'Dieu et mon Droit' (God and my right) were embossed, said so.

The soldiers in France had one religious concept firmly

embedded in their heads, the idea of heaven and hell: hell was the Western Front, heaven was home. The unspoilt countryside of northwest France wasn't so very different from that in many parts of England, and if men happened to be resting near the coast it would have been just about possible to see the white cliffs on a sunny day. Leave for men in or out of the line was something they could barely hope for. 'You have to remember we'd been with men, men only for years. Good pals as they might be, you were sick and tired of seeing the same faces.' recalled one veteran.

After 1916, the army tried to regulate leave and in theory a list of those who were due to go home was kept, leave being given by strict rotation. With upwards of two million soldiers in France at any one time, even seven days' leave per year per man would mean, in theory, forty thousand men pouring through the coastal ports each week, and hundreds of boats devoted almost entirely to transporting fit and healthy soldiers away from the firing line. In reality, the figure was far lower, as most soldiers in the firing line did not last long enough to become eligible for leave. Even for those who survived, there were no guarantees of getting away 'to see a bit of civilization'. One veteran who served in France for all but six months of the war received one single week's leave in England after recovering from wounds in 1915, then one three-day leave from France in 1917. Nor did compassion play any part in leave. When this same veteran heard that his father was seriously ill after an accident, his appeal for special consideration fell on deaf ears.

'You only got a leave if you survived a year in France. As a private soldier, a ranker, you were very lucky to be alive after a year,' asserts Andrew Bowie. 'I was out in France from 1916 to '18 but I never got a leave from the line, and why? Because I never got enough service, because I was home wounded and when I went back my year started over again. It was a great thing to hear of anyone going on leave. It was a talking point. It came up with the rations that so many men could go on leave, if they'd had so much service, but if you'd had only six months in France, forget it, no chance. That's what made the men wild, because the officers were getting their leave every three months, but the poor rankers had to wait a year. It was a sore point, that.' Officers undoubtedly received more leave, owing, in part, to the enormous strain of leading a platoon, company or a much higher command. In letters home, one officer was fairly sure he could get Christmas leave, despite having served just over two months at the front, an un-attainable dream for all privates and NCOs.

In theory, a man was not meant to know he was due for leave until the actual day arrived. In practice they often knew two, three, even five days in advance. Infantryman Jack Rogers had been awarded leave well before the actual day. 'I was given leave the day before my twenty-fourth birthday, so I could be home on the day, 21 March 1918. I'd written to my mother telling her not to send a cake or anything like that because I was on my way home, when on the 19th, the army cancelled all leave.' The German March offensive began on 21 March, on which day Jack Rogers was captured. He did not return home for another nine months. Both Jack and his family might have wished they had never known about his leave but of course, if no prior warning was given in France, then there could be no advance notice at home. It seems likely that a few soldiers did return home to discover that their families had gone away to visit relatives elsewhere.

Leave, as and when it did come, arrived in the form of a white pass issued, stamped and dated by the battalion orderly room. Once it was given, the soldier was on his way, although he still had to run the gauntlet of army administration, being told to report first to Brigade Headquarters where he obtained a railway warrant in order to proceed on leave. From there, he reported to the Corps Reinforcement Camp where any outstanding pay would be settled with the Railhead Disbursing Officer before the soldier made his way to the station, reporting to the Railway Transport Officer and then catching a train to the port of embarkation. At any time his pass could be inspected. Somewhere along this chain, soldiers were meant to have a bath and a clean set of clothes from the quartermaster, although there is plenty of evidence that men often did not receive the latter. All men were given a chit confirming that they were free from lice and scabies.

Length of leave varied from three to ten days and did not take into account any distance that a soldier might have to travel to get home. Leave began at embarkation for England, and ended with arrival at the port from which the men were due to return to France. Three days might be of use for a soldier who lived in Canterbury or Folkestone but was of little use to men who came from northern England, never mind Scotland. At such a distance, any attempt to get home would invariably lead to disappointment whether a soldier managed the journey or not, for he would have to depart almost as soon as he'd arrived. It is hardly surprising that no small number of men took an extra day, accepting the

7260 Pte Ford Ew

You will report to Headquarters. 124ª Infantry Brigade. at 7 pm on 5ᵗʰ inst., to obtain Railway Warrant in order to proceed on Leave.

On 6ᵘ inst. you will report at the Corps Reinforcement Camp. before 12 noon. On 7ᵗʰ inst. you will report to the R.T.C. GHYVELDE. at 1.45 pm. and thence by train to Port of Embarkation, where M.O⁺ certificate must be produced when demanded.

Pay may be obtained from RAILHEAD DISBURSING OFFICER at Reinforcement Camp, on production of a Furlough Pay Roll.

CERTIFIED THAT Nº 251832 RANK C.Q.M.S. NAME Smallcombe W.
REGIMENT Nº 1. R.E Workshops HAS BEEN GIVEN
A BATH AND ISSUED WITH CLEAN CLOTHING BEFORE PROCEEDING ON
ON LEAVE. HE IS FREE FROM SCABIES.

DATE. 13-11-17

MAJOR. R.E.
O.C. Nº. 1. R.E. WORKSHOP,

The permission to go on leave and confirmation of
cleanliness and good health.

consequences of their actions for a few more precious hours at home.

Thoughts of home were never far away from any soldiers in the line, although their enjoyment of it was often at variance with anticipation. While families were greatly missed, going home often left the soldier with a great sense of dislocation. Civilians could have little real knowledge of life at the front, and ignorant questions, however kindly meant, sometimes left soldiers feeling bewildered, and it was often with resigned relief that they were on their way back to France, to comrades who understood. 'Father in particular was immensely proud of me and took me everywhere,' remembered one veteran. 'I didn't enjoy it, not one bit. Of course, relatives asked what conditions were like but you didn't want to scare them so I said, "Oh, we manage, we get along."' Many soldiers just wanted to be left alone. Some slept their leave away, others ate ravenously, some liked to go for walks, others stayed at home, every man had his own way of using his leave, but for almost all, the time passed too quickly.

Arthur Barraclough received his leave while lying in a base hospital. He had been badly shell-shocked after a very near miss. 'Shells were flying over the top until one landed bang in the middle of us, and when the smoke cleared, there was only two of us, the lance corporal and me, the other two lads had completely disappeared. My memory blanks after then; it must have been shell-shock. Anyway, I was in hospital in France and the doctor came round, and he just said to me, "Hello, how long have you been out here?" I said "Fifteen months". He told me it was time I had a leave, and he put my name down for the next boat for

England. And that's how I got home after fifteen months without a leave. I went to hospital in Manchester and then Wigan. Wigan was the best place, they were real grand people were Wigan people, all the theatres and pictures were free to wounded soldiers. We all wore a blue suit in hospital, so we could get a bit of privilege when we were out.'

The warm welcome, could not keep the war at bay for long. 'One day, while I was in this hospital, a couple of people came round with a list of missing soldiers,' Arthur explains. 'They asked if we knew anyone called so and so, and so and so, and they called one of these lads' names out who'd been with me, so I said, "Yes, I know that lad, he's dead." They asked, "Are you sure?" and I said, "As sure as I can be, he just got blown to bits."

Although shell-shocked, Arthur was then given the task of breaking the news to the man's family. '"Would you like to go to Chesterfield?" they asked me. "That lad you just named lived in Chesterfield and it would be a great pleasure to us if you could go and tell his mother, tell it to her nice, that he isn't a prisoner of war or anything like that, that he is dead and won't be coming home."'

The man had lived in a mining district. 'I found the house,' remembers Arthur, 'and told them they wouldn't have to expect him coming home. I said he was killed, but didn't tell them how it happened. They had been hoping he was a prisoner, but I had to say to them, "Sorry, no, I know for a fact he won't be coming home." It was a bit of a hard do for them. He was only a young man like myself, about twenty. They were heartbroken really, but they thanked me for going to tell them.'

Returning to the Western Front was exceptionally hard. The exultation at receiving leave was now replaced by a stomach-churning dread as men realized that they might well never see their families again, and, even if they did, they would have to survive another year in the line or hope for a Blighty wound. A few soldiers chose to say their goodbyes at home, not able to bear the awful scenes at the railway station where families collectively bade tearful farewells, intermingled with scenes of near hysteria. One child's final memory of her father was watching him walk towards the brow of a hill, turning and waving goodbye. He had insisted that he must see her leave, not the other way round, so he ushered her away with a gentle wave of the hand. He did not survive the war. Other families sought to cover their pain by false joviality, one veteran recalling his mother dancing round with the little blood-painted sword he had carried when a boy. Even for those soldiers who found life back in Britain difficult to accept, there was nevertheless a need to prepare themselves once more for the crucible of the Western Front, to walk away from the North Yorkshire Moors, or the rolling South Downs, to return to the shell-pocked landscape of France and Belgium, and all that entailed in terms of bombs, bullets, gas and fear.

CHAPTER NINE

THE INDUSTRIAL WAR

Artillery was the big killer of World War One. Approximately fifty-eight per cent of all injuries were inflicted by hundreds of balls of lead or hot shards of shell case flying over the heads of advancing infantrymen or tearing strips out of the enemy front line. Once infantrymen took to the trenches, they were to be assailed by all manner of devilishly new or rapidly improved modes of weaponry, that had rarely, if ever, been seen on the battlefield. Poison gas, flame-throwers, trench mortars and tanks were all introduced, as both sides sought new ways of breaking through the enemy line so as to return to open warfare, where victory would be achieved by one side over the other.

One of the fascinating aspects of the conflict of 1914-18 was the rapidity with which the old world of lightly armed, mobile warfare, in which the infantryman and cavalry horse were king, was replaced by an impersonal, industrialized war in which damage was done to, rather than done by, the front line soldier. The irony was that while the infantryman rarely saw his enemy, it was increasingly unlikely in any case that either would be the direct cause of the other's demise. For the first time, death could be dealt out at a great distance by men who were never seen. As 2nd Lieutenant Norman Collins wrote, 'Bombardments were terrible for both sides. We felt we had more in common with the German infantry sitting perhaps one hundred yards away than we did with our own or their gunners, who never seemed to shoot at each other but were always intent on bombarding us. This was especially true with our heavy artillery which was situated, in some cases, miles behind the line. We were under the same condition as the Germans, they were in muddy trenches, they were suffering under intensive shellfire. We didn't feel any real animosity towards them.'

During the war, almost four shells were fired by British guns for every man, woman and child living in the United Kingdom, nearly thirty shells for every man under arms. It was a colossal amount of ammunition and weighed more than five million tons. One small bombardment commonly used more shells than had been fired by British artillery during the entire Boer War. At their maximum in 1918, British guns fired no fewer than one million rounds every week except one. In a four-week period between August and September 1918, the figure was 9.8 million. Little wonder that the infantryman cowered at the foot of his trench in shock and awe at the cacophony of sound that passed overhead.

'The big stuff, when they were firing 16-inch shells, they

CLOCKWISE

Morning, 11 October 2001: the chosen volunteers parade before beginning a week's intensive training.

Carl Jackson waits to be issued with his equipment.

A BBC crew films foot drill as taught to No. 3 Section on the parade ground, Catterick. Sgt Gillingham oversees progress.

The 24 volunteers and Khaki Chums parade before embarking for France, 19 October.

ABOVE: Digging the trench: the entire construction took just 28 days.

RIGHT: The front line takes shape.

BELOW LEFT: The Khaki Chums helping to put the final touches to the trench.

BELOW RIGHT: Live shells and hand grenades found during the excavation of the site.

LEFT: The entrance to Lt Robert Yuill's dugout.

BELOW LEFT: Trench supplies, including a stretcher.

BELOW RIGHT: Arthur Halestrap with men from the Khaki Chums, visiting the trench just before the arrival of the volunteers.

ABOVE: Volunteers 2001:
Carl Jackson waits to go on duty; Pte
David Fawcett on the Lewis Gun,
keeping up observation of no man's land.

BELOW LEFT: The daily grind that is
front line life is evident from the picture.
© BBC/Stephen Morley

BELOW CENTRE: Eating from their dixies
in the reserve trench. © BBC/Stephen Morley

ABOVE LEFT: Pte Darren Womack writing
a letter by moonlight. © BBC/Stephen Morley

ABOVE RIGHT: 'Gas, gas!' The men Stand
To as gas drifts towards the front line.
© BBC/Stephen Morley

BELOW RIGHT: Sleeping in the line
between 12 noon and 4 p.m. each day.
© BBC/Stephen Morley

An impromptu football game during 'rest'.

The volunteers relax in an *estaminet* behind the lines.

OPPOSITE

FAR LEFT: Pay parade held in the company orderly room.

FAR RIGHT: Pte Thompson, sentenced to field punishment no. 2, runs round the courtyard in full kit.

RIGHT: Shaving, a daily routine for all ranks.

A typical 'shell' explosion close to the trench. © BBC/Stephen Morley

The final morning: the surviving volunteers go back to the billet for breakfast and a welcome return to civilian clothes.

generally landed beyond the front line. For the front line they had the smaller shells, and they were the ones that would get you. The big stuff was meant for the artillery lines and transport. Even so, when even a small shell lands maybe twenty yards behind you, the ground shakes,' recalls Andrew Bowie.

As a signaller, Andrew would usually be in a dugout which might, if he was lucky, be built well enough to withstand direct hits from smaller shells. For the infantryman stuck in the trench and under fire there was little he could do but crouch as low as he could at the bottom and wait. Different soldiers had different techniques for dealing with shelling: one man noted that he tried to write poems while under fire, another recalled how he simply stared fixedly at his boots, clearing his mind of any thoughts whatsoever. There was nothing to be done but to endure as one veteran remembered: 'All we could do was to sit quietly on the firestep in the dark and listen to the bits of earth crashing down on our tin helmets, just hoping nothing dreadful would hit us. You just shrug your shoulders and get as much into your tin hat as you possibly could. If you walked from one place to another you wouldn't be any better off, so there was nothing to do except sit down, be terrified, and wait until it was all over.'

Barrages could be so intense that it became no longer possible to identify the flight of a single shell, there was just a wall of noise; veterans recall a 'continuous drumming', 'a solid canopy of steel'. Not all shelling was heavy, and men such as Arthur Halestrap, who arrived in the line in early 1918, quickly learnt to identify shells, ignoring those which were passing safely overhead. 'Every size shell had a different sound, with a different whine to it, and we would speculate on where these shells were going to drop: "Oh that's over there, or over there." And we knew when they were going to affect the horses and we were prepared for that, always. I wasn't especially versed in the shell types. I just knew by the sound of them that they were heavy shells from heavy guns, or lighter guns; that was all.'

'A heavy one, you could hear him going over, and once you hear a shell going over, that's OK, he's not going to hit you. But it's the one you don't hear. If a whizzbang was coming, there was not time to react,' recalls Arthur Barraclough.

It was a whizzbang that accounted for Harry Patch as he was leaving the line with his Lewis Gun team in September 1917. 'Heavy shells make a "whump" sound but the light shells, the whizzbangs, they used to come over quickly with a "zuppppp, bang, flash". That was it. The only thing I saw was a flash when the shell burst, and the concussion of that shell bursting threw me to the ground. I didn't even know I was hit at first, but then the pain came and I looked down and saw my tunic was torn away, and I saw some blood.'

The fact that you heard a shell didn't necessarily mean you would escape, as one veteran recalled. 'I heard a shriek, and I knew a lot about the shriek of shells by this time and I thought "My God, this one's got my name on it." I recognized it as a coal box, a 5.9-inch shell. The screech got louder and louder. I knew it was going to drop very near me. My body tensed up as the shell burst on the metalled road just behind me, and I pitched forward. The shell must have passed over my shoulder almost.'

Not every shell that landed on British trenches was the

enemy's. Firing over a distance, the gunners relied on accurate information about the occupation of trenches As telephone communication was frequently cut during action, and runners often killed or wounded, other ways of signalling were used. To aid more precise gunnery, assaulting soldiers carried marker flags or wore a piece of thin polished metal, triangular in shape, and carried on the back. The intention was that reflective glints from the sun would help observers pinpoint progress during and after an attack. Even then, it was perfectly possible to shell your own men in the mistaken belief that the trench was still in enemy hands. Another problem occurred when shells fell short. This might be due to faulty ammunition or incorrectly set fuses. It might be due to wear in the barrel and particularly to the rifling, which gave the shell spin and therefore distance; as the rifling deteriorated, so the guns increasingly lost their accuracy and range. The term 'friendly fire' was unknown, but the notion that your own side could pitch a shell into your trench as accurately as any German was hardly reassuring, as Arthur Barraclough recalls: 'Our own shells started coming over and landing bang in the middle of our trenches, and it created a terrible lot of trouble. The sergeant in charge just shouted "Come on, I want a volunteer to go and try and find these guns, they've been fired too much and the barrels have worn." Well, the first thing you learn in the army is you never volunteer for anything; they learned you that when you join up, they whispered it to you. So nobody volunteered. Anyway, I must have been near to him because he said, "Barraclough, you get through, get on to that trench and get down it and find where the shells are coming from." Well, that were a job wasn't it, at night? I had no idea where it was. I had to climb out and go so far, then stop because the trench had been blown in. So I had to scrape my way on, crawl along like a snail on the top until I found the trench, then drop into it. Then it was blown in again, so I crawled out and made my way through to the reserve trench. They were shelling all the while and it took a long time. I was absolutely mucked up to the eyes. Then a voice came out of the dark, "Who goes there?" and of course I told him what I wanted. This fella took me to the officers' mess, and the officer in charge. I remember it was all lit up and he just said to someone, "Oh get in touch with that battery so and so and tell them what's happening." That were it. I had to go back the same way and I had to make sure I made no noise because there were snipers on the job all the time; anyway by the time I got back it had all stopped.'

No soldier ever got truly used to shelling, but most managed to steel their nerves in the face of its awesome power. However, as one man wrote in a letter home, the war wasn't war as it had once been known, 'It is absolute murder now. There is too much machinery about it,' he complained.

Shells weren't the only threat that pitched down out of the sky. Aircraft too played their small part in ratcheting up the pressure on the infantryman. At the outbreak of war, aircraft had been so primitive that their only use had been observation, the pilots armed with little more than the revolver they opted to carry on board. The Royal Flying Corps' sixty-three aircraft that safely struggled across the Channel in August 1914 had, by the end of the war, grown into a force of 22,000 aircraft across the globe under the newly established Royal Air Force, including squadrons of heavy bombers capable of hitting German cities such as Cologne, Mainz and even Berlin. Aircraft development was swift on both sides, the air advantage swinging from one to the other and back again as new planes were introduced. By the end of September 1916 it was the German air force that was in the ascendancy as the Albatross D-I and D-II set new standards in combat. In mid 1917 the Albatross was replaced by the more famous Fokker Triplane.

'They used to fly on top of the trenches nearly knocking your nose off, firing like mad,' remembered Arthur Halestrap. 'With the shape of our trench, with fire-bays, most of the bullets would miss. We tried to fire back but shooting with a rifle was a million to one chance. Before you could pick your rifle up they'd be gone.'

A few enemy aircraft were shot down by such ground fire. The most notable casualty was the highest scoring ace of the war, Baron von Richthofen, who was almost certainly brought down by Lewis Gun fire. Rifles could be effective if used in unison, and at the very least could drive enemy aircraft away. Either way, shooting at aircraft was fun and Arthur Halestrap wasn't averse to having a go. 'The Germans were shelling at intervals, then at regular times in the morning and in the evening an observation plane would come over and of course we would take pot shots at it with our rifles. This airman was so low that we could see him using his revolver. I was shooting on one occasion and, as the plane went over, I suddenly felt a bang on the table beside me and there was a bullet hole in the wood; the bullet had just missed me by an inch. No-one was hurt in these exchanges and in fact we took it all as a joke and we enjoyed it really. That's the truth. We enjoyed taking pot shots at this airman and I suppose he enjoyed taking pot shots at us.'

Not all infantrymen were as comfortable with enemy aircraft and some were downright terrified of their sudden appearance and distinctive noise. Neither did all pilots choose to be so devil-may-care in engaging infantrymen on the ground; most preferred to drop bombs from a more comfortable height, though, as one veteran recalled, they would be constantly peppered by anti-aircraft fire from the ground. He estimated that he had seen some five hundred puffs of smoke in the sky in one half-hour, as shells burst around enemy planes. German airmen responded by dropping aerial bombs manually from four thousand feet or less, or, occasionally, clusters of vicious aerial darts. It was primarily the job of the Royal Flying Corps to engage the enemy and dominate the airspace, just as soldiers were expected to dominate the ground. With regular combats overhead bullets flew in all directions, most falling harmlessly to earth. A man would be very unlucky to be hit by a spent bullet. But although rare, such an occurrence was by no means unique. One veteran, Stan Clayton of the Royal Engineers, recalled such an incident, when he was walking with a friend who was killed instantaneously by a bullet passing through his shoulder down into his chest. At the time they were well behind the lines and had only just turned away from watching an inconclusive aerial combat.

'There used to be right battles between their planes and ours,' remembers Arthur Barraclough. 'Several times a week, one of ours would go up and just fly around, and in a minute or two Jerry would go up and they'd have a battle. We saw some wonderful scraps, but we rarely knew who the victor was. Sometimes you'd be stood watching and shout for it, but we often didn't know which were ours and which was Jerry's. They always seemed to have manned balloons up and if they saw one of our planes flying around, they'd send a signal and one of theirs would go up. They'd go round and turn and twist, it was really good watching them sometimes. We were told the Germans were winning and it seemed that nine times out of ten it were our plane that went down.'

'Just once I got to watch an aerial battle between German planes, which had been shooting down our balloons, and the RFC, who had gone up to intercept them,' remembers Arthur Halestrap. 'The sky seemed to be full of planes weaving about and at different heights. From time to time we saw at least two planes shot down and then we saw bits of planes falling. I was rather surprised at that because, as they were falling, I could see them tumbling in all different directions and other bits, like parts of wings, just floating down. There were several of us watching this; it was directly overhead and it was interesting, as I had never seen an aerial battle before.'

Although it was not possible for the makers of the 2001 documentary to shoot down enemy aircraft, one feature that could be recreated for the volunteers was gas. Originally, it had been proposed to use a mild form of CS gas, more generally used in riot control. The strength of the CS would have been enough to make the volunteers feel very uncomfortable if they were tardy in getting their gas hoods on. Eventually, the proposal was dropped for health and safety reasons; however the pretence was continued that CS would be used.

The panic and bewilderment that resulted was widespread. 'When they started shouting "gas, gas, gas", we had only fifteen seconds to get our gas masks on and the hoods over our heads,' explained one volunteer. 'It was one mad frantic rush; everything was just thrown out of the way.'

'There were four of us in the crater when the gas alarm went off,' said another volunteer. 'The word went up, "Gas, gas, gas, gas". I put my helmet on but Paul was panicking, he was saying "I haven't got it, I don't know where it is!" He thought it was under his greatcoat, so he took that off, but he didn't have it. "What the hell are you going to do?" we asked. Eventually I wrapped him up on the inside of my coat and covered him over and told him to stay there until it was all clear. I kept him in my coat until the end of the gas alarm because he's only little. He was really panicking because everyone was talking about the CS gas.'

In fact the dread of poison gas, one of the most feared weapons of the industrial war, was out of all proportion to the number of injuries it actually caused; indeed only five per cent of gas casualties failed to return to the front. With hindsight, its greatest effect during the war was to create among the front line troops exactly the sort of panic and bewilderment seen in the modern volunteers. Gas was first used as an offensive weapon by the Germans on 22 April 1915 near Ypres. Billowing across the front line trenches, it spread terror amongst the French territorial and colonial troops on whom it was used. The gas was chlorine, a greenish–yellow gas that caused terrible nausea and retching, the victim finding it almost impossible to breathe. In extreme cases the gas attacked the lungs, filling them with liquid so that the soldier effectively drowned.

The attack tore a four-mile gap in Allied lines, forcing British soldiers to move up and fill the vacant line, where they used jackets and towels to fan away the remaining gas. The assault set alarm-bells ringing and, to their credit, the military authorities reacted swiftly: four days after the attack, printed instructions were issued advising soldiers what to do. 'If no better means of protection are available, take a pocket handkerchief or other small piece of cloth, roll it into a ball and hold it in the mouth drawing the breath in and out through it until the cloth is quite moist.' The damp cloth was a partial protection against chlorine, reducing, it was estimated, the poisonous effects by half. There was another, less appealing option, too. This was to urinate on a sock or field dressing and hold it over the mouth and nose, the urine neutralizing the chlorine in the gas.

The first 'masks' to reach the soldiers in the line were copied from a respirator taken from a German prisoner. This was a pad of cotton waste held in a gauze bag and dipped in a solution of sodium carbonate and hyposulphate. Within a week of the discovery, masks with slight modifications were being produced around the clock and sent out to the men in the line.

The next development came with the H(Hypo) Helmets, more commonly known as Smoke Helmets. These were in fact hoods made from a single layer of flannel. They were dipped in a solution of hyposulphate, pulled over the head and tucked inside the tunic. Their main drawback was that the mica eyepieces proved brittle and liable to crack; yet, between May and the end of August 1915, two million were produced. Hoods remained the basic anti-gas protection for the next year, with modifications to counteract advances in gas technology. A cellulose acetate eyepiece replaced the mica windows, while shortly afterwards the P(phenate) Helmets were produced, hoods with glass eyepieces and made with two layers of flannelette instead of one. The PH (phenate-hexamine) Helmet, which would have been carried by the 10th East Yorks, was introduced in January 1916 as a response to the Germans' first use of phosgene gas, an almost odourless (mouldy hay was its faint smell) and colourless gas, which was fatal even if inhaled in small quantities. The PH Helmet or Hood was standard issue until the small Box Respirators were brought into service in August 1916, and even then the PH Hoods were widely used until early 1917 and were kept as a back-up until the end of the war. Arthur Barraclough wore his in 1917. 'The mask was like a sack which you put over your head and pushed down the top of your tunic. In the middle of the mask there were a tube. Now this tube, you could only blow out, you couldn't draw in. You drew your breath through the mask itself and then breathed out slowly through this tube. The helmet was soaped with something, it smelled of disinfectant, in fact several of the lads couldn't stand it, they'd just throw them off because they couldn't breathe with them, hardly.'

Early on in the war, gas was released from cylinders, the gas cloud being blown, where favourable conditions permitted, towards the enemy lines. This was almost as hazardous for the sender as the receiver. Once the British had got over the shock and

AR LORNE
after
Pte. A. SHIRES R.A.M.C.

DIRECTIONS FOR USE & CARE OF TUBE HELMETS.

DESCRIPTION.

These Helmets are the same as the "Smoke Helmet" already issued, except that stronger chemicals are added and a "Tube-valve" provided through which to breathe out. The Tube-valve makes helmet cooler and saves the chemicals from being affected by breath.

N.B. Wearer cannot breathe in through the Tube-valve, this is intended for breathing out only.

DIRECTIONS FOR USE.

Remove paper wrap from mouth-piece of "Tube-Valve." Remove cap. Pull helmet over head. Adjust so that goggles are opposite eyes. Tuck in skirt of helmet under coat collar and button coat so as to close in skirt of helmet. Hold the "Tube" lightly in lips or teeth like stem of pipe, so as to be able to breathe in past it and out through it.

Breathe in through mouth and nose, using the air inside the helmet. Breathe out through tube only.

DIRECTIONS FOR CARE OF TUBE-HELMET.

(1) *Do not remove the Helmet from its Waterproof Case except to use for protection against Gas.*

(2) *Never use your Tube-Helmet for practice or drill. Special helmets are kept in each Company for instruction only.*

WITHDRAW THESE INSTRUCTIONS FROM THE CASE AND KEEP FOLDED IN YOUR PAY BOOK.

Introduced in 1915, the Tube Helmet or PH Hood was the primary protection against gas for over a year. The hoods, although replaced by the Box Respirator in late 1916, were often kept for emergencies until the end of the war.

moral outrage caused by the Germans' gas attack, they retaliated with the first of their own at the Battle of Loos in September 1915. In the event, the wind changed and blew the gas back on to the soldiers, inflicting many casualties. It was clear to both sides that gas attacks were too dependent on wind conditions, so the mode of delivery was changed. The British modified the 3–inch Stokes Mortar to carry gas and developed the Livens Projector, which could fire a gas canister up to three thousand yards. These projectors, looking similar to the ends of outflow pipes, were dug into the ground two yards apart and buried up to the bottom lip. The gas canister, which weighed some 61lb when fully loaded, was placed in the projector and fired electrically towards the German lines. The canister split open on impact and released a cloud of gas. By 1918 the Livens Projector was considered the best method of saturating the enemy with gas.

Gas could not be used in all circumstances. Intense sunshine would rapidly evaporate it, while heavy rain would also destroy its action; if it was too cold, the gas would not vaporize. The optimum weather conditions were fog or cloud with an eight to ten m.p.h. wind, with the release at night or early morning.

As well as chlorine and phosgene gas, both sides widely used tear gas, a painful irritant which had no long-term effects. In 1917, mustard gas was introduced, possibly the best known of all the gases, and in the last year of the war it was responsible for ninety per cent of gas casualties. This wasn't really gas at all but brown liquid, and it smelt of garlic or violets. On the skin, mustard gas caused huge blisters which, if burst, made fresh blisters wherever the liquid ran, while eyelids swelled and closed, copious mucus leaving men blind for days, weeks, and sometimes for good.

In reality gas was more feared than fatal. Its psychological effects were so great that a network of gas alarms was built along the Western Front. In the trenches these were improvised: a school bell or an upturned shell case would be rung, a piece of railway track hit. There were rattles, not dissimilar to those used at football matches in bygone years, and there were gongs. For a general alarm there were the Strombos Horns, fitted with two compressed-air cylinders. Ideally, there were twenty horns available per mile of front line and, when sounded, they could be heard for thousands of yards.

Wind vanes were located in trenches to give a quick indication of whether gassing was imminent; however, once gas had arrived, methods of reducing its impact were developed. Simplest of all were the anti-gas fans, of which two hundred per mile of front was the recommended number. These were simply used to waft the gas away. More technical were the Vermoral Sprayers. Introduced in 1915, they lasted out the war, forty-eight being allocated to each division. A two-man team held the canister of bicarbonate of soda; one pumped to release the liquid while the other sprayed it on to the gas, helping to neutralize it.

The gas, being heavier than air, sank to the bottom of shell holes and trenches. For the occupants of dugouts this could be especially dangerous. As a protection, two damp gas curtains were installed, one attached to the roof at the top of the dugout staircase, another at the foot. These were released during an attack, the bottom nine inches of the cape draping on the stair below, creating an air lock. This worked well, but not in every scenario, one veteran recalling how he was gassed after retreating to a dugout with a man whose uniform had already been splashed by mustard gas.

Andrew Bowie was in a dugout when he was gassed near the town of Péronne in March 1918. 'I was on the phone and we knew there was gas around, but I had to take my mask off to speak. I didn't know I was being gassed, I was inhaling it, unconsciously, until I finally collapsed.

'You start to choke and gasp for breath and then it gets so bad it gives you the impression that somebody has got a corkscrew and is turning it around in your chest. The pain becomes intense. Anything that has water or is moist is attacked, your eyes gradually close, your lips swell and feel like sausages in your mouth, and, if your legs are sweating, you'll get blisters. You go through hell, I can tell you. You are vomiting, you can't vomit, you try to vomit, you can't vomit, and your eyes burn all the time.'

Andrew Bowie was lucky enough to be evacuated in time to save his life. 'We were bundled into a vehicle and the men were crying. There was a big corporal next to me, about sixteen stone, shouting for his mother. We ended up in a dressing station behind the lines, where a doctor bandaged my eyes, but I was still choking, panting all the time. I could just see below the bandage, and I was in a field and there were a lot of us, I couldn't count them. From there we went to the base hospital, then across the Channel and on to Birmingham War Hospital, where I remained blind for about nine days. The hospital was a former asylum, and opposite me were two big windows; I could gradually see the light coming through, and I eventually got my sight back.'

During the war, British forces suffered 185,706 gas cases, or around six per cent of battle casualties. In all, 5,899 men, or just over three per cent of those injured by gas, died, although many thousands more had their lives blighted to a greater or lesser degree. My father, when a young lecturer in the late 1950s, rented a room from a middle-aged couple in Nottingham. The husband, Captain Wilfred Parsons, had been badly gassed in the war and had been forced to retire early from teaching. His last years were spent sitting in front of the fire, with constant bronchial problems, until, forced to take to his bed, he died in his early sixties. Some had less serious but chronic problems: one veteran, gassed by chlorine in 1915, continued to have sudden and heavy nosebleeds until the late 1960s, when the effects finally wore off. In some other cases, gas victims were given a low life expectancy but in the end lived long and full lives. Andrew Bowie was cheerfully told, by one doctor, that he would only live until he was about thirty years of age. 'He was a bit out there, wasn't he?' says Andrew with a grin. At 104 he is 'a medical freak', as his doctor confirms, but thousands more died broken men.

It is hard to imagine how anyone who went through the First World War could not have been traumatized by what he saw, suffered or did. But make no mistake about it, there were those who were exhilarated by the experience. Lieutenant Richard Hawkins was present when he overheard the following exchange: 'Maxwell said to my colonel one day, "You know, Carr, I don't think you really enjoy this war, do you?" Carr said, "My God, I do not, I think it is a dreadful business." "No," Maxwell said, "I thoroughly enjoy it." This was absolutely true and eventually he was promoted to brigadier and was killed walking over the top. He shouldn't have been walking over the top, he should have been behind at his headquarters. One time up at Armentières the guns were about to open up and Maxwell said to one of his officers, "Where d'you think we can get the best view of this wonderful barrage they're going to put up? I think probably in the front line." And off he went.'

There were many such firebrands who, to mere mortals, seem larger than life and a mite odd, too. Adrian Carton de Wiart, another senior officer, showed the same traits, and, despite having lost an eye and a hand in action, insisted on returning to the fray. It is perhaps unsurprising that Maxwell already held a Victoria Cross from his service in the Boer War, while de Wiart won his during the Somme Battle.

It wasn't just the officers who enjoyed the bombs, bullets and other paraphernalia of war, as one private mentioned in an interview. 'I'm glad I served in the war, of course I am, and I stuck my age on, didn't I, I could have waited till I was old enough to join up, but I didn't. I loved to hear the artillery and the machine guns, I can't tell you why, but I did. I used to sweep the German parapets, just pressed the button, brrrrrrrr, and they done the same to us. That was a bit of fun, oh yes.'

For many soldiers, the First World War was the best time of their lives, even those who detested what they went through. One veteran, Hal Kerridge, was 'glad' to have served. 'I wouldn't have missed the experience, and nearly every old soldier will tell you the same; they hated it, they abhorred it, they loathed it, but they wouldn't have missed it. It's an experience that can make or mar you for life, but I have no regrets.'

It was, of course, perfectly possible for the war both to mar and to make the man. Richard Hawkins always asserted that 'We all had great fun really, tremendous fun, enjoyed ourselves. I personally enjoyed the ruddy war, I don't know why.' But he acknowledged, too, that 'You couldn't help being a bit frightened, I think, but you couldn't show it, got to bottle it up, that's why it put such a strain on you. After the war I was troubled for a good many years by a difficulty in speaking. It was hardly a stammer, it was a stuttering, but it was awfully difficult in business. You would go to a meeting and have to say something, and it was a tremendous stress on the nervous system, which had been pretty well shattered after nineteen months in the front line. Nineteen months is too long, it ruined my digestive system, really, and my nervous system for a good many years afterwards.' Despite his nerves, Richard rose to become managing director of Bellings, the electrical goods company.

The one thing every soldier looked back on with pride and joy was the remarkable comradeship of the war, the like of which few, if any, ever found again in civilian life. 'We tolerated each other and understood each other,' asserts Andrew Bowie. 'Men would swear at each other, swear about each other, but the true fact was there was always that other bond of friendship; we were still friends. We accepted things, and our role in the army. We would do anything for each other. We might call someone a bloody so-and-so one day, but if we heard that chap was badly wounded in the next bay everyone would go at once to see what they could do for him. Your pals are almost family, a very rough family, mind.

'The comradeship was terrific, that's one thing they couldn't take away from you, comradeship,' Andew Bowie continues. 'You felt that you were great pals and you would feel naked if you didn't have them with you. That was a great feeling which did not exist in civilian life. I teamed up with Macdonald and later Jock Ewart. Everybody would have their own pals, the teetotallers got together, and those who liked a drink. There was a brotherly love within the signallers, and it was the same with the machine gunners. I was a bomber when I went out first time, and you shared everything with your group.'

Such closeness and interdependence, of course, carried their own risks. 'Comradeship was a necessity, and it was a difficult thing to accept if you lost your pal. You had to get over it, but there was no way of having any feeling with anybody else; it was your personal loss. Mind, you often didn't know they were good until you were parted from them. Jock Ewart, who was killed in the offensive in March 1918, had both his legs blown off, I heard, and he was a sprinter, one of the fastest men in Britain.'

Not all devotion was based on personal friendship: there was a comradeship in arms, as Arthur Halestrap discovered. 'On one occasion I was on detachment with one other man. We'd become separated from the rest and were trying to make our way forward to link up with everyone else. He was a much older man than me, a Yorkshireman, and we were looking for somewhere to rest for the night. There had been a lot of shelling about, and the only place we could find to sleep was in a shell hole, so we walked around until we found one that we thought was warmer than the rest. All the gas had evaporated and it seemed softer when we got into it and warmer at the bottom than some of the others. So we took out our groundsheets and got down together lying side by side, and this man said to me "I'll give you my body heat." and he put his body next to mine and put his arms around me.'

Comradeship helped control fear but fear was a great leveller, and only a man with no imagination whatsoever could fight without any thought as to the possible consequences, should he be hit by a shell fragment, or impaled on a bayonet. Comradeship undoubtedly helped men to suppress their darkest anxieties, and drove them on in dire situations. Great faith in God helped others to cope, believing that death or injury was His will. And then there was rank fatalism. If your name was on that bullet then there was nothing you could do about it anyway, so why worry? Everyone had methods of coping, but in truth fear was always present, as Harry Patch affirms. 'Anyone who tells you that in the trenches they weren't scared, he's a damned liar: you were scared all the time. You couldn't deal with the fear. It was there and it always will be. I know the first time I went to the line we were scared; we were all scared. We lived hour by hour, we never knew the future. You saw the sun rise, hopefully you'd see it set. If you saw it set, you hoped you'd see it rise. Some men would, some wouldn't.'

Joe Yarwood learnt how to keep going. 'I kidded myself I was a bit of a Christian and I always liked to go to Communion because I thought it might help ward off feelings of fear and the wind up. It was really rather romantic because you'd go to Communion, and there was the clergyman with his surplice, and showing below there would be his riding boots and spurs, and it seemed rather incongruous. But I always made a point of going when I was in France, just for the reason that I didn't want to freeze up, show cowardice; we were quite desperate not to show that we were frightened in front of our comrades. You wanted to keep your self-respect and you can't do that very easily if you're continually whingeing.'

The fear of 'freezing up', as Joe put it, haunted men. Letting comrades down, showing cowardice; at a time in history when there were clear definitions of how a man should act and behave, failing the test of manhood or manliness was always in the back of a soldier's mind, and bravado, when displayed, only underlined the true fears. For Arthur Barraclough, it was men who had a little too much to drink who were the cause for anxiety.

'Did I get the wind up? I don't know. You get that used to chancing your neck. You know why you're there and you know what you're doing. Sometimes you could get somewhere near a village where there were army canteen pubs – they used to put tents up – and some of these lads used to come back fresh and these were the fellas who put the wind up me. I used to think, "I hope that fella doesn't come near me," because they'd no sense when they get fresh, half drunk, standing up, cursing the Jerries. I remember one or two fellas that always got rum, I don't know where they got it from. Every time when there was going to be an attack they used to get badly fresh. But they couldn't miss out on the attack, they were forced to go along with the rest and I used to think, "I'm not going to stick with them, it's false pluck." That's all it used to be, they used to be frightened to death so they'd get drunk to try and take the fear away.'

The army's issuing of rum was not solely to warm a soldier's toes: rum took away inhibitions, and, as Arthur Barraclough says, it helped stifle fear. When Andrew Bowie was working as a company signaller in March 1918, he received a message that could cause nothing but anxiety. It said, 'Report troops massing on your front, stand to earlier than usual, all ranks and ratings must be in the front line.' 'I took the message to Captain St Clair Grant, and he was a big tall fellow and he read it, and his hands began to shake, and he said, "Signaller, how about a wee tot of rum," and he gave us both a tot. We were at the point of a salient, a most precarious position, as the Germans were on two sides and could almost have fired into the back of us. The next morning everybody, including the signallers, stood to, but it was quiet, not a sound, and there was no attack.'

Shell-shock was the bottom line, when a man's resolve finally gave out, but there were many stages before a man might reach his nadir. 'I would get a butterfly in my stomach and my hands would shake, so for a moment or two I would have a job to co-ordinate my nerves to do anything,' says Harry Patch.

Battle fatigue, or the slow attrition of one's nerves, could cause a breakdown. The cumulative effect of sleep deprivation, fear or anxiety could send a man over the edge, and the sight of a man grovelling in the dirt, crying for his mother, shaking un- controllably or even sitting perfectly mute was a terrible sight for any soldier to witness, and only helped to confirm the sense of a man's own vulnerability. On most occasions a shell-shocked man was removed from the line, as he would only be a danger to the men around him, although some officers believed in quicker 'cures', as Lieutenant Richard Hawkins recalls. 'After the battle of Thiepval we were withdrawn to a cellar in a chateau. One of the boys there had a bit of shell-shock and kept running across the road, and Maxwell said to me, "Give him a damn good kick up the backside as he passes you, he'll be all right," and he was, he was all right.' Such a wake-up call as a boot up the backside might well bring a man back to reality, but his new-found resolve was surely only a temporary state.

The incidence of shell-shock grew as industrialized warfare found ever better ways to pulverize soldiers. There were under two thousand cases of behaviour disorder in 1914, and over twenty thousand in 1915, albeit with a far larger army in the field. But such figures are possibly the tip of a much greater iceberg, as soldiers 'recovered' in the field or were treated by the Medical Officer in the line, ensuring that the soldier's complaint was not entered in the medical statistics. Brigade Signaller Arthur Halestrap once saw such a recovery as he took part in an attack on the Hindenburg Line in 1918. 'When we had the orders to go over, the shelling was still very heavy. We looked round and the corporal said, "Oh dear, he's not good," and the third man with us was lying at the bottom of the trench, gibbering; he'd lost control completely, he was absolutely shell-shocked and his teeth were chattering and he was moaning, because the barrage was so fierce. The noise of the guns and the shells bursting, it's impossible to describe, a barrage of that sort, the different tones of the shells, the high whine of the machine gun bullets, and small arms and the heavy shells coming over: it was a medley of sound, all mixed together. And there this man was, at the bottom of the trench, and this corporal looked at me and shrugged his shoulders and said, "Come on, we'd better get on with it." We went on without this man and came back for him afterwards. He'd recovered and didn't remember a thing about it. And the corporal said nothing to him and neither did I.'

Andrew Bowie had been at the front on and off for eighteen months without any apparent wear and tear on his nerves. 'We were coming out of a quiet part of the line one night. I was in charge of the signals section, three of us, and I asked the captain beforehand if we could go out of the line on our own; we generally did that, the signals section, because we could read maps and I knew the rendezvous, sunken road so and so. And he said, "Yes, signaller, take your men out." Going out, we came to this wire put up by the South Africans, and just as we were passing through, the Germans decided to send a salvo over. I was carrying a Fuller phone on my back, and one of the party, a nervous type, shouted "Andrew, I'm stuck on the wire." I went back to help him and pulled him off the wire, but in doing so I got stuck. But his silly fool ran on, he didn't think about me. This fellow had been at the Battle of Loos in 1915 and had come back again to join our lot, and he had shell-shock, not severe, but he was the nervous type.

'Another salvo came and went over my head, and there I was stood upright, stuck. The next lot came over and exploded; the force of the percussion threw me out of the wire, dashing me on the ground. I didn't know what to do, but I got up and tried to walk and picked up the Fuller phone and made for a railway line.

I knew there was a ditch, and I flung myself in, being stung all over the backside by nettles, and lay there panting.'

Happily one of Bowie's close friends did not let him down. 'Then I heard Jock Ewart's voice, "Andrew, where are you?" He had come back to find me. I made a noise of some description and he picked me up and brought me out.

'I had a touch of shell-shock, I can tell you, nerves. I lost my voice for a week or so and could just make husky noises for "yes" and "no", just gasping. The doctor wanted to send me to hospital but I wouldn't go, because if you got to hospital you would come back to another battalion, and you'd lose all your friends.'

Most soldiers could tell that their nerves were fraying at the edges; shaking hands was a clear indication to Harry Patch. Men were often embarrassed by even the mildest reaction to war's strain, one recording the shame he felt as he cringed in front of other men, all too aware that they were looking at him. For officers, like St Clair Grant, a quick tot helped to calm the nerves. If none was available, a face-saving rationale for the shaking was made, that there was a real nip in the air, even if the air was anything but cold. But for many men there was no need to save face, they were so mentally damaged that reality rarely impinged upon their haunted lives. According to Denis Winter in his book *Death's Men*, over fifty thousand men received war pensions for mental disorders caused by the war However, so notorious were the awarding panels, that far more men deserving of a pension received nothing. Thousands were left to cope on their own with the trauma caused by the war, and many took their lives in the 1920s and '30s, unable to stand the mental anguish any longer.

Others spent a lifetime in institutions, locked up in their own worlds, and the spectacle of a long-term psychiatric patient suddenly reliving life in the line, a day or two before his own passing, was not unknown. In June 2001 the press reported the death of the last psychiatric patient from the war. A former private in the Black Watch, David Ireland died in hospital in Scotland, aged 103. He had been inside since 1924, effectively all his adult life.

CHAPTER TEN

GOING OVER THE TOP

Every time before we set off, over the top, I just stood up a minute by myself: 'Dear God, I'm going into great danger, would you please guard me and help me to act like a man. Please bring me back safe,' and I used to go out there without a fear, and here I am. I didn't say it out loud. My pals got to know and they did all sorts of daft stuff to get drunk, well, I didn't need it because I trusted, you know, in my prayers.

ARTHUR BARRACLOUGH, AGED 104

As summer 1916 gave way to a wet and cold autumn, so the quiet period for 10th Battalion East Yorks came to an end. On the night of 18–19 September, four parties of twenty-five men, one from each company, took part in a major raid on the enemy trenches near Béthune. For a week beforehand, the battalion had maintained a non-offensive policy to lull the enemy into a false sense of security. To take the Germans by surprise, no preliminary bombardment would take place, although explosives known as Bangalore torpedoes would be used to blow up the enemy wire. In the event, half the torpedoes failed to explode, leaving two groups of raiders to cut their way manually through the wire. But two parties could get into the German trench straight away and were able to inflict heavy casualties, take eight prisoners and capture a machine gun. In the raid, the 10th Battalion lost only one man killed.

Congratulations poured in from brigade headquarters and up the chain of command, as useful intelligence was gained from the prisoners. When the divisional general came to give a speech a few days later he thanked the men, before mentioning that a return to the Somme Battle was on the cards. Two weeks later the battalion did indeed entrain for the Somme, and for the same trenches, in front of the village of Serre, where the brigade had lost so many men three months before.

The battalion did not go back into the trenches immediately. For most of October it took part in brigade exercises, practising attacks in the morning before the men played sports, namely football and rugby, in the afternoon. The Commercials' rugby team consisted of better soldiers than players, for they were trounced 46–0 by the Tradesmen (11th Battalion), leaving it to the football team to restore their spirits.

On 20 October, the battalion arrived at their new billets in the village of Hébuterne, just behind the British lines, nine miles north of the town of Albert. Hébuterne today is a large, sleepy village with houses strung along either side of a wide main road. It was rebuilt in the twenties and thirties, and was and remains the adopted 'twin' village of Evesham, because of the link with the Worcester Regiment, battalions of which served there in 1915 and 1916 for an extended period of time. To the west of Hébuterne is the military cemetery containing many graves of men killed after August 1915, when the British arrived on the Somme, and who were buried by the Field Ambulance units that worked to bring back the wounded.

In October 1916, the village was surrounded by gun positions that shelled the German lines and, as a result, was constantly under counter-fire as well as desultory shelling. A favourable wind also ensured Hébuterne was the unwilling recipient of gas attacks, giving the place a bad reputation amongst the troops. Given the perennial danger, communication trenches were dug, branching out from the village's main road towards the front line. These trenches were given friendly names such as 'Whiskey', 'Women' and 'Welcome'; in contrast, the village was largely reduced to ruins, although not flattened like so many other places within the battle zone. There were still warm, comfortable cellars to rest in, which afforded protection from the shelling. The village remained the unit's rest rest for the next two and a half months, but for now, there was little time to settle in. The very next day – 21 October – the 10th Battalion were due to go up the line.

Going over the top might have been a collective act, but, for every man who was about to launch himself into no man's land, there was always a terrible sense of personal vulnerability. A few had premonitions that they would not survive, most felt sure they would be wounded, and with that sense of foreboding there was invariably a need to come to terms in a very private way with personal thoughts and emotions. The countdown to going over the top was agonizing for most men, like waiting for the hangman's noose, as one veteran put it. No-one quite knew how he would react, and many were as frightened of showing cowardice in front of their friends at such a critical moment as they were of the wounds they expected to receive. A junior officer was as likely as anyone to be killed or wounded in an attack, but as 2nd Lieutenant Norman Collins recalled, he was grateful at that moment for his rank. 'Knowing one's duty took one's mind off the horrible things. You are very aware of the example you are setting the men and if they saw you funking it – showing fear – they wouldn't think much of you.' Responsibility helped steel the nerves.

Although men would usually know by the activity around them that an attack was imminent, the knowledge didn't make the thought any easier, as Andrew Bowie recalls. 'The great thing about going over the top was the anticipation. Prior to our attack, about a week or so beforehand, they talked to us about taking a particular objective. It was all done in model form, showing us the terrain we were to go over, and we learnt the contours of the land to a certain degree, though it all looked different when we got there.

'You knew you were going over the top for definite maybe a day or two before, because orders would come round to clean up your equipment, "Machine gunners, make sure all the panniers are full", "Signallers, make sure all the signalling equipment is in order." Bombers had to have a full supply of hand grenades, it went down the line, you knew there was something in the air. They didn't actually say you were going over, but that was what it amounted to. You were numb and you knew that it would be the end for somebody.'

As the hours ticked down, the pressure built up. In his dugout, Norman Collins shared a drink with his batman. 'The night before the attack, he came to see me and asked if I could provide him with the means of buying a small bottle of whisky – quite illegal of course, but I gave him the money to do it. He would be going over the top with me and he was likely to be killed, as I thought I would be. I thought my chances of coming back were very small, but it doesn't deter you because you have no choice, no alternative.'

Andrew Bowie did not have the luxury of a dugout; he wasn't even in a trench, but in a line of shell holes crudely linked together. 'You go into a sort of coma, just thinking, thinking, and you know what you are thinking, will it be the last time? and if you come through, you are lucky. I didn't write a letter home before going over the top, I accepted the situation as it was, but a lot of people did, I think married men would, naturally, they would feel it was their duty. When you are single your thoughts are more fluid.

'We had made a scraping in the ground, and that was our little home, maybe two feet deep and about six feet long. In the dark our company captain came along and said, "Could I have a seat, I have been out on the tapes." Before an attack they put a tape out, like starting a race, because there were just shell holes, no defined trench line. So we said, "Yes, we've just made a little hole, you can have a rest." But then he suddenly changed his mind, he said "No, it's all right, signallers, I'll go on," and that was the last time I spoke to him. I think he was dead half an hour later when the attack opened up.'

By far the worst time was in the minutes before the order to go, as the men waited with fixed bayonets. 'I was in the trench with a cigarette, my last cigarette, in my fingers and I was shaking like a leaf,' recalled one veteran. 'Then we had to go and at that moment I lost all feeling, I wasn't nervous at all.'

'As the time to go approaches, you're looking at your watch to see the hour,' remembers Norman Collins, 'and then you're looking in front to see when the barrage will open, and then you look and see that your men are equipped and ready to go, and that nobody's turned around and gone back.'

Fear did not necessarily override the ability to think. Many veterans recall some sort of plan in their minds once they had to go. Some men believed that the best way was to shoot straight up the ladder as fast as they could because as the German machine gun swept the top of the parapet, it was better to get a bullet in the chest, thigh or leg than one through the head. Other men, like Ted Francis and his brother Harry, preferred to hang back just for a moment. 'Harry and I, on the sound of the whistle, we didn't jump up and get over – those that did got mercilessly cut down by machine guns and killed, but we waited till the machine gun had passed our trench and then dashed over quick.'

The signal to go was usually a whistle or the sergeant encouraging the men with a shout of 'Right, lads'. Men often recalled distinctly hearing either, or indeed both, as the devastating bombardment that preceded an attack fell unnervingly quiet. For a few seconds there was a 'terrific silence', wrote one man, as the guns that had been smashing the German front line lifted to dish out their barrage onto the enemy's second and third lines.

'I can't recall anything I said, something absolutely ridiculous, probably. Even so, the men looked to me for encouragement, and you made jokes if you could,' says Norman Collins. 'I suppose I might have blown a whistle, but it didn't mean anything, so you sort of shepherded the men over. You're working in a very small area, the rest of the Front is nothing. You quickly look to see if a man who had dropped is dead or not, or if there is anything you could do for him, but you hadn't time to stop. When you saw men wandering about, which did happen, it was the officer's job to form them into a fighting unit, no matter what regiment they were in. Then you encourage them, right and left, to go with you, all go together, and you keep looking as they fall occasionally.'

For three weeks, the 10th East Yorks ventured in and out of the trenches near Serre, holding the line or, when out at rest, preparing for an attack on the village. This was repeatedly postponed owing to the weather. During this time, the men continued to suffer casualties, before the date of the attack was finally set for 13 November.

On the morning of the attack, the Hull Pals were to be on the extreme left of the general advance, in trenches to the north of Serre. The assaulting units were to act as a flank to men of another division, who were to launch an attack on the village of Serre itself. However, once again the bulk of the 10th Battalion was to be held back, while the 12th and 13th Battalions led the way, with the 11th Battalion in support. Some eighty-five men of the 10th Battalion provided carrying parties to the front line and this proved extremely hazardous, as German artillery pounded the British communication trenches to stop reinforcements and supplies coming up. Two Lewis Gun sections of the 10th were also attached to the 12th Battalion and went over the top, occupying the German front line all day.

The assault was launched at 5.45 a.m. in thick fog and was initially successful, the Hull Pals taking large sections of the enemy's first and second lines. However, as on 1 July, the attack faltered, then failed, as the Germans launched strong counter-attacks. Throughout the day the fighting continued but the men were beaten back to their front line trenches, owing to the neighbouring division's failure to take Serre village on their right, which had left the Hull Pals' flank exposed to murderous enfilading fire.

Further south there had been success, with Beaumont Hamel, Beaucourt and St Pierre Divion being taken, leaving Serre as the only first-day objective to hold out for the entire Somme Battle. Serre remained in German hands until they voluntarily retreated to the Hindenburg Line the following year. In the assault, the 12th and 13th Battalions of the Hull Pals had suffered 244 killed and a far greater number wounded; almost every company officer had been killed, wounded, or taken prisoner. The 10th had suffered just seven dead and perhaps a dozen or more wounded. Now, added to their official designation of the 10th East Yorkshire

Regiment, and to their popular title, the Hull Commercials, there came one further name: 'The Lucky Tenth.'

Few other units were as fortunate. Andrew Bowie: 'Three of us went together, and when the attack started, one was hit straight away. "Andrew, Andrew, I'm hit!" He was hit in the shoulder and blood was gushing out. I took his equipment off and put a field bandage on. "What do I do now?" He was excited, the boy; I said, "You get back to the duckboards and go down there to the artillery lines, they'll look after you." He was just a new boy to us and it was his only chance, as he would bleed to death otherwise.

'We didn't get fifty yards. I couldn't measure time but I would think the whole attack was finished in half an hour. The Germans were above us and that made it easy for them, and with their machine guns rattling, we were just targets. There seemed to be a blast of fire straight away, there was no battle. I saw men dropping down for safety as well, because you can't imagine how intense the fire was.'

There were always those who went hell-bent for the enemy line, 'I'll get that bloody German style' as one veteran described it, adding 'but if you tried to go full steam ahead when everything was going hammer and tongs, you knew you didn't stand a cat in hell's chance.' As they advanced, soldiers recalled their complete surprise and wonderment at the sound of the bullets that buzzed past their ears without finding a target. Like many survivors of the war, one veteran used his brains as much as possible. 'You didn't do anything daft going over the top, you went quietly over, keeping as low as possible, and where there was a bit of shelter you took it, you learnt to be very canny. A lot of lads dropped on purpose till it got less rough, and then advanced.'

Every man had his own way of coping with action. Some soldiers walked forward like automatons, and afterwards had only fragmented memories of the attack, others found themselves jolted back to reality only when a pal was wounded, although there was little they could do, other than perhaps offer a moment's encouragement. In an attack, the infantry were under strict orders to push on and not stop to help a wounded man, for it was the job of the stretcher bearer to deal with casualties. Even so, many veterans recall with clarity those moments when a wounded man might grab their ankle, pleading for help, even if it was just to drag him into a shell hole, or to give him a sip of water, or a cigarette.

And then there are those men who remember every detail, the memory is seared in the mind. Recollections could be irrelevant or mundane. Second Lieutenant Norman Collins recalled the thick mist during his attack and how, 'when the mist rose and the sun came out, the sun shone on the shell holes full of water and they were all different colours; the chemicals I suppose.'

Often the memory is too terrible ever to forget. Harry Patch took part in an attack near Ypres. 'I came across a lad from A Company from my regiment and he was ripped open from his shoulder to his waist by shrapnel, a terrible wound. When we got to him he said, "Shoot me", but before we could draw a revolver, he was dead. And the only word he uttered was "Mother". Only in the last two years has Harry been willing to talk about this incident.

He continues: 'Two or three Germans had got up out of the

trench, and one of them came towards us with a fixed bayonet, he couldn't have had any ammunition otherwise he would have shot us. My right hand was free; I'd just changed a magazine. I drew my revolver, which I carried as No. 2 on a Lewis gun, and I shot him in the right shoulder. He dropped his rifle and he came stumbling on, no doubt to kick us to pieces if he could. I had four seconds to make my mind up. I had three live rounds in that revolver. I could have killed him with my first, I was a crack shot. What shall I do? Four seconds to make my mind up. I gave him his life. I shot him above the ankle, and above the knee. I brought him down. I didn't kill him. For him the war was over. He would be picked up, interrogated, passed back to a prisoner of war camp, and at the end of the war he would rejoin his family. Six weeks later, a countryman of his pulled the lanyard on a field gun and killed my three mates. If that had happened before I met him, I would have damn well killed him.'

If the attack was successful, and advanced the line by even a few hundred yards, then the wounded could be helped, including, in time, the German shot by Harry. A failed assault made life far more problematic, not just for the wounded lying out in no man's land, but for those uninjured men who were cut off and forced to shelter in shell holes. Andrew Bowie's assault had barely got going. Even so, he had advanced far enough for a shell hole to be his only refuge, with little apparent chance of escape.

'I was on the extreme right of the battalion and I had fixed on a big shell hole where there was a sergeant of the Seaforth Highlanders and two of his men already in. I joined them, as did my pal Macdonald with whom I had gone over the top, and there we sat in the mud, heads down. We could hear the machine guns still playing occasionally and I could also hear the wounded crying out for water. I was getting desperate because Macdonald, who had been out east and had had malaria, was having shivering bouts and was in a terrible state. When it got dark, he said, "Oh Andrew, try and find a way out," but I told him that in the dark I didn't know north from south and that we could walk into the German lines. We sat there for a long time when a sergeant who was in the shell hole with us said, "Well, there is one way you can try to get out. Put your two rifles together and put your two groundsheets over the top and pretend you are stretcher bearers."

'We did what he said and we came out right under the noses of the Germans, the two of us, the only two left from the battalion as far as we were concerned. Walking back, we saw an old German pill box, and behind it lay a lot of our boys wounded. The stretcher bearers were wiped out too, so the lads remained there and probably died there. Afterwards, I noticed that the top of my tunic was cut clean off by a piece of shrapnel, and was hanging loose. You would have thought it was cut by a razor, and it missed my throat by a fraction of an inch.'

For any loss of territory there was usually a pay-back. Counter-attacks were often mounted, or a violent shelling of the lines. Arthur Barraclough took part in a successful assault at Cambrai in November 1917 and was just starting to make his way out of the action when he was wounded. 'I was going back when all of a sudden Jerry sent a terrible barrage over, umpteen big black coal-boxes we used to call them, full of shrapnel, nails, anything that would do damage. There was one or two with me when we got hit, and we all three got hit together. Not serious, we could walk. Somebody said, "Well, there's a dressing station just there." There was a first aid man nearby, every battalion had them, and he attended to all three of us. I'd got a big gap in the muscle of my leg and he put a bandage on which stopped the bleeding.

'We advanced six miles and came through this village which hadn't been cleared up when all of a sudden snipers opened fire. We were walking shoulder to shoulder and these bullets were going past my nose. One of them went into the young officer in between me and this other lad, a bullet going clean through his cheeks. This lad, he was only a young officer, and he said 'Oh!' I said, "What's up?" I told him, "Oh aye, you're lucky." The bullet had gone through his face and out the other side, leaving a hole in either cheek. He were lucky, if it had been an inch higher he would have been dead, it would have blown his brains out. It didn't even knock him out. Anyway we could do nowt about it, and there was nowhere to stop so we'd to keep going.

'They kept shooting these bullets across and the lad on the far side got hit in the knee. How they were missing me, I don't know. We struggled on until we came to an open area, and there was a small van so we all went up to it and there's two or three fellas sat in it. I said, "What's this carry on?" "Oh, we're picking up the wounded," they replied. We said, "Oh, that's good," and the three of us crowded into this little van. I couldn't believe it because this van was well in the line of fire. Anyway, there was room for us to get in and they brought us back to reality, to some village where we got our wounds properly dressed. It were the only time it ever happened that I saw a van like that so close to the fighting.

'We were moved back to a village, even though it was still in the firing line. You see, after the main attack goes in, there's another lot comes and collects prisoners, they clear up, straighten things out, looking down cellars and empty houses, checking there's no Jerries down there. Anyway, they'd set up the dressing station in this cellar and we just had to go down some steps in pitch dark, and I think there were a couple of candles, nothing else, and we found a chap tending to everybody and anybody of the wounded.

'But I'll never forget that little van, it were like angels coming.'

CHAPTER ELEVEN

WOUNDS AND MEDICS

We needed another stretcher bearer and then we spotted a nice-looking German officer, ginger moustache. 'Get hold of the end of that stretcher,' he was told. 'Nein, nein,' he said, 'German officers don't carry stretchers with private soldiers.' Sale said, 'Get hold of the end of that stretcher!' 'Nein.' So dear old Sale stuck his boot under this young officer's backside and off he chased him, down into shell holes, through the water. He reached him again and kicked his backside several times, after which he decided he would take the end of the stretcher after all.

LIEUTENANT RICHARD HAWKINS,
11TH ROYAL FUSILIERS

After any attack, whether successful or not, there would be

Army Form B. 104—81.

No. 9S/Q22968.
(If replying, please quote
above No.)

R. W. SURREY Record Office,

HOUNSLOW. Station.

3 . 10 . , 1916.

Sir,

I regret to have to inform you that a report has this day been

received from the War Office to the effect that (No.) 7260

(Rank) Pte (Name) E. W. Ford

*Strike out
words that do
not apply.

(Regiment) R. W. SURREY. was {
*dangerously
*severely
*slightly
}

wounded in action with the Expeditionary Force, France,

on the 17 day of 9 1916

I am at the same time to express the sympathy and regret of the

Army Council.

Any further information received in this office as to his condition

will be at once notified to you.

Remaining at Sub.   I am,

Sir,

Your obedient Servant,

Major for Lieut.
C Infantry   Colonel.
Officer in charge of Records.

(4 27 1. W 13031 —273 100,000 8/15 H W V(P)   Forms/B. 104—80/2

Wounded in action: the official notification. Ernest Ford
lived into his ninety-ninth year.

wounded men strung out across the battlefield in desperate need of medical attention. Wounded men could cling to life, and sometimes suffered many days' waiting, often in the vain hope that stretcher bearers would rescue them. For those lying out after a successful attack, rescue might be quick if they were close to their own lines, or someone or something indicated their presence in a shell hole; an upturned rifle with the bayonet stuck in the ground was one favoured sign. However, for men caught between opposing lines, the chances of rescue were often slim. 'I could hear other men calling out "Stretcher bearers!" but you could call stretcher bearers for ever, there were not that many about,' recalled one veteran.

Sergeant Walter Popple, of the 8th King's Own Yorkshire Light Infantry, lay for three days and nights in no man's land after he was shot during his battalion's attack on 1 July 1916. The bullet wound to his left shoulder was serious but not immediately life-threatening, and after a while he was able to make himself as comfortable as he could while he waited for help.

Such soldiers, who were lightly wounded, were not totally bereft of medical treatment. Everyone carried what looked like a small pouch lightly stitched on the inside of the tunic, containing what was known as the First Field Dressing. This was, in fact, two surgical dressings within a bandage, in the middle of which was a small bottle of iodine. The iodine vial was broken and poured on to the wound, the bandage keeping the dressings in place, with the iodine helping, in theory, to staunch the flow of blood. Preferably, another man would be on hand to give assistance, but even for a soldier on his own such a dressing would have proved useful for a clean bullet wound to the shoulder. The problem for Walter Popple was that he had just one dressing. As the days passed, bursting shrapnel inflicted seven more wounds to his legs and the back of his shoulders. Only on the fourth morning did he finally drag himself across no man's land, after he drew the inevitable conclusion that he had to save himself or die. Walter Popple lived to the ripe old age of ninety-two, although the terrible recollections of that day drew tears until he died.

Another casualty that day was Frederick Francis of the Border Regiment. He, too, was shot, although his stomach wound was more serious. As he lay out in the open all night he kept shouting out for help: 'Will anybody come and get me in?' Strangely, he seemed all on his own. 'I never remember hearing anybody else; I seemed a lone bird. In the end I heard a voice, "We're coming for you now," and I saw a stretcher thrown over the parapet. They rushed out and put me on to the stretcher before lifting me over the parapet and into the trench, the Germans turning their machine guns on to us all the while.'

Fred Francis had clearly been close to his own line, but it took until the second day for his plaintive calls to be answered. Stretcher bearers worked as hard as they could, but local conditions dictated how many men they could bring in. All wore a brassard on the arm with the letters SB, indicating their role, and they worked tirelessly, often through appalling mud and shellfire, to bring in the wounded. On many occasions the Germans allowed these men to work in the open to rescue wounded soldiers; Andrew Bowie's miraculous escape from a shell hole was made possible only because the Germans mistook him for a stretcher bearer.

Not all Germans were so accommodating. Walter Popple's battalion suffered grievous casualties on 1 July (at least 539 killed or wounded) because they were exposed to withering machine gun fire. However, the figures were higher than they might have been owing in no small measure to one enemy soldier, who picked off the wounded as he sat in a funk hole forward of the front line. Under such conditions the work of battalion stretcher bearers and men of the Royal Army Medical Corps (RAMC) was made well nigh impossible. It is notable that the only double Victoria Cross winner of the Great War was a member of the RAMC, Captain Noel Chavasse, who saved numerous wounded soldiers under fire. He was wounded each time he won the VC. The second was awarded posthumously.

It was not the fear of death that played on soldiers' minds so much as the fear of horrific injury. Death was ever-present, as was the evidence of death, and many men had a morbidly curious desire to look at the dead, with that feeling of 'there but for the grace of God go I'. Surviving veterans will commonly affirm that while they always had the feeling that they would survive, they also fully expected to receive a wound. The best kind was the 'Blighty' variety, a word derived from the Hindi word *bilaik*, meaning 'home'. In other words, the soldier looked forward to an injury severe enough to ensure he passed through the base hospital and on to a hospital ship for England, but not one likely unduly to affect his long-term prospects in life.

Ideally the Blighty would be a clean wound obtained during a

12

Short Form of Will.

(See instruction 4 on page 1).

If a soldier on active service, or under orders for active service, wishes to make a short will, he may do so on the opposite page. **It must be entirely in his own handwriting and must be signed by him and dated.** The full names and addresses of the persons whom he desires to benefit, and the sum of money or the articles or property which he desires to leave to them, must be clearly stated. **The mere entry of the name of an intended legatee on the opposite page without any mention of what the legatee is to receive is of no legal value.**

The following is a specimen of a will leaving all to one person :—

In the event of my death I give the whole of my property and effects to my mother, Mrs. Mary Atkins, 999, High Street, Aldershot.

(Signature) THOMAS ATKINS.

Private, No. 1793,

Date, 5th August, 1914. Gloucester Fusrs.

The following is a specimen of a will leaving legacies to more than one person :—

In the event of my death I give £10 to my friend, Miss Rose Smith, of No. 1, High St., London, and I give £5 to my sister, Miss Sarah Atkins, 999, High Street, Aldershot, and I give the remaining part of my property to my mother Mrs. Mary Atkins, 999, High Street, Aldershot.

(Signature) THOMAS ATKINS,

Private, No. 1793,

Date, 5th August, 1914. Gloucester Fusrs.

Signature of Soldier

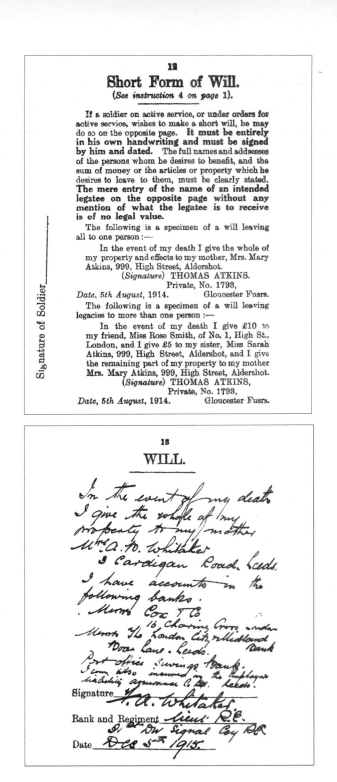

13

WILL.

[handwritten:] In the event of my death I give the whole of my property to my mother Mrs A. M. Whitaker 9 Cardigan Road. Leeds. I have accounts in the following banks. Messrs Cox & Co 16 Charing Cross, Messrs The London City & Midland Bank Boar Lane. Leeds. Post office Savings Bank. I am also insured in the Employers liability assurance Co. Leeds.

Signature *H. A. Whitaker.*

Rank and Regiment *Lieut. R.E.*
D.W Signal Coy R.E

Date *Dec 5th 1915.*

The form of will as found in a soldier's paybook.

quiet time in the line, a single casualty when the medical services were not over-stretched. The wound would be small and in some non-vital extremity such as the hand or lower leg, and inflicted in the summer time so that the roads to hospital would be easily negotiable. The worst scenario was too terrible to contemplate: stuck out in no man's land, alone, after a failed attack, in a shell hole full of water and mud, and close to the German lines. It would be a vicious shell-wound, serious enough to be life-threatening but not enough to kill quickly. Rescue was unlikely except perhaps by the Germans, the only realistic, if faint, alternative.

Removing the wounded from no man's land or the firing line was one of the most arduous jobs, both emotionally and physically. The haunting cry for 'Stretcher bearers' would be relayed along the trench and met with a rapid scuttling of feet, hastening from the support line, down the communication trench and into the firing line. Usually the first men on the scene were the battalion's own stretcher bearers drawn from the regimental band, who had been taught basic first aid. They attempted to staunch any blood-flow and apply a field dressing; however, stretcher bearers from the regiment or even the RAMC had precious little room to manoeuvre. 'We were hardly allowed to touch the wounds. If they had a bad open wound you'd just cover it up and get them out,' recalled one veteran.

Speed was of the essence. Under quiet conditions and in dry surroundings there would be enough stretcher bearers to deal with the regular, low-level attrition suffered by most battalions holding the line: a man sniped, a shell falling plumb into a fire-bay, a burst of shrapnel catching a working party. The problems grew exponentially when the trenches were in poor condition, mud oozed through the duckboards, revetted walls collapsed, or communication trenches proved too narrow to be negotiated with speed. Then, wounded men would have to be lifted above the height of the trench, subjecting the casualty to further injury, or tilted dangerously round corners, increasing the pain and heightening the chance that he might succumb to his injuries. Even when the case reached the Regimental Aid Post (RAP), a dugout in the support line and the first port of call for treatment, a difficult and tortuous manoeuvre might still have to be made to carry the stretcher underground.

Waiting in the RAP was the battalion's own Medical Officer, a man attached from the RAMC. His job was to deal quickly with injured soldiers, splinting fractures where necessary, re-dressing wounds, and giving morphia injections. Only *in extremis* would he ever attempt surgery, even of the most primitive type.

Unless heavy shelling prevented evacuation, the casualty rarely spent more than a few minutes at the Aid Post, RAMC stretcher bearers being called forward to take the wounded soldier further down the line. One veteran of the 94th Field Ambulance, serving the 31st Division (including men of the East Yorkshire Regiment), remembered the routine. 'As a rule we didn't go in the front line, we were left in the second line. It was a monotonous job and there were long periods when there was nothing happening and you were bored to the pants. Very often the regimental men were the people who did first aid to their own wounded and then we'd pick them up from there. The first case I ever took out of the line was a man shot through the head. We had to lift him down on to a stretcher and then take him off. We found we couldn't carry the stretcher down the trench as it was too narrow; it had been dug by the French and they hadn't done the job properly, so we had to carry that poor devil out with great difficulty, one fellow walking behind hanging on to the casualty's wrists, for we found that there was a tendency for them to snatch their bandage off. I felt sorry for the poor fella and put my tunic under him, which he promptly vomited over. When I got back to headquarters I had to indent for a new tunic, and when the colonel heard he told me I was a bloody fool and that if I did it again I would have to pay.'

Stretcher-bearing teams worked to their strengths A left-handed man would take the right-hand corner of the stretcher, as his left hand, the dominant one, could carry more than his right. The strongest man would often take the leg-end of the stretcher, as this always seemed to weigh more. They encouraged each other to keep going when desperate for a rest; however, as one stretcher bearer noted: 'I lost all feeling once I got into the line. My one object was to get the people out and be done with it. Some of the other men thought I was heartless, but it was the only way to survive.' Another concurred that: 'In point of fact you were just working like an automaton: you had to keep going backwards and forwards and you didn't bother to think a lot about things. Our job was to get rid of the wounded as quickly as possible. Keep going, keep going, keep going.'

During offensives, the trickle of casualties turned into a flood. At the time of the Somme Battle around 316,000 wounded men passed through Field Ambulance units, or around 2,250 per day.

With so many casualties it was not unusual for infantrymen out on rest to be sent forward, with no medical training, to evacuate the wounded, struggling for many hours through shellfire to rescue a man. In the worst scenarios a twelve- or even fifteen-hour slop through the mud was not impossible.

'Some of the wounded would groan and kick up an awful row, which was rather nerve-pulling,' recalls stretcher bearer Bill Easton. 'To make carrying easier, we had slings which we put round our shoulders and over the stretcher's handles. If anybody was too restless we used the slings to tie them on. Others were so badly wounded, you'd practically pick them up in pieces. If they were still alive, you had to cart them away, and you knew jolly well that they'd die at any time. We didn't think anything of struggling for perhaps two or three hours down to a Dressing Station and on arrival finding the man had died. It made you hardened to the sights; it had to.'

Once out of the trenches, the casualty was taken to an Advanced Dressing Station, often in an old concrete emplacement, or in the ruin of an old house or barn. Here, tetanus jabs were given to most men, while Field Medical Cards, akin to luggage labels, were written out, giving the number, rank, name and unit of the casualty, and the wound or disease suffered. This card was placed in a green cover (red for more dangerously wounded) and attached to the breast pocket button. The Advanced Dressing Station was a critical point of contact with the wounded, for it would take a long time to remove men to the next port of call, the Casualty Clearing Station, perhaps twelve or fifteen miles away, and generally out of the range of enemy artillery.

FIELD MEDICAL CARD.

(N.B.—USE LEAD PENCIL.)

NUMBER *15066* RANK *L Cpl*

NAME *Sweatland* UNIT *2 Glost*

Wound or Disease *Shell Shock*

Condition (if any) requiring } special attention

Medical Unit from } *1 M.F.A.* which transferred }

Date *25.7.16*

The red edged envelope will be used for cases dangerously or severely wounded and who require immediate attention.

The reverse is to be used for notes on special cases (history, operations, special treatment, or other necessary information); also on cases requiring or receiving special treatment during evacuation.

If a more detailed history is necessary, a Medical Certificate (A.B. 172) or Medical Case Sheet (A.F.I. 1237), or other statements of case may accompany.

In spite of shell shock, this soldier was back on duty
within days.

A slow and bumpy ride in an ambulance awaited critically injured men, and while the CCS was capable of receiving many hundreds of casualties a day, it was out of necessity that some basic surgery was undertaken at the ADS, to stabilize the patient or, if possible, relieve a man in great pain.

In the moments after being hit by shrapnel, Harry Fatch had had the presence of mind to apply his field dressing. 'After that I must have passed out. I don't remember how long I lay there. The next thing I knew, I was in a Dressing Station. They had taken the bandage off and cleaned the wound and put another bandage on. I stayed there for what was left of that night and the next day, and the next evening the doctor came. As shrapnel wounds went, mine was just a scratch. He could see the shrapnel in the wound and he asked me, "Shall I take it out? Before you answer yes, we've no anaesthetic in the can, it's all been used on more seriously wounded than you." So I thought for a minute or two and the pain from it was terrific, and I thought, "Well, perhaps a couple of minutes' more pain might be worth it," so I said, "Carry on." Four people got hold of me, one on each arm, one on each leg and the doctor got busy. I'd asked him how long he'd be and he'd said "Two minutes", and in those two minutes I could have damned-well killed him. Well, anyway, he got hold of it with tweezers, and pulled it out, two inches long, about half an inch thick, with a jagged edge.'

Although the majority of injuries were caused by artillery, at least thirty per cent were from bullets. Unless they were ricochets, most bullets left clean entrance and exit wounds, although there was always the risk of dangerous abscesses or gangrene, if the bullet carried dirt into the victim. Shrapnel, on the other hand, could cause devastation to the body. Without immediate treatment, the medical prognosis would be dim, as nearly all wounds went septic after six hours. For serious cases such as stomach wounds, treatment within such a short time-frame was vital or the patient was likely to die. Removing dead tissue was also important to avoid the risk of gangrene, which killed around half of its victims, although for this there was a slightly longer window of up to thirty hours.

The pressure on the ADS was such that it was a common sight to see dozens of men patiently waiting on stretchers on the ground as the more seriously wounded were attended to. Still close to the firing line, these men, and the orderlies who cared for them, were frequently at risk of being killed or wounded by shelling.

Joe Yarwood recalled one particularly devastating incident involving the 94th Field Ambulance in 1918. 'We were using an old brewery as an Advanced Dressing Station, but were due to be withdrawn because the German advance was so rapid. We didn't have the facilities to move everyone, so the colonel came down and was asking for volunteers to stay behind to be taken prisoner with the wounded. As he talked I heard this stinking shell coming and I dived into the lee of a house as it burst. I was uninjured, but as I came round the corner I was shocked by the scene. Colonel Stewart was lying dead, the adjutant had his leg blown off and was hanging on to the artery to try and prevent himself bleeding to death. Lieutenant Quartermaster Addey-Jibb was killed and I lost two comrades, real comrades I was very fond of, Arthur Hartland and Wilf Uren. There were a number of casualties too amongst the RAMC, while quite a few wounded soldiers at the ADS had a fresh dose from the shell.' The rescuers as well as the rescued were now casualties.

The effects of trauma were relatively little understood during the war, and men who had often suffered serious injuries, the loss of a hand or even an arm, were still expected to walk out of the line if possible. In a major action perhaps thirty per cent of the wounded would be 'walking', enabling the stretcher bearers to deal with the dozens, perhaps hundreds, of more critically injured, as one veteran recalled later. 'I met one poor devil he had been a walking wounded case and he was an elderly man too, and I felt very sorry for him because his wound was bleeding, and the whole of his chest was covered with a thick mat of congealed blood. I thought he would go down any minute with loss of blood.

I couldn't help him because I'd already got a case with me, but I got him carried out because, had he collapsed, he might well have died.'

A combination of slow medical treatment with the paucity of help in difficult times, led to a great number of men dying of minor wounds. Furthermore, in the absence of antibiotics, even slight injuries could lead to the loss of limbs, particularly when men could not receive treatment in the first critical hours after injury. Many bled to death (transfusions being in their infancy) or subsequently contracted gas-gangrene in the wound. One in three casualties died in the First World War, while during the Second World War this ratio fell to one in seven as advances in medicine and a better understanding of 'shock' brought wounded men within the frame of medical help far more quickly. The Falklands War was admittedly on a minuscule scale by comparison with the First World War, and the cold conditions helped wounded men cope with injuries and shock, but it is nevertheless remarkable that not one casualty who reached the Casualty Clearing Stations sub-sequently died of his injuries.

The first hint of normality greeted the wounded once they finally reached the CCS. Shelling could still be clearly heard, the explosions lighting up the sky in the near distance. Like a hospital's Accident and Emergency Department, the CCS was the first place where casualties could be properly sifted between those who were dangerously ill, and those who were not. For those men who were less seriously wounded, the presence of female nurses and Sisters was a great comfort, for most had not seen women for weeks (and women who spoke their own language possibly not for months). 'You'd smile and tell them that everything would be all right, even if they were not going to live,' recalled one nurse, Marjorie Grigsby. 'Usually, if they were conscious, the first thing they wanted was a cigarette but then, after a puff or two, the cigarette fell from their mouths, for they were generally too ill to smoke.'

The CCSs were small mobile hospitals, typically made up of tents and one or two huts, or housed in an abandoned building such as an old school or asylum. Six operating tables would be available at times of greatest pressure, ready to cope with a rapid escalation in the number of casualties. Young nurses of the Voluntary Aid Detachments (VADs) helped out as best they could, as one recalled. 'I attended operations, and there were always body parts to remove. I will forever remember the first leg I had to carry, because I was shocked to find how much a leg weighed. I carried it in a bucket with the foot sticking up. It wasn't very nice.'

Sometimes, even for the less dangerously wounded, the CCS could still save lives. Arthur Barraclough was injured by shellfire during an attack at Arras in 1917. 'You could hear shells coming sometimes and once I heard one drop very close. I just had time to put my hand up to cover my face, and as I did so a shrapnel ball went into the muscle in my arm, the mark is still there. I met another lad and he looked at my wound and he said, "Oh, I can see shrapnel in there. I'll pick it out for you if you want." I said, "You can hell as like. I'll get it bandaged up, never mind about picking it out." When I was in the CCS later, the doctor said I was dead lucky: he said if that shrapnel had gone the slightest bit further I'd have bled to death. The main artery's in there and the shrapnel was just touching it. He told me, "If anybody had mucked with that, you'd have had it." So I was a bit lucky there.'

For ease of transportation, a CCS was usually located near a main road or train station. Ambulance Trains were the primary mode of evacuation to the base hospitals, and men rarely spent more than a day or two at the CCS before being sent down the line. The more seriously injured made their way to England while the rest recovered near the coast in France, too frustratingly close to Blighty for most to bear.

At the CCS, medical attention had been paramount, while 'patient care' was left to the base hospital or England. In all, 1.16 million men were evacuated back to Blighty during the war. Partly owing to the sheer volume of work, partly owing to the soldiers' shock, few casualties knew much about the extent of their injuries. One veteran, Fred Tayler, was boarding a train for the boat to England when, just by chance, he heard bad news. 'I had an operation but I didn't know what they had done. I was taken to a ward, and the next day a train arrived to take the wounded down to the base. My particulars were taken and I was wheeled out to the ambulance train. As they lifted me up, a corporal receiving the patients asked "What's this one?" and a chap looked at a label on me and the answer came "Amputation". Well, that was the first I knew that my leg was off, it was quite a shock.' Tragically for Fred, his injury and subsequent amputation had occurred just weeks before the war ended.

During the First World War the medical services made super-human efforts, restoring to some form of health nearly eighty per

The King commands me to assure you
of the true sympathy of His Majesty and
The Queen in your sorrow.

He whose loss you mourn died in the
noblest of causes.   His Country will be
ever grateful to him for the sacrifice he has
made for Freedom and Justice.

Milner

Secretary of State for War.

One of the many thousands of such messages, sent as
comfort and reassurance that loved ones had died in a
worthy cause.

cent of all the casualties who passed through their hands. As a corps, they had grown in number from just under 20,000 in 1914 to over 144,000 in 1918; during that time they had used over 7,000 tons of cotton wool, 108 million bandages, and 1.5 million splints. Of the men evacuated to England, two-thirds were able to return to France in some semblance of good health. Helping the wounded had itself cost many lives. A total of 4,039 men of the RAMC were killed in action, and two to three times that number were wounded.

CHAPTER TWELVE

THE TRENCH 2001

My grandfather and my great-grandfather both fought in the First World War and my motive for coming here was to see if I could put up with a little bit of what my relatives went through. At the end, when we walked through the gates at the billet and everyone from the BBC and local people, too, stood there clapping us, I had tears in my eyes. I felt so proud that I had done my best by my grandfather and my great-grandfather. I didn't do it for money and I didn't do it for fame and I didn't do it for anything other than to prove to those people from my life, who are dead now, that given a go I could carry their name forward with pride.

CARL JACKSON, HULL PAL 2001

The experiences of the new Hull Pals were recorded, in the main, on the final night they spent in the trenches. I had arrived back in France expecting to watch any activity from a distance, but as little filming was due to take place that night I was able to don a helmet and greatcoat and pass up the communication trench to the front line as a last-minute draft. The noise of shelling could still be heard, the odd Very light was bursting in the sky and the occasional bout of rifle fire broke out, but as the night wore on it became distinctly quiet. Some of the men were able to sleep, others, on duty, manned the firing line or held a crater blown earlier in the week, forward of the trench. In the dark, armed with an unobtrusive tape recorder, I was able to talk to several volunteers. The experiences they told me were fascinating, not least because several stories echoed, to a greater or lesser degree, those told me by veterans in the past.

'When it starts raining, the rain drops on your metal helmet and it starts pinging, tinc, tinc, tinc. So what we decided to do was put empty sandbags on top of our helmets to stop the noise, because after a while it starts to become annoying, especially if it's raining heavy, because you start to feel as if you've got your head inside of a bell sometimes. The sandbags were useful because they stopped the water going down the back of our necks, too. Other chaps put their feet inside them to keep their feet warm, it's common sense.'

While I have never heard of soldiers draping sandbags over their helmets, hessian covers were provided during the war to ensure helmets did not reflect sunlight, and many a soldier tied sandbags around his feet; this demonstrates how, given the same circumstances, men adapt in similar ways. And like their forebears, the volunteers weren't above the odd dirty trick, contriving little ways of going on sentry duty late at the expense of the next man on. 'We worked at finding five minutes later to go on, or then, if you were on duty, you might try and call the next bloke on five minutes earlier. You'd pick on the one in your section that didn't complain or one that was keen as mustard.'

The volunteers stuck to the task as it presented itself; indeed, as time passed, they became even more determined to see the project through to its conclusion. As volunteers were 'killed off' in the latter stages of filming, so it became harder to convince them that their death was necessary and that they would have to leave the line. A hot bath, clean clothes, a solid meal and a few beers would tempt most civilians from a muddy existence, but the last men to 'die' appeared shell-shocked and upset that they had been suddenly plucked from amongst their surviving comrades.

Had the volunteers broken, no doubt critics would have pointed to their lack of resilience as proof that modern man is not as hardy as his forefather. The flip-side of that particular coin is that the men of 1916 had to keep going; once they had enlisted, they then served under the full weight of military discipline and law and could have been shot had they walked away. There was no gun pointed at the modern volunteers; they could have upped sticks and gone home at any time. In the end only one volunteer was 'transferred' to another platoon, in other words sent home. He was unwilling to apply himself to the task in hand, while his constant moaning had become excessive. His departure was not mourned by the other volunteers.

Most documentaries of this type are riven with on-screen problems and issues. There were occasional gripes and grumbles about food, about the cold, but no more than would be expected from any group of volunteers, whether in 1916 or 2001, and once in France there were no incidents which could have unravelled, or seemed likely to unravel, the filming of *The Trench*. As one volunteer said, there was a genuine motivation: 'The idea that I'm representing Hull is with me all the time, especially when you're down. When we were out of the line, after the football game, we had an hour off and we visited a cemetery nearby and it brings it all back to you, why you are doing it, it's a morale-injection, it really is, because they did it for real, and they paid the ultimate sacrifice. We moan and groan about the food, and that our feet are cold, but we're still intact, we can still go home. And when you look at the ages too, eighteen years old, twenty-four years, younger than us.'

One incident is worth recording. At the pay parade, it was found that Pte Thompson had deliberately not shaved, as much to probe military authority as anything else. Sent before the commanding officer, Thompson was asked why he had not shaved, and was duly sentenced to Field Punishment No. 2. This punishment entailed running round the farm courtyard in full pack with his 9lb rifle held aloft. Thompson had tested the officers' resolve and they had not been found wanting. He might and could have refused the punishment and in the end no further sanction could have been handed out. The point was, he didn't.

Along with this dedication, the volunteers soon learnt the importance of relying on each other. 'It's not about being the best soldier. It's about standing together with the men from your section. No-one can hide anything, what you see is what you get. You've got nothing to gain by trying to be anything better than what you are. We're all out here for the same reason. We have only known each other three weeks, but we've really bonded in that time.'

Such friendship helped the volunteers get through the times when morale was low. 'There's been great comradeship, that's what's helped us stick it. As soon as anybody's seen anyone else down, they've gone straight over and had a word with them to cheer them up, because we've all had our moments. Later on, when you were really down you thought "Lucky bugger" about one of the lads who was "killed", you really did, you thought it would be great to get a Blighty, then at least you would be out of this shit.'

The comradeship grew as time passed, to the extent that reality had the potential to blur. 'You do lose yourself in the thing. Out on patrol, it's totally different than in here, it sounds daft, but when it's dark you do get a buzz. When you're out there, you don't want to die. Out in the crater we were saying that if they come for us, we'll fight.' Apparently 'there was an idea to form a snatch party and grab one of us from the trench, but Taff said, ' No, you can't do it because all these lads are on edge, you try that and someone will get injured." If someone jumped in here with a German uniform on, he'd probably get filled in, he honestly would.'

As with all soldiers, nicknames abounded. In 1916 it would have been 'Ding Dong' Bell, 'Nobby' Clarke, and 'Chalky' White, in

2001 it was 'Dan' for Pte Ackroyd, 'Judith' as in Chalmers; then there was 'No Votes' because he's a county councillor, while other names such as 'Attitude' were used for more opaque reasons.

Given the length of time at the front, it was perhaps surprising that tempers were not lost. 'One of our mates in section three, he was really fed up, and he found it hard going. He was constantly talking on and on, so we nicknamed him "Jabber jaws"; anyway, he started saying "I'm sick of this, I'm sick of this cheese, I'm sick of this place, I don't want to be here," and he's moaning and groaning. We were marching on our way into the trench in single file, and he was about five or six people behind me and somebody had said "Jabber" to him and he just went off on one. He threw his helmet on the floor and said "Right, that's it, I've had enough, I've got a first name you know, I'm just sick of it." He just threw a fit until he calmed down again.'

Two of the best known were the smallest volunteers, Palmer and Thompson, collectively called the 'Bantams'. As a team, they sought to undermine authority whenever the opportunity arose, once sneaking alcohol into the line for the men, or on another occasion stealing extra blankets.

'We won't forget Palmer and Thompson bringing us the blankets. Thompson comes across as a rogue but he's got a heart of gold. It was chucking it down with rain and we were all freezing, and he and Palmer took the risk by themselves, the two little Bantam lads, and each of them brought a stack of blankets, and they covered us up. Asleep or hardly awake, they covered us up to make sure that next morning we were warm and dry. I woke up and saw Palmer tucking us in like a mother, and it really

274   THE TRENCH

touches your heart, and that's when you bond with someone.'

Such living comradeship would be broken by death, and during filming a total of five volunteers were removed from the line, representing the five Hull Pals killed in action during the same period in the line.

'When someone's killed off there is a sense of loss, but not a great one because we know we'll see him next week.' Even so, it was touching how volunteers were missed and efforts were made to remember those lost, regardless of the fact that a reunion with everyone together was never more than a week or two ahead.

'Joe out of Section One asked me to do a memorial for Jonathan Baxter, so I just knocked together a memorial seat in the front line. Then, as the first one went well, I was asked to do something for Private Wilson. So I did a plaque for Wilson, who went over the top and didn't come back. Then, after he died, we dug a sap at one end of the trench, and it was the officer's idea to call it Wilson's Sap.'

Because the men were starved of information, rumour and superstitions, usually based on nothing more substantial than a flight of fancy, took firm root in the minds of the volunteers. Lance Gadd, the first volunteer to 'die', had been carrying the medical bag. This bag had been handed by chance to Steve Wilson, but as he had become the second to be killed, the medical bag was from then on to be avoided at all costs. A football match played while the men were out on rest generated more superstition. The rumour went around that the rattle, for use as a gas alarm, was to be avoided as the holder would not survive.

'That's what has kept us going, rumours. It's like when the

patrols go out, the first patrol is getting it, you're going home. There was rumours about everything, like what day we were going home, it's Monday, then Thursday, then Friday and rumours about what we're having for tea; someone said we were getting custard one night.' It was about the only rumour that proved correct.

To allay fear and worries, it was important that the volunteers had the opportunity to write home to their families and to receive parcels from home. As with all mail from the front, letters were vetted by Lieutenant Yuill, who found that, while he had to strike out one or two things on the first day, such as place names and one request for alcohol, little else had to be lost.

Mail was sent out via the BBC in Bristol and delivered, slightly less efficiently than had been the case in 1916. Letters were posted not just to the volunteers but to the Khaki Chums. Realizing the importance to morale, Sgt Gillingham had sent a general e-mail to friends prior to leaving England asking for letters of support to be sent to the Chums out in France, in much the same way as women in England were encouraged to write to the soldiers abroad during the war. A bundle of letters duly arrived, including one from America and another from the inhabitants of the Belgian village of Ploegsteert, where so much fighting had taken place during the war.

A letter from a loved one at home was a great boost for the soldiers in the line regardless of the year, 1916 or 2001. Similarly, the absence of a letter would be the cause of worry, as Private Steve Wilson recalls. 'When the first mail drop came out, I was really expecting a letter because my wife said she'd write to me, but nowt came; then the second drop there was nowt there either and I was really gutted, I was proper gutted. If she says she's going to write, she usually writes, so I'm wondering what's wrong.' To cheer Pte Wilson up, the other volunteers all got together and wrote him a letter purporting to come from his family back home, only with soldiers' typical bullish humour, and accompanying presents. 'It was so funny. There was a tin of corned beef, and one of these chalk stones they'd carved with a knife, just like trench art, and they'd put on it "From Withernsea", a town on the Yorkshire coast. It was really appreci-ated until I did get that letter from home.'

Writing letters home gave insights into family letters written during the war but misunderstood until today. 'I talked to one chap about my great-grandad's letters and I said, how can he write about sending cigarette cards home to his son when he's going through all this shit. But the first letter I wrote home was telling my wife about things, and you just totally blank what you're doing, you're in a different world when you're writing this letter. I now know why he was writing that stuff, because you just want to blank what you're going through out of your head. I was telling her about how things will be when I get back. It's a little fantasy: that when you're writing it you are back there in Hull, and then you put your pencil away and realize "Oh God. I'm still here." I was saying to Paul last night, "Hey, Paul, just think, my wife and your wife will be looking at the moon as we're looking at it now." You think these crazy things.'

Escapism was found to be very important for all the men, even if only for a few fleeting moments, and was perhaps one of the main differences between the volunteers of today and the soldiers of 1916. The availability of time and space has been a by-product of twentieth-century technological advances and sociological changes. Fewer hours at work, smaller families, larger homes and, with the growth in car ownership, the accessibility of the countryside, all this has helped make modern man much more aware of his freedoms and possibly less able to tolerate constant close confinement with others.

'Every man needs five minutes to themselves, whatever you are doing: my first ten minutes on sentry duty was for myself, I knew no-one was going to come and disturb me. In this time you reflect on your life and home and all these things at home that gave you trouble before. Then you think, "I'm stood here in a cold field with a rifle in my hand and I'm looking out for an enemy and it's really surreal!" You take everything into account back home and how simple it all is, and how simply you could solve it up against what you are going through now. Those ten little minutes mean so much to you, it's escapism, and it's a great feeling.'

Free time, as much as there was, was used constructively. Taking some of the lumps of chalk that stuck out of trench walls or which lay on the parapet, the men worked with their knives. It was another five minutes of peace, although, by the look of some of the art, the work must have taken far longer.

'The chalk is so easy to carve, it's like cheese and it's so moist, it's soft. I did a scroll with "Hull Pals" on it. I made a dice and I'll keep it as a memento and I'll put it on my desk in my office and look at it and remember this time.

'We won't see the Lieutenant again; we might see each other, but he's not from Hull. So we made him a little keepsake and I put on it "Lieutenant Yuill, Hull Pal", and on the back "From Three Section". I reckon he'll be quite chuffed with that; as soon as he sees that it'll remind him of us lot, won't it?'

At the end of the shoot, the volunteers and the Chums left the trench, firing off any remaining ammunition in a thirty-five-rifle and one Lewis Gun salute. They then marched off to the billet for a well-deserved breakfast before returning their uniforms and equipment to the quartermaster. That afternoon, they took a cross that they had made to Oppy Wood Memorial near Arras, where the battalion had suffered its first grievous losses in May 1917. Only after paying their respects did they head for the hotel in Cambrai, where a post-operations bash was laid on before they left for Hull the following morning.

The trench was suddenly empty, but not de-personalized as it had been before the arrival of the volunteers. Chalked on the wall as one made one's way up the communication trench was the warning 'Go Back', then a few yards further, 'I said Go Back', then a little further, 'You are not listening, are you?' Then 'Last Chance?' before, 'Too late!' Once in the line, there was to be found the odd parcel wrapping with name and address, and an envelope with sentry duty hastily written on the back: 'Tug 11–12, Dave F 12–1, Colin 1–2, Bob 2–3, Dan 3–4, Paul 4–5, Dave S 5 to Reveille.' Elsewhere there was an empty bully-beef tin that had not been launched into no man's land, and a couple of pieces of trench art still stuck in the wall. The memorial seat to Pte Baxter remained, and at one point a lucky horseshoe had been left above a dugout. But by far the most poignant details were those names and notes chalked up on the many bits of wood: Hull names like 'Holderness Road' and 'Beverley Road'. There were the names of wives and children too, Joe, Eric, Pat, Nick, Sue, Luke and Paul, Susan and Harry, Mark, Jessica and Faith, underlining how much they evidently missed them, while one private showed his unit pride with a 'God bless Two Section', neatly written on a cross-beam.

It is hard not to imagine that similar scenes would have been found in abandoned trenches eighty-five years ago, before they were slowly filled in. In the case of our trench, local people were invited to see the cause of all the disturbance on the day following the conclusion of filming, while a party of school children was expected the day after. And then that would be it. The BBC were contracted to destroy the trench system rather more quickly than it was built; indeed, within two weeks the land had to return to its former undistinguished appearance. It seemed a shame to every-one, including the designer who talked of pouring petrol the whole length of the trench, hosting one huge funeral pyre rather than letting it be dismantled bit by bit. At the last moment local people bought the field and will ensure, after all, that The Trench will be preserved. It will be as good an example as any of how a trench might have looked, minus the names, of course; they will be washed away with the first good soaking.

CHAPTER THIRTEEN

THE 10TH EAST YORKS

During the winter months of 1916–17, the 10th Battalion East Yorks continued to undertake tours of the line and to provide men for the endless working parties. The winter had ended any fighting for the time being, and both sides shivered the weeks away, the 10th Battalion receiving an evening rum ration, 'a thing unheard of previously', as the battalion's War History notes. Indeed, the cold was so bad that, while on a route march, the battalion's band was slowly put out of commission as the instruments froze one by one.

The usual training continued, but as the war-footing recommenced, games of tug-of-war gave way to competitions in route marching, which in turn gave way to musketry and practice attacks.

In February 1917, the Germans retired from the Somme to a new, seemingly impregnable position, known as the Hindenburg

Line. The village of Serre was abandoned to the British and to the Hull Pals, who were able to explore freely the German trenches they had once fought so hard to win. As the Germans withdrew, a scheduled attack by men of the 10th Battalion on the village of Bucquoy was cancelled owing to insufficient ammunition; the 10th had been 'lucky' again, although for the last time.

On 3 May 1917, the battalion took part in an attack on Oppy Wood, their first big attack and the one for which they are best remembered. But the attack, part of the Battle of Arras, was something of a diversionary assault, a bit part in the larger strike at the enemy, and no great results were anticipated. For the brigade as a whole, it was costly. Even before going over the top, the men had been spotted and heavily shelled, and when they finally attacked, under the protection of a rolling barrage, they found the wire in front of the enemy trenches uncut. All four company commanders were injured, and in the smoke and mist the men became disorientated. When the attack was over 125 men of the 10th Battalion had been killed or wounded.

Although another assault was made on Oppy Wood in June, the 10th Battalion was placed in reserve and did not play an active role in the fighting. Throughout the summer the battalion went in and out of the line near Vimy Ridge, which the Canadian Corps had taken in April. The summer months were again taken up with training, a period relieved only when in July the King arrived to review the battalion.

The men continued to supply working parties to the line, and took part in company and battalion training while out on rest. In September they were involved in another successful raid on

enemy lines, but it wasn't until the German offensive the following March that they were once again actively involved in heavy
fighting. In the intervening months, the battalion had lost just
seven men killed. When the Germans attacked in March 1918, the
battalion was in rest near the town of St Pol. At first, the men did
not realize the seriousness of the situation, and on a day when the
Germans were smashing through the British lines, the Hull Pals
were playing football.

Later, when the men were moved forward to join the fray, they
were shocked to see army canteens on fire, burnt to stop them
falling into enemy hands. In an attempt to halt the enemy advance,
the Pals were set to work improving shallow trenches around the
French village of Ervillers. Ahead there was much confused fighting, and it was not long before British soldiers retreated through
the Pals' lines. The 10th Battalion stood their ground and fought
bravely, but in the end were forced to take part in a general fighting retirement and were mentioned by Field Marshal Haig as
showing 'exceptional gallantry'. In three days the unit had lost 211
officers and men, killed or wounded. The remnants of the
battalion were reinforced with young eighteen-year-old boys in
April. They fought on throughout the month as part of the desperate struggle to halt the enemy, in what was known as the Battle
of the Lys. Again, casualties showed the severity of the action:
ninety-nine men were killed, most in a three-day period in mid-
April, and hundreds more were wounded or taken prisoner. Some
twenty-two of those killed were original 1914 recruits, a high per-
centage of the last remaining volunteers still serving with the
battalion. The German offensive finally blew itself out in June

and July and the front line was re-stabilized. In August, the exhausted German army was turned, and over the next four months began a retreat that was to culminate in the Armistice in November. Throughout the intervening months, the 10th Battalion was never far from the fighting and continued to suffer grievously. The battalion was unrecognizable as the one which had gone to the Somme in 1916, its ranks being filled by boys sent out from Britain, many of whom had no connection with Hull, but were simply drafted into the battalion to make up the numbers. In the last six months of the war, amongst a total number of 217 deaths, only eighteen were original recruits from Wenlock Barracks in 1914; this shows how far the battalion had become Hull Pals in name only.

News of the Armistice reached the men of the 10th Battalion East Yorkshire Regiment at 2 a.m. on 11 November, nine hours before the cessation of hostilities. The War Diary noted: 'Battalion Runners carried the news to the Companies at 6 a.m., when such a heavy bombardment was in progress so very near at hand that most of our men turned over for that last hour in bed well nigh incredulous! Later, when the men began to stir and to discuss the momentous news, there was a surprising lack of enthusiasm. The war had continued so long that we had come to know army life pretty well – civilian life would mean taking a fresh plunge – besides breaking up what seemed lifelong friendships.'

One lifelong friendship was about to be broken that morning between a private and the battalion he had joined in September 1914. Pte Robert Bernard Stead, No. 1172, an original 10th

Battalion Hull Pall, died in hospital on 11 November 1918. It is not known whether he knew about the Armistice, or cared.

The sound of gunfire continued right up to 10.59 a.m., when sound-ranging recorded the last spluttering gunfire on tape, as a seismograph monitors the shaking in an earth tremor. Then there was silence. Ironically, the first and last shots of the war took place round the Belgian town of Mons. Just north of the town is Casteau village, where there is a hotel on the walls of which is a bronze plaque. This marks the place where elements of the 116th Canadian Infantry arrived at 11 a.m. that Armistice morning. Almost directly opposite, forty yards away, is a stone memorial commemorating the first engagement of the war, when British and German cavalry clashed in the village almost four years and three months earlier.

Another soldier feeling a 'lack of enthusiasm' that Armistice morning was Arthur Halestrap. 'We were on detachment and we were following an infantry unit. We knew the Armistice was about to happen. I listened to the signal on my radio set and said, "That's it". At the time, we were in a bombed-out factory and we had to wait there until we received orders. As soon as the Armistice took place there was such a silence, it was a silence that knocked one silly, it was so sudden. Straight away we felt that we had nothing to live for, no objective. We didn't know what to do next or where we would go, and that is rather an eerie feeling. We asked, "Well, now what happens?" There was nothing whatever to look forward to, a queer feeling that.'

In London, in complete contrast to the Western Front, there were joyous celebrations. Eighteen-year-old Patricia Wilson, the daughter of Major Carver, heard the news early that morning. 'My mother and I were staying in London. We had taken a flat at Queen Anne Mansions, as my father was, by that time, working in the capital. On the eleventh we knew the war was coming to an end, and even in those days there was a sort of ticker machine and I remember this was down in the hall. At about 10 a.m. I said to my mother, who was reading the paper, "Do come over and look at this," because the ticker said that at 11 a.m. that morning the war would be over. Queen Anne Mansions is quite close to Buckingham Palace and my mother said we must go round, and we rushed to the Palace where we met others who had gone there as well. Then the King and Queen came out on to the balcony. I was in the crowd looking up at them, although the numbers weren't that large because people hadn't had time to get there. I remember we had taken a whole lot of German tanks and they were lined up as war trophies all the way up to the Palace. Oh, the crowds were cheering and throwing their hats in the air, it was a lovely party.'

The tragedy of war did not automatically finish on 11 November. The last original member of the battalion to die was not in fact Pte Stead, for four days later another, Pte Clarence Bilbe, died in the flu epidemic that swept Europe that winter.

And in the celebrations there were new casualties, too. Andrew Bowie was at a railway station in France on 12 November. 'There were about a dozen of us larking about, and a train went through and there were some fellas who, for fun or devilment, had climbed up on top of the carriages. They were shouting and cheering and waving to us, so we waved back to them. About half an hour later, the stationmaster came and asked if we'd seen the train that had gone through with "les soldats anglais" on top. We said "Yes". "Well," he said, "they're all dead." The train had gone under a low bridge and they were all cut off, half a dozen killed just like that.'

Of the original volunteers who had enlisted during those two heady days of September 1914, at least 285 did not survive the war, a quarter of the original volunteers. They included at least six of the thirty men that Patricia Wilson had seen that early morning, when, as a fourteen-year-old, she had accompanied her father to Wenlock Barracks, Hull. A further 423 men who were later sent as drafts died serving with the 10th Battalion, and this does not include a further thirty-six officers who were also killed during the 1914–18 period.

The figures hide many individual tragedies. A third of those who died have a given age at the time of death. Of these only a very few were aged thirty or over, while the average age at the time of death was twenty-three. The casualty figures reveal that around twelve per cent of the battalion enlisted under-age, the youngest casualty, Private Harry Jipson 10/1351, being killed in action in August 1916 aged just sixteen.

Two months after the war was over, a picture was taken of the remaining original members in a park at St Omer in France, when it was noted that, in all, 125 men were still serving with the 'Lucky Tenth', including just one officer, R. C. Hewson, who had risen from being a lowly subaltern to command the battalion. Hewson had won the Military Cross, one distinction among many in the 10th Battalion. In all, the battalion was awarded two

Distinguished Service Orders, with one bar, twenty-two Military Crosses, and one bar, thirteen Distinguished Conduct Medals, and fifty-eight Military Medals, with three bars.

On 26 May 1919 a cadre of men from the 10th Battalion, amongst others, paraded at the station in Hull. Then, to the strains of 'Home, Sweet Home' and 'The Yorkshire Lass', they marched to the Guildhall where they were addressed by the Lord Mayor, who told them, 'You have fought a fight, you have gained a victory, you have won a peace.'

The same year, Major Carver took his family to the battlefields to see where the 10th Battalion had fought. His daughter commented: 'My father said that he must take us and show us where he had been in France, so he took my mother, myself and brother. He wanted to show us all the places where there were still trenches, and we went to see where my cousin was buried, who had been in the artillery and was killed. The trenches and the atmosphere, it shocked us. My mother didn't like it at all, and you couldn't help but feel it was too soon.'

In the years after the war, veterans looked back on what they had seen and done with a mixture of emotions. Some, like Ted Francis, were angry for a long time. 'At the end of the war I looked back on my childish dreams of gallant deeds by men on horseback. I thought "Oh what a fool I was to take all that in." If anyone detested the army it was me. I hated all its terrible laws and the discipline they dealt out to poor lads of eighteen and nineteen, and never more would I be connected in any way with the army. The war was something I wanted to forget, to put behind me, to put all my thinking ability into my job. That is the reason that I worked for forty years with not one word to anyone about the war.'

Others, like Joe Yarwood, looked back on the war as a 'unique' experience. 'We were lucky to have taken part, luckier still to have come through it without any serious injury. And you felt satisfaction that, if only in a very humble degree, you had served your country at a vital time. Looking back, I think it was one of the most interesting experiences of my whole life. I am extremely fortunate to have taken part in it, and I'm being quite sincere about that.'

Arthur Barraclough and Harry Patch have never been back, and have refused every invitation to go. Arthur does not appear haunted by his memories; Harry is. 'I was asked recently if I wanted to go back to France and I said "No, never",' Harry Patch insists. 'I never want to see Flanders again, nor see the trenches. I don't want to see any of it. Brings back too many memories. Far too many.' Even at night he still sees the shell explosion that took his friends in 1917. 'All I remember is the flash, and when I'm lying in bed at night and the nurse switches the light on outside my room, if I'm half asleep and half awake, I'm back on that battlefield; there's the flash.'

Arthur Halestrap has come to terms with his war better than most and will keep returning to the battlefield as long as he can. 'Whenever I go to the Menin Gate at Ypres, where so many names are commemorated, I think about all the tens of thousands of men of my generation who volunteered their liberty and their lives for an ideal, which was the maintenance of the British way of life; and I don't think those men should be forgotten, not because they died but because of what they sacrificed their lives for.'

SELECT BIBLIOGRAPHY

Adams, Bernard, *Nothing of Importance: A Record of Eight Months at the Front with a Welsh Battalion*, Tom Donovan Publishing (reprint), 1988.

Andrews, Albert, *Orders Are Orders: A Manchester Pal on the Somme*, privately published, 1987.

Barnes, Barry, *This Righteous War*, Richard Netherwood Ltd, 1990.

Bilton, David, *Hull Pals*, Pen & Sword Books Ltd, 1999.

British Trench Warfare 1917-1918, reprinted by The Imperial War Museum and the Battery Press, Nashville, 1997.

Brown, Malcolm, *Tommy Goes to War*, J.M. Dent & Sons Ltd, 1978.

Carrington, Charles, *Somme Memoirs*, Stockwell, 1928.

Carver, R. B. et al., *A History of the 10th (Service) Battalion The East Yorkshire Regiment (Hull Commercials)*, A. Brown & Sons Ltd, 1937.

Cliff, Norman D., *To Hell and Back with the Guards*, Merlin Books, Braunton, 1988.

Ellis, John, *Eye-Deep in Hell: Trench Warfare in World War One*, Pantheon Books, 1976.

Gliddon, Gerald, *When the Barrage Lifts*, Gliddon Books, 1987.

Graves, Robert, *Goodbye to All That*, Penguin Books, 1984.

Horsfall, Jack, and Cave, Nigel, *Serre*, Pen & Sword Books, 1997.

MacDonald, Lyn, *Somme*, Papermac, 1984.

Middlebrook, Martin, *The First Day on the Somme: 1 July 1916*, Penguin Books, 1984.

Mitchell, Major T. J., *Official History of the War Medical Services, Casualties and Medical Statistics*, 1931, reprinted by the Imperial War Museum, 1997.

Rogerson, Sydney, *Twelve Days*, Gliddon Books (reprint), 1988.

Simpson, Andy, *Hot Blood and Cold Steel*, Tom Donovan Publishing, 1993.

Statistics of the Military Effort of the British Empire during the Great War 1914–20, HMSO, London, 1922.

van Emden, Richard, *Veterans: The Last Survivors of the Great War*, Pen & Sword Books, 1998.

Winter, Denis, *Death's Men: Soldiers of the Great War*, Allen Lane, 1978.

INDEX

Accrington Pals, 33, 68, 77
Advanced Dressing Station (ADS),
    260, 261, 262, 263
aircraft, 214–16
Aisne, river, 41
Albert, 62, 63, 67, 134, 238
ambulances, 260–1
Ambulance Trains, 266
ammunition, 26, 102, 120–2, 210,
    282
Armentières, 226
Armistice, 284–6
Army Cinema, 183
Army Postal Service, 149, 150
Arras: Battle of, 282; bodies, 54;
    pilgrimages to battlefield, 4;
    shellfire, 265; war damage, 182
artillery, 49, 209–10, *see also* shelling
Ashurst, George, 65
Australian forces, 190

Bairnsfather, Bruce, 197–8
Bangalore torpedoes, 238
Bapaume, 62, 63, 182
barbed wire, 47, 53, 70, 112–13

Barraclough, Arthur: on air battles,
    216–17; arrival at front, 37; on
    barbed wire, 112–13; on bullying,
    80, 82; on canteens, 189;
    enlistment, 19; on foot care, 163;
    friendships, 84; on gas masks, 220;
    on German dugouts, 35; on going
    over the top, 237; grandson, 4; on
    leave, 205–6; on lice, 173, 174, 176;
    memories, 289; on mules, 129–30;
    on nervousness, 87; on patrols,
    106–7; on rats, 171; on rum, 144,
    231; on sentry duty, 116; service
    with Duke of Wellington's, 101; on
    shelling, 212, 213–14; on snipers,
    91–2; training, 26, 82, 84; on Very
    lights, 114–15; on washing, 136,
    175; on water bottles, 135;
    wounded, 4, 248–50, 265–6
Barraclough, Simon, 4
baths, *see* washing
battalions: allegiance to, 77, 78; front
    line duty, 98–9; Kitchener, 98;
    numbers of men, 76; rotation of
    duties, 100–1; snipers, 91

Hull Pals (*cont.*)
  (1916), 69; German offensive
  (1918), 283; Kitchener units, 10;
  march round Hull (1914), 30;
  names of units, 14; recruitment,
  14, 284; at Richebourg St Vaast,
  179–80; at Robecq, 179; Serre
  attacks, 243–4; Serre occupation,
  282; Serre trenches, 50, 51, 101,
  238; training, 33, 67; 31st Division
  (92nd Infantry Brigade), 33
Hull Pals, The (Bilton), 10
Hull Sportsmen, 14
Hull Tradesmen, 14
humour, 196–8

Ireland, David, 235

Jackson, Carl, 269
Jackson, Edward, 20
Jipson, Harry, 287

Kerridge, Hal, 226–7
Khaki Chums: experience of mud,
  163–4; kitting out volunteers,
  22–4; re-enactment of Somme life,
  3, 6; training of volunteers, 17, 18,
  21–2, 27–8; trench construction,
  55–6, 163
King's Own Shropshire Light
  Infantry, 66
King's Own Yorkshire Light
  Infantry, 253
kit, *see* equipment
Kitchener of Khartoum, Horatio
  Herbert, 1st Earl, 11
Kitchener's New Army, 11–20, 24–5,
  29, 78
kitchens, field, 129

La Boisselle, 37, 61, 62

La Grande Mine, 61
Lancashire Fusiliers, 64
latrines, 22, 102, 139–40
Lauder, Harry, 193
Lauder, John, 193
leave, 201–7
Le Cateau, 78
Leipzig Redoubt, 65
Le Sars, 64
letters, 149, 152, 154–7, 276–7
Lewis Machine Gun, 99, 212, 215,
  244
lice, 24, 151, 172–4, 176–8
Lincolnshire Regiment, 54
listening posts, 47, 102
Livens Projector, 222
Lochnagar Crater, 60–1
London Regiment, 79
Loopholes, 92
Loos: battle, 24, 222, 233; trenches, 43
Lys, Battle of the, 283

machine guns, 42, 92, 99, 104
magazines, 195
mail, 149–50, 276–7
Mailly-Maillet, 182
Malins, Geoffrey, 64
Mametz: front line, 62; Wood, 65
manual of trench warfare, 39–40, 91,
  99, 105, 112
marching, 17, 70, 88, 281
marker flags, 213
Marne, river, 41
Marshall, Smiler, 94, 143, 144, 170
Mary, Queen, 267, 286
medals, 255, 287–8
Medical Officers, 258
medicine and duty (M&D), 32
Menin Gate, 289
Merville, 180
Military Cross, 287–8

rats, 170–2

Regimental Aid Post (RAP), 258

regiments, 78–9

reserve lines, 47

rest: billets, 52–3, 184–8; removal from line, 183–8; removal from trenches, 180–3; types of, 180

Richards, Frank, 65, 97

Richardson, Lt-Colonel, 29, 31, 32, 33

Richebourg St Vaast, 179–80

Richthofen, Baron von, 215

rifles: arms inspections, 120; cleaning, 28, 120, 122; Lee Enfield, 33; outdated, 31, 33; rules for use in trenches, 57, 104; skills, 28; training, 33; *see also* bayonets

Ripon, 32

Robecq, 179

Robertson, Sir William, 19

Robin Hood Rifles, 79

Robinson, Walter, 73, 243

Rogers, Jack, 202

Rogerson, Sydney, 95

roll call, 102

Rose, G. K., 111

Rouen, 26

Royal Air Force, 214–15

Royal Army Medical Corps (RAMC), 255, 257, 258, 266, 268

Royal Berkshire Regiment, 110, 121

Royal Engineers, 6, 26, 37, 56, 134, 149, 216

Royal Flying Corps, 214

Royal Fusiliers, 142, 145, 251

Royal Garrison Artillery, 135

Royal Green Jackets, 23

Royal Scots, 166

Royal Warwickshire Regiment, 107, 197

Royal Welch Fusiliers, 97

Royal West Kent Regiment, 195

Royal West Surrey Regiment, 184

rum, 100, 120, 140–5, 231, 281

rumours, 275–6

St Omer, 287

St Pierre Divion, 244

St Pol, 283

Salisbury Plain, 83

Salvation Army, 189

Sanctuary Wood, 43

sandbags, 91, 102, 119, 129–30, 270

Sassoon, Siegfried, 65

Scarborough, naval bombardment, 31

Schlieffen Plan, 40

Schwaben Redoubt, 61

Scottish Division (9th), 52

Seaforth Highlanders, 25, 106, 191, 247

sections, army, 76

sentries: dry standing, 122; duty, 103–4, 117, 121, 271, 278; first night, 73; front line trenches, 100; German, 93, 107, 109; machine guns, 117; patrols, 109; sleeping, 116

Serre: attacks on village, 37, 68, 101, 243–4; battlefield, 51; front line, 62; German retreat, 244, 282; map, 38; military objective, 37; trenches, 38, 50, 51, 238

shaving, 21, 136, 138, 272

Sheffield City Battalion, 68

shelling: attitudes to, 211, 214; bombardments, 210, 211, 248–9; defences against, 49, 211; friendly fire, 213–14; recreation of, 57; size of shells, 210, 211–12; sound of, 211–12, 232–3; transport convoy, 87; wounds, 257, 262, 265

shell-shock, 231–5